ENCOUNTERS WITH THE LAND AND PEOPLE GOD LOVES

ISRAEL
The Miracle

INSPIRING
COMMENTARY
by
75
CHRISTIAN
LEADERS

GENESIS 123 FOUNDATION

The Bible is full of miracles and prophecies. It is in our generation that we see so many of those prophecies being realized, in the most miraculous of ways. The Christian leaders writing in this book describe these miracles at length, but the biggest miracle is their cooperation, even loving relationship, with the Jewish publisher, Jonathan Feldstein of the Genesis 123 Foundation, whose mission is to build bridges between Christians and Jews based on their mutual values of the God of Israel, the People of Israel, and the Land of Israel. This beautiful book will be an adornment on many coffee tables, but more so on the hearts of Christians and Jews who are open to God writing His love there. Blessings to the writers and the readers!

GIDON ARIEL, *Co-founder, www.root-source.com*

In *Israel The Miracle*, Jonathan Feldstein and the Genesis 123 Foundation have compiled a remarkable anthology of exquisite photographs of the Holy Land and commentary by a distinguished assembly of individuals that eloquently speak of God's love for His beautiful land and His people. And nobly testifies to the spiritual connection between Christians and Jews, forever linked by God's promise of the Messiah. The next best thing to actually being in Israel is to bring this book into your home! Read it. Share it. Display it. It's impossible to walk past it and not be drawn to it!

JOE BATTAGLIA *is an author* (The Politically Incorrect Jesus), *broadcaster, and co-executive producer of the nationally syndicated radio program Keep the Faith, and president of Renaissance Communications.*

I am honored to endorse *Israel The Miracle*. Essays from 75 devoted advocates share gleaming insights about our spiritual homeland during its 75th Sapphire anniversary year. God reveals His design for Jerusalem in Isaiah 54:11 to use blue sapphires for its foundation. Israel is the only place on earth where rare deep blue Mt. Carmel sapphires are found. Israel itself, shining as a rarity, is the only nation on earth where God declares in Leviticus, "The land is mine."

ARLENE BRIDGES SAMUELS *is the Weekly Feature Columnist for The Christian Broadcasting Network Israel, and previously on the staff of American Israel Public Affairs Committee and Mercy Ships.*

Israel The Miracle is an extraordinary book that is much more than just a collection of beautiful pictures. This captivating centerpiece will impress your guests and set the perfect tone for in-depth theological conversation. When I first looked through this book, I was struck by its stunning images of the Holy Land. However, *Israel The Miracle* is more than a visual treat. It presents serious theological issues in simple, easy-to-read segments, including topics such as the legality of Israel, prophetic fulfillment, and the coming Messiah. I highly recommend this brilliant book to anyone who wishes to understand and study the Bible.

PASTOR ROBBIE COLEMAN *holds a Master of Ministerial Leadership and pastored for thirty-four years before the Lord refocused his ministry to the Jewish people. He currently serves as Director of Zion's Bridge.*

Israel The Miracle is an astounding testament of the enduring significance and global influence of Israel. The book gently unravels the profound narratives of 75 distinguished leaders and influential figures from across the globe, each sharing personal encounters and reflections on the "land of milk and honey." Enveloped within its pages are thought-provoking and emotion-stirring essays that invite the reader into the hearts and minds of these notable figures, providing unique insight into what makes Israel so special and irreplaceable in their eyes. The spectrum of authors is indeed remarkable, collectively painting a rich, diverse, and complex tapestry of voices that truly bring to life the miracles of Israel. Thanks a gazillion times Genesis 123 Foundation for changing the game.

MAJOR DAUGHTER *is a non-profit leader, top 100 mentor, award-winning speaker, broadcaster, and creator and president of MDNTV.*

This book compiled by my friend Jonathan Feldstein and the Genesis 123 Foundation is a powerful presentation of the wonderful images from Israel. If you have been to Israel, you will be thrilled to see some of the wonderful places and locations in the country. If you have never been there, you will be inspired by the images of so many powerful and wonderful places.

PASTOR JOHN K. JENKINS, SR., *Senior Pastor, First Baptist Church of Glenarden*

As prominent Christian leaders come together, representing cultural and ethnic diversity from around the world, we celebrate in unity the miraculous Jewish State of Israel and the historic compilation of *Israel The Miracle*. As a civil rights leader and advocate for life from the womb to the tomb, and beyond, I honor God's chosen people and the Holy Land of Israel. *Israel The Miracle*, is a beautiful reflection of the body of Messiah functioning in unison as depicted in 1 Corinthians 12:12–27, as we stand united in the divine embrace of God's love and grace.

ALVEDA C. KING, PhD, *author, actress, producer, pro-life and civil rights leader, daughter to slain civil rights activist Rev. A.D.*

What a timely, inspirational, and educational book *Israel The Miracle* is, in the year the modern nation State of Israel celebrates its 75th anniversary! Read and be inspired by the personal narratives of 75 well-known Christian leaders, on the land God loves and the people He has chosen to be "a light unto the nations" A perfect mix of pictures and prose, not only will this book be a beautiful addition to your coffee table library, but also give you solid scriptural insights into God's never-ending love for Israel.

PAUSHALI LASS *is an Indian-German international speaker, author, mom of five, and bridge-builder between Christians, Jews and Muslims.*

Israel certainly is a miracle, and this book is an incredible testimony to the resilience of a people and their land. It is also an important must-read for everyone who loves Zion, allowing people to understand the deep roots of their support for Israel. *Israel The Miracle* is a book that does this not only through words, but with beautiful, sweeping illustrations. The photographs are simply stunning and are a testimony to the everlasting variety of sights from the Holy Land. Indeed, Israel's significance runs deep, and entire families can share this experience by reading together, enjoying the beauty of Israel's nature and people. Don't miss this opportunity to explore a book that is both meaningful and moving for Christians and Jews alike. We share our love of the Land of Israel and pray for the success of the people of Israel, together. What a beautiful work.

RUTH JAFFE LIEBERMAN *is a political advisor in Israel, co-founder of the Yes! Israel Project, creating personal ties for advocacy work between DC and Jerusalem. A licensed tour guide, she's also studying an advanced degree in archaeology.*

The strong support which Israel receives from Christians uplifts the spirits of the people of Israel and strengthens the Jewish state. It is such a blessing to be a partner with brothers and sisters of faith from around the world in celebrating the open fulfillment of biblical prophecies happening before our eyes in the lan of Israel today. In the remarkable essays that fill *Israel The Miracle,* Jonathan Feldstein, the Genesis 123 Foundation, and the authors have captured all of these sentiments. May Jonathan, the Genesis 123 Foundation, the authors, and all readers be the recipients of much divine blessing as a result of this spectacular project.

RABBI DOV LIPMAN *served as a member of the 19th Knesset and is the founder and CEO of Yad L'Olim, an NGO that helps Jews from around the world make Israel their home.*

Israel The Miracle is a unique retelling and gorgeous depiction of the miraculous story of the Land of Israel. It is also proof that Israel changes lives. No wonder so many Christian visitors have returned home as Israel lovers. This beautiful book reminds us of Israel's beauty and eternal significance, and makes us long to visit there again.

DR. SUSAN M. MICHAEL *is USA Director for the International Christian Embassy Jerusalem and author of* Encounter the 3D Bible, *a gifted teacher and international speaker having traveled Israel for over forty years.*

Gateway Church has made Israel a priority, and, as a result, we have seen God do miraculous things in and through our ministry. That's why I'm thrilled my friend Jonathan Feldstein has compiled these 75 commentaries about the miracle of Israel. This book is sure to strengthen your faith in God and give you a greater love for Israel.

ROBERT MORRIS, *Senior Pastor of Gateway Church and bestselling author*

Israel The Miracle is a captivating and insightful read that seamlessly bridges the gap between Judeo-Christian alliances and our understanding of Israel. This book illuminates the profound bond shared by Jews and Christians throughout history, while highlighting Israel's awe-inspiring resilience and growth. It's not just a book, but a journey that enriches one's perspective on spirituality, history, and geopolitics. A must-read for anyone seeking to understand the miracle that is Israel.

HANANYA NAFTALI *is a prominent Israeli speaker and influencer in the fight against antisemitism, terrorism, and assault on the State of Israel.*

Israel The Miracle provides a believer in the God of Abraham, Isaac, and Jacob an opportunity to pause and reflect on what it means to be living in sacred history when prophecies are "in fulfillment." This is an incredible love letter from our covenantal partners in the kingdom of God.

DAVID NEKRUTMAN, *Executive Director for The Isaiah Projects and Jewish adviser to* The Chosen

Israel The Miracle captures the heart and soul of the land that God gave the Jewish people. But it's more than just another book about how this miracle happened; it's a look at God's goodness and grace as seen through the lens of the beauty of the land and the people to whom He gave it. I know you'll love seeing how God's supernatural hand brought His people home to the land that He gave them so long ago!

TODD SCHUMACHER *is the founding pastor of Church of the King, a life-giving church with multiple campuses in southwest Louisiana.*

I love Israel. There's a renewing power that comes with visiting there that fills my soul with every visit. I've felt what it feels like when you walk in the footsteps of Jesus. *Israel The Miracle* is a powerful depiction of that reality, expressed by dozens of Christian leaders from all around the world. Many of these are my good friends. More than just a book that you read, it's a visual experience to enjoy. It is truly beautiful. I pray that this book will expose readers to the people of Israel, the land in which Jesus lived, and His people.

MICHAEL W. SMITH *is a muti-platinum singer-songwriter, worship leader, and actor.*

iStock.com/VRnCmS

COPYRIGHT

Dedication

This book is dedicated to the generations that came before, passing down Jewish and ancient tradition to us, as part of a legacy for future generations. And to hundreds of millions of Christians who love and support Israel and the Jewish people, with whom we share the God of Abraham, Isaac, and Jacob, and who see in Israel and the Jewish people the fulfillment of God's promises, and prophecies. We serve an incredible God and we pray this book will build lasting bridges between us for generations to come.

Jonathan Feldstein
Jerusalem, Israel

CONTENTS

—— *Please see authors bios on pages 222-232* ——

Israel, you are the chosen people of the Lord your God.

There are many nations on this earth, but He chose only Israel to be His very own.

DEUTERONOMY
— 7:6 —

I wish my parents were alive to share the fruit of this project with them. Other than being proud of me as their son, they'd be inspired. They gave me my earliest foundation in Judaism—our people, our faith, and our history—including my deep connection to the Land and State of Israel. When my father lived and grew up in Israel, it was a very different and often hard place to live. My mother was able to see us thriving in Israel: happy and prospering, even though she was personally sad that we "kidnapped" her grandchildren and moved them across the world. They'd be inspired by the reality of Christian support for Israel and my role as an important bridge between Jews and Christians.

As much as I am defined by the foundation my parents gave me, I knew when I met my wife that she was my partner to our future, personally and as a people. She's always been my better half in many ways. Even as the mother of our six children, to our son and daughter-in-law, and grandmother to three beautiful grandchildren, she has supported me on this journey, even sometimes suffering as a result.

My family understands how important what I do is. We have been blessed by establishing deep relationships with many Christian friends who have become like family. But they also bear the biggest sacrifice—my travels take me away from home, and them, much of the year, every year. Because my "work" is a calling and a passion; I pray that as much as it takes time away from my family, it's a model to them as well. I'd be nowhere without them in my life, especially my wife and partner of 31 years, Lori, with whom I am blessed abundantly to share our growing family. I pray for many, many more years to see our family flourish, with the added measure of doing so as part of the prophetic return of the Jewish people to the Land of Israel.

I am extremely grateful to the authors, photographers, and artists who contributed to this book. They are recognized within these pages. Their words have made my heart race and brought tears to my eyes. The images make me more in love with this country and my people. The weaving of these has resulted in an extraordinary, historic work of art. None of this would be possible without their thoughtfulness and generosity. I pray that as you interact with this volume, you come away with an appreciation of that and for each of their unique participation.

This book would not have been possible without the incredible team at HigherLife. Their professionalism, many hours of work, and tremendous enthusiasm for the project have been invaluable. I could not have done it without them. It was a team effort for which I am grateful. Special thanks to Michelle Buckley for her overall hands-on efforts; Marcy Pusey, whose editing was invaluable and whom many of the authors complemented for improving their essays; Virginia Grounds, who interfaced with all the photographers and artists and much more; and Bill Johnson as the graphic designer whose work speaks for itself. Tim Synan was my go-to person for just about everything, orchestrating all the many elements of the book with great detail and being available at all hours of the day, every day of the week. When I reached out to David Welday, president of HigherLife Publishing, to propose the concept in late 2022, he embraced it, improved upon it, and has been a hands-on proponent of the project from that moment, ensuring that we realized its completion at the high standard that it is. His professionalism and kindness, pulling together the best team possible, have been a blessing.

I am grateful to God, our Creator, for allowing me to be born into the Jewish people, our rich history and traditions, to serve Him, and be a direct inheritor of His Covenant with Abraham, Isaac, and Jacob. I am grateful to God for the privilege of living and raising my family in the covenanted Land of which we are each part owners, for living at this moment in history when the Jewish people have been restored to our Land, where we are prospering and thriving, and seeing prophecies relating to Israel taking place before our eyes, even through my family.

I thank God for calling me to build bridges between Jews and Christians in the 1980s at a small church in Cleveland, Tennessee, and for giving me the opportunities I've had to do this over the decades and through the Genesis 123 Foundation. It's not only a privilege serving Him, but a delight and a pleasure, something that makes me a better person, and a better Jew.

Jonathan Feldstein
Jerusalem, Israel
2023 (corresponding to the year 5783 since Creation)

INTRODUCTION

"The Lord said to Moses, 'Speak to the people of Israel, that they take for me a contribution. From every man whose heart moves him you shall receive the contribution for me. And this is the contribution that you shall receive from them: gold, silver, and bronze, blue and purple and scarlet yarns and fine twined linen, goats' hair, tanned rams' skins, goatskins, acacia wood, oil for the lamps, spices for the anointing oil and for the fragrant incense, onyx stones, and stones for setting, for the ephod and for the breastpiece. And let them make me a sanctuary, that I may dwell in their midst.'" (Exodus 25:1-8)

Jewish tradition teaches that all the materials used to build the Tabernacle and adorn the high priest were given voluntarily. The people of Israel were so eager to participate and have a share in creating a sacred resting place for God's presence, and to provide a place for worship, that those in charge had to appeal to Moses (36:3–6) to cease the contributions. People contributed simply for the sake of loving God, not for anything in return.

We set out to publish this book to be both inspiring and beautiful—something that would remind us of God's presence and inspire worship and gratitude. We asked 75 Christian leaders to share why Israel is so important, on the occasion of Israel's 75th anniversary of independence. Each one did so without asking anything in return.

We trust you will find this book to be breathtaking on every page. It's also incredible that we asked 75 pro-Israel Christian leaders to come together to share what's significant about Israel to them, and we received not a single redundant essay. It shows the depth and breadth of how and why Christians relate to Israel and the Jewish people as they do, and for many others, why they should. And just like building a sacred space in the Tabernacle, each author did so voluntarily, graciously, with love. They have helped create a new kind of sacred space.

We could have invited many more people to write essays, but we wanted to keep to 75 in honor of the nation's 75th anniversary. Some were unable to participate for a variety of reasons: time constraints, personal crises, other deadlines, and more. On their own, and in the capacity of their own ministries, many will no doubt use the milestone of Israel's 75th anniversary to express their words independently. We don't mean to leave anyone out and invite you to write and "nominate" others who are not part of this project now, for meaningful projects in the future. Please let us know who your inspiring Christian leaders are who understand and celebrate the significance of Israel at www.IsraeltheMiracle.com.

It's a blessing, and something not to be taken for granted, that while not everyone could participate in this project here, at this season, everyone who is participating is a serious Christian leader who demonstrably supports the Land, people, and State of Israel, and each is rooted in the God of Israel. Some of our contributors are widely known primarily in their own nation. Some are known internationally. Others are less famous, but no less pro-Israel in their own communities and ministries. While not widely known, they are no less inspiring. They represent millions of others who, like them, are relatable role models.

I had the unique privilege of being the first person to read all these essays. As I read, my heart was often stirred, pounding through my shirt, over and over. We asked our authors to write something about why Israel is significant to them, personally, with very loose parameters. I was blessed and overwhelmed by how each contribution was both unique and inspiring.

I pray that as you read and view these pages, your heart will be stirred by the complement of inspiring words, and stunning images. I pray that you and your loved ones, from old to young, will read and meaningfully interact with these pages. I pray that whether you've been to Israel dozens of times, or never before, this book will add a new dimension to your understanding of and connection to Israel. I pray that this will be a volume you cherish, because of the historic milestone of Israel's 75th anniversary, and this book is the first time anything like this has ever been done. I pray that you'll be moved to connect with and learn about Israel more deeply and that you'll come to visit soon.

Jonathan Feldstein
Jerusalem, Israel

The Dead Sea

Dear friends:

This year, Israel is celebrating its 75th year of independence as a sovereign nation in our ancient homeland. It is this Holy Land, where we have built our modern nation-state, which serves as a living bridge to the shared ancestry between Jews and Christians.

The vivid paths of Christianity and Judaism are intertwined through the centuries. Our shared roots derive from a faith we continue to rely upon for guidance, sustenance, and strength. Though the history of Christianity's relationship with the Jewish people has its share of persecution and bloodshed, today the covenant with our Christian brothers and sisters is one of the key pillars of support for our national project.

The story of the State of Israel is one of courage, devotion, and acts of political daring. It is a tale of a people searching for a sanctuary, and finding support from friends both old and new. You celebrate with us in times of joy, and sustain us during times of crisis.

It is an honor to appear in the beautiful pages of this timeless book, which details the bonds between our two faiths. We are grateful for your devotion to our cause, and for your pursuit of friendship between our two peoples.

Sincerely, *an Shalom!*

Isaac Herzog
President of the State of Israel

State of Israel
Ministry of Tourism

Shalom!

Israel is more than just another place on your bucket list. First and foremost, it is a unique spiritual experience. There are places that just must be seen– and primarily experienced – in order to understand what everyone is talking about.

Israel is one such place – and especially in the context of our Judeo-Christian heritage – it is THE place, one that without actually visiting, a true understanding of the Bible, its background and its message, will be impossible.

The Ministry of Tourism of the State of Israel, under my leadership, is aiming to go the extra mile in making the Land of the Bible accessible and meaningful for visitors from around the world. We are working hard to promote fast and effective infrastructure development, to add more hotel rooms and to improve the tourist experience. The bond between Jews and Christians relies on the ability to visit and to fully experience the Holy Sites of our mutual heritage.

"Israel the Miracle" is an outstanding compilation of meaningful words by top Christian leaders sharing their own experiences in Israel and among its people.

I would like to convey my appreciation to the Genesis 123 Foundation for this historic work that contributes to deepening the relations between Christians who have already visited Israel, and those who have not yet visited, but we hope will do so in the nearest future.

Sincerely,

Haim Katz
Minister of Tourism

EVIDENCE OF GOD'S EXISTENCE

by

DR. PAT ROBERTSON

During the final editing of this book, we were saddened by the news of Dr. Pat Robertson's death. We are blessed that he is part of this book, and that these may be his last public words on Israel. In his memory, with great respect, and because he was the giant he was, we have elected to place this essay first.

One day in the late nineteenth century, Queen Victoria of England asked her Prime Minister, Benjamin Disraeli, this question:

"Mr. Prime Minister, what evidence can you give me of the existence of God?"

Disraeli thought momentarily and then replied, "The Jew, Your Majesty."

Think of it. According to Disraeli, the primary evidence that God exists is the existence of the Jewish people. This is a people who, in 586 BC, were deported to Babylon yet returned after seventy years to rebuild a nation. They were again brutally massacred and dispersed by the Romans in AD 70, yet after countless centuries of Diaspora, expulsions, pogroms, ghettos, and attempts at genocidal extermination, they have clung to their faith, their customs—and now, after some 2,500 years, have returned to the Land promised by God to their ancestors.

A new nation that began in that Land in 1948 was named after their ancestor Jacob, whose divinely appointed name, Israel, means "Prince with God." And to fulfill another ancient prophecy, God moved on the heart of Eliezer Ben-Yehuda, whose son Ehud told me that while his father was living in Eastern Europe, Eliezer heard a voice and saw a light directing him to bring forth for the Jewish people a pure language—Hebrew—the language of the Torah and the ancient prophets.

The survival of the Jewish people is a miracle of God. The return of the Jewish people to the Land promised to Abraham, Isaac, and Jacob is a miracle of God. The remarkable victories of the Jewish armies against overwhelming odds in successive battles in 1948, 1967, and 1973 are clearly miracles of God. The technological marvels of Israeli industry, the military prowess, the bounty of Israeli agriculture, the fruits and flowers, and the abundance of the Land are all incredible testimony to God's watchful care over this nation and the genius of this people.

Yet what has happened was foretold by the ancient prophet Ezekiel, who, writing at the time of the Babylonian captivity, declared this message for the Jewish people:

"I will take you from the nations and gather you from all the countries and bring you into your own land…. You shall dwell in the land that I gave to your fathers, and you shall be my people, and I will be your God" (Ezek. 36:24, 28).

Evangelical Christians support Israel because we believe that God inspired the words of Moses and the ancient prophets of Israel. We believe the emergence of a Jewish State in the Land promised by God to Abraham, Isaac, and Jacob was ordained by God. We believe that God has a plan for this nation and that He still intends for them to be a blessing to all the nations of the earth. We support Israel because it is an island of democracy, individual freedom, the rule of law, and modernity amid a sea of dictatorial regimes, the suppression of individual liberty, and a fanatical religion intent on returning to the feudalism of eighth-century Arabia.

Mere political rhetoric does not account for the profound devotion to Israel in the hearts of tens of millions of evangelical Christians. You must realize that the God who spoke to Moses on Mount Sinai is our God. Abraham, Isaac, and Jacob are our spiritual patriarchs.

Jeremiah, Ezekiel, and Daniel are our prophets. King David, a man after God's own heart, is our hero. The Holy City of Jerusalem is our spiritual capital. And the continuation of Jewish sovereignty over the Holy Land is further evidence that the God of the Bible exists and that His Word is true.

We should also note that, as Christians, we serve a Jew that we believe was the divine Messiah of Israel, spoken of by the ancient prophets, who entrusted the worldwide dissemination of His message to twelve Jewish apostles.

Today, Christianity, with well over two billion adherents, is expected to see that number swell to nearly three billion by 2050. Of these, more than six hundred million are Bible-believing evangelicals and charismatics who are ardent supporters of the nation of Israel. Israel has millions of Christian friends in China, India, Indonesia, Africa, and South America, as well as North America.

To our Jewish friends, we say: We are with you in your struggle. We are with you as a wave of antisemitism is engulfing the earth. We are with you despite the incredibly hostile resolutions of the United Nations. We are with you despite the ongoing threats of terrorism against the nation and people of Israel.

We evangelical Christians say to our Israeli friends: Let us serve our God together by opposing the virulent poison of antisemitism and anti-Zionism that is rapidly consuming the world.

On Christmas day in 1974, I had the privilege of interviewing Israel's prime minister, Yitzhak Rabin, on *The 700 Club*. Rabin lamented that after Israeli military victories, the nation had been stopped from achieving a peace treaty. That was over forty years ago. Israel seems as isolated and alone today as it did then. As I concluded my interview, I asked Prime Minister Rabin a final question: "What would you want the United States to do now for Israel?"

He replied without hesitation, "Be strong! Be strong!"

That evening, I went to dinner with several hundred people who had accompanied me from the United States. We met in the large dining room of the InterContinental Hotel on the Mount of Olives in Jerusalem, whose floor-to-ceiling windows gave a stunning view of the illuminated Temple Mount. As I related to the group the substance of my meeting, I began to recall the feeling of sadness from the prime minister—the sense of his nation's isolation.

I made a solemn vow to God that evening, that despite whatever happened in the future, the organizations I headed and I would stand with Israel and the Jewish people. I am proud to say that I have kept that vow each year since 1974.

Now, on the celebration of the 75th anniversary of Israel's independence, I would deliver to Israel the message Yitzhak Rabin had delivered to the United States on Christmas Day in 1974.

For you are the living witnesses that the promises of the Sovereign Lord are true. "Be strong! Be strong!"

Roman Yanushevsky/Shutterstock.com

Omri Eliyahu/Shutterstock.com

ISRAEL, THE SYMBOL OF HOPE

by

PASTOR E. A. ADEBOYE

From a Christian perspective, one of the things that makes Israel a miracle is that it is a symbol of hope.

The origin of Israel's name, as found in Genesis 32:24–28, suggests several things to conclude that if one encounters the God of Israel, there is hope for such a one.

In Genesis 27:1–45, Jacob had obtained the blessings meant for his brother, Esau, by deception. In response, Esau promised Jacob death as soon as their dad died.

Jacob fled (Gen. 28:1–5) and had been away for years. He was returning from exile and informed Esau that he was returning home. The response he got frightened him greatly (Gen. 32:1–7).

Then, alone and at his wit's end, he encountered God. The encounter led to a change of his name from Jacob to Israel (Gen. 32:24–28).

By the following morning, when he came face to face with his brother, the tide had turned dramatically (Gen.33:1–11).

It is through this historical event that the name Israel came to the world. We can safely conclude that the God of Israel can bring hope to the hopeless.

1. He can change an enemy to a friend.

   He can make an enemy to be at peace (Pro. 16:7).

   Or prosper you in the presence of your enemy (Ps. 25:5).

2. He can change sorrow to joy overnight.

   Joy comes in the morning (Ps. 30:5).

   He has the ability to wipe away all tears (Rev. 21:4).

3. He can give someone or a relationship a new beginning.

   He promises to do new things (Is. 43:18–19).

   And what He promises to do, He will do (Num. 23:19).

   Because His Word is forever settled (Ps. 199:89).

   Once He speaks, it is done (Ps. 33:8–9).

For Christians, Israel is the birthplace of our Lord, Saviour, and Christ. It is written, *"Christ in you the hope of glory" (Col. 1:27).*

This confirms the prophecy of Isaiah to us in Isaiah 3:10— *"Tell the righteous that it shall be well with them...."*

The miracle of Israel is that it says, in essence, "Tomorrow will be all right."

THIS IS THE LAND THAT GOD HAS GIVEN TO YOU

by

KAY ARTHUR

An olive grove outside the Old City of Jerusalem

As a young woman and new Christian, I was invited to Tennessee Temple University in Chattanooga, Tennessee, to watch a film about Israel. During the film, I began to sob.

A veil dropped from my eyes as I realized who the Jewish people were to God—how central Israel is to God, His Word, and all Christians. I began devouring God's promises to Abraham, Isaac, and Jacob in His Word. God promises the Land of Israel, a covenanted Land through which so many of God's prophecies are revealed, to the people of Israel.

I was fifteen years old when Israel's first Prime Minister, David Ben-Gurion, declared independence. United States President, Harry Truman, was the first to recognize Israel's independence. I knew this was important but didn't realize how important. But through my lifetime, I have been privileged to see so many of God's promises to Israel realized. Israel has restored its ancient biblical language, Hebrew, which is taught in schools, spoken in courts, prayed in synagogues, and is even the language of parking tickets and birth certificates.

Through Israel, we witness God's divine love for His people.

As soon as I stepped off the plane on my first visit to Israel, my heart was overwhelmed.

I was standing on holy ground. The Land is holy because it is set apart; it is sacred. From that moment, I realized how important and powerful it is to teach the Word of God in the Land. My husband, Jack, and I started bringing tours to Israel, which we did for decades, so as many people as possible would understand God's Word as it relates to Israel.

Wherever I go and with whomever I can, I share one central message: "This is your Land and God has given it to you as an everlasting possession."

Israelis look at me in amazement—that a gentile knows about, much less cares about, Israel and the significance of its existence. Sharing

Guy Zidel/Shutterstock.com

Haifa, Israel

this simple biblical truth opens doors, builds relationships, and gives Israelis a sense of appreciation and encouragement. This blesses all of us.

Truly one of the greatest joys God has given me is the gift of my Jewish friends in Israel—being able to go to Israel, meet them, get to know them, and love them. I was even privileged to live among them for a short while.

I have been blessed to see Israel through the lens of my Israeli friends, hearing their stories and those of their relatives who came back to the Land and fought for their independence.

I have spent countless hours reading and discussing the Word of God with Jewish friends, a gift beyond measure. My beloved friend, Esther Schlisser, and I would sit in wonder that we—a gentile and a Jew—could spend hours together dialoguing about the Scriptures. It was a miracle I experienced firsthand in the Land and among God's chosen people.

As Christians, we need to remind Israel what God said to Joshua through Moses in Deuteronomy 31:7–8: *"Be strong and courageous, for you shall go with* *this people into the land that the Lord has sworn to their fathers to give them, and you shall put them in possession of it. It is the Lord who goes before you. He will be with you; he will not leave you or forsake you. Do not fear or be dismayed."*

As we celebrate Israel's milestone anniversary of seventy-five years of independence, we pray that Israel stands strong in the truths of God's Word and that the leaders of the world will not persuade Israel to go against His precepts. It is God's Promised Land, deeded to the Jewish people. God Almighty has set the boundaries.

Let's pray all the earth will know Israel is God's beloved, and all the nations will come to know that Jerusalem is the praise of all the earth.

"To the world You were just 'a Jew' … but now they know you are Israel, My Beloved."

(Israel, My Beloved, Kay Arthur, 1996, page 444)

Tel Aviv coastline

A sunrise over Masada

The Orient Hotel in the German Colony in Jerusalem

GERMAN SETTLERS IN ISRAEL
by
HONORABLE MICHELE BACHMANN

"Then they shall know that I am the Lord their God, because I sent them into exile among the nations and then assembled them into their own land." —Ezekiel 39:28

Nearly a century before the rebirth of Israel in 1948, God called a community of Christian believers in Germany to leave their comforts, abandon their livelihoods, risk their lives, and prepare for Israel's prophetic regathering.

The beautiful Orient Hotel in Jerusalem tells the story of the first stirrings of God's plan to return the Jews to their homeland following some 1,800 years in exile. The hotel rests at the edge of a German colony, built and established as an offering by the German Templers of the mid-nineteenth century.

The Templers believed they were called to the Promised Land of God's people to prepare the way for Israel's return. In 1867, the Land of Israel was desolate and deserted, mostly uninhabited and totally inhospitable. Mark Twain famously reported in his bestselling book, *Innocents Abroad*, written during his excursion beginning in 1876 and published in 1869:

We rode a little way up a hill and found ourselves at Endor, famous for its witch. Her descendants are there yet. They were the wildest horde of half-naked savages we have found thus far…. The hill is barren, rocky, and forbidding. No sprig of grass is visible, and only one tree….

The further we went the hotter the sun got, and the more rocky and bare, repulsive and dreary the landscape became…. There was hardly a tree or a shrub anywhere. Even the olive and the cactus, those fast friends of a worthless soil, had almost deserted the country. No landscape exists that is more tiresome to the eye than that which bounds the approaches to Jerusalem.

In 1867, a group of twenty-five pioneers who were impatient for action attempted to settle ahead of their Templer cohorts. A year later, fifteen of those twenty-five earlier migrants had perished due to the harshness of the environment.

Later, a more prepared community of Templers arrived on the Land. They drained swamps infested with malaria and other diseases. They planted fields and vineyards for later settlers to inherit. They produced food and oil, building materials, and buildings. They created an economy and eventually opened the first hotels in the Land.

This humble group became renowned for their greatness, their excellence, and their sacrifice to cultivate a land worthy of God's plan to restore Israel to its Land of Promise. Thanks to their radical obedience and an unbending "yes" to God, the Templers will forever be celebrated as participants in God's plan to redeem and restore Israel.

Photo by Richard C. Lewis

A statue in Chicago of George Washington holding the hands of Robert Morris and Hyam Solomon

AMERICA'S LOVE FOR ISRAEL:
FROM THE PILGRIMS TO THE PRESENT

by

DAVID BARTON

From our earliest days, the United States saw ancient Israel as a model for our nation, heavily influencing our culture, institutions, and legal codes.

In the early 1600s, when America was forming its first colonies, Governor William Bradford undertook the study of Hebrew, explaining:

> Though I am grown aged, yet I have had a longing desire to see, with my own eyes, something of that most ancient language and holy tongue in which the Law and oracles of God were written; and in which God and angels spake to the holy patriarchs of old time; and what names were given to things from the creation…. My aim and desire is to see how the words and phrases lie in the holy text; and to discern somewhat of the same, for my own content.

Notably, he wrote much of his colony's history in Hebrew.

Another early governor, John Winthrop, made many of the laws of Moses the basis of their legal code. In fact, their reliance on ancient biblical laws resulted in America's first anti-slavery law. Citing Exodus 21:16, man-stealing became a capital crime in 1641, punishable by death. Consequently, in 1646, when a shipload of slaves arrived in Massachusetts, they were freed, and the slave traders imprisoned and punished.

Because of the early colonists' love for the Bible and God's chosen people, America's earliest Christian settlers openly welcomed Jews into their colonies.

By 1658, Jewish synagogues were established in Christian colonies in Newport, Rhode Island, and in Savannah, Georgia. In 1719, a Jewish synagogue started in Richmond, Virginia, and in 1750 in Charleston, South Carolina.

In the American War for Independence, Christians and Jews fought side by side. Famous Jewish military patriots included Colonels David and Isaac Franks, Francis Salvador (the first Jew to hold political office in America and the first to die in the War for Independence), Isaac Moses (a blockade runner), Major Benjamin Nones (a leader in the Battles of Savannah and Camden), Mordecai Sheftall (patriot leader in Georgia), and Hyam Salomon.

In fact, in Chicago's business district is a large statue of George Washington holding the hands of Robert Morris and Hyam Salomon—a Christian and a Jew, and the two men most responsible for arranging the financial support necessary to keep his troops in the field.

When America declared its independence in 1776, Congress formed a committee of three individuals (Thomas Jefferson, Benjamin Franklin, and John Adams) to determine the official seal for the new United States. According to John Adams:

> Mr. Jefferson proposed. The Children of Israel in the Wilderness, led by a Cloud by day, and a Pillar of Fire by night.

And Founding Father Elias Boudinot, President of Congress, started the "Society for Ameliorating the State of the Jews," making personal provision to bring persecuted Jews to America where they could have an "asylum of safety."

Many of America's Founders openly praised the Jewish people. Declaration of Independence signer, John Witherspoon, noted:

> To the Jews were first committed the care of the Sacred Writings....[Y]et was the providence of God particularly manifest in their preservation and purity.

John Adams was also effusive in his praise of the Jews, declaring:

> As much as I love, esteem and admire the Greeks, I believe the Hebrews have done more to civilize the world. Moses did more than all their legislators and philosophers. I will insist that the Hebrews have done more to civilize men than any other nation.

In the period when American independence was won, and our Constitution was written, the most frequently-cited work during that time was the Bible, and the most quoted book was Deuteronomy.

When a parade was held in Philadelphia to celebrate the adoption of the Constitution, signer of the Declaration, Benjamin Rush, happily reported:

> The clergy formed a very agreeable part of the procession.... The rabbi of the Jews locked in the arms of two ministers of the Gospel was a most delightful sight. There could not have been a more happy emblem.

When George Washington was inaugurated, his ceremony contained seven different religious activities, planned by fourteen religious leaders, including Christian ministers and Jewish rabbis.

During Washington's presidency, when Thomas Paine penned his famous *Age of Reason* attacking Christianity and Judaism, Christian and Jewish leaders joined to defend the Bible.

During the Barbary Powers War (1784-1816), in which Muslim terrorists captured and enslaved American seamen because of their Christian faith, Christian

President James Madison dispatched American Jewish Diplomat Mordecai Noah to negotiate with the Muslim terrorists to secure the release of captured Christians.

Many of America's Founding Fathers openly affirmed to Noah their Zionistic views. As John Adams told Noah two centuries ago:

> I could find it in my heart to wish that you had been at the head of a hundred thousand Israelites ... and marching with them into Judea and making a conquest of that country and restoring your nation to the dominion of it. For I really wish the Jews again in Judea an independent nation.

In 1844, American consular offices were established in Jerusalem. One of the American Middle East diplomats to visit there was Lew Wallace, famous American Civil War general (and author of the best-selling novel *Ben-Hur*), who worked with Jewish rabbis around the holy city.

America became the first to rec-

ognize the reconstituted State of Israel in 1948. Today's Bible-based Christians remain some of the world's staunchest defenders of the Jewish nation, remembering God's clear promise:

> *Now the Lord said to Abram, "Go from your country and your kindred and your father's house to the land that I will show you. And I will make of you a great nation, and I will bless you and make your name great, so that you will be a blessing. I will bless those who bless you, and him who dishonors you I will curse, and in you all the families of the earth shall be blessed." (Genesis 12:1–3)*

> *He remembers his covenant forever, the word that he commanded, for a thousand generations. (Psalm 105:8)*

37

PUCKER UP, WE'RE LANDING IN ISRAEL

by

KEN BARUN

I was born just six weeks before Israel declared independence. It was the first time the Jewish people restored sovereignty in Israel in nearly two thousand years. My birth was much less eventful than Israel's, and for years I was oblivious to the struggle of what I later would call my true homeland.

I remember the stories my grandfather, Izzie, shared about his arrival from Kyiv to Ellis Island—just past the outstretched arm of the Statue of Liberty. So began our family's arrival in the New World, another stop in thousands of years of Diaspora. Even so, Israel always felt like home, even though I'd never been there.

As I matured, I began to relate to the struggles of the Jews, starting with Abraham, Isaac, Jacob, Moses, Jesus, and His disciples. In modern history, people like Ben Gurion, Jabotinsky, Begin, Meir, Sharon, and Peres battled to ensure the Jewish people's survival in their covenanted homeland.

Despite being ridiculed, harassed, and constantly threatened by cultural and religious extermination, the Jews continued to achieve everything from curing diseases, writing award-winning novels, and winning more Nobel Prizes than any other group in the world—let alone reestablish their own thriving and inspiring state. They didn't only achieve, they excelled.

One day, as I rummaged through my father's old clothes, I found two pistols. I'd never seen a gun. My dad wasn't happy that I'd found them. He said in almost a whisper, "Son, you must never tell anyone about this." He explained that he and several friends collected weapons as part of a network of Jews who sent guns and ammunition to enable Israeli freedom fighters to maintain independence for the State of Israel. My connection to Israel became deeply personal.

Growing up in a close-knit Jewish community, I was insulated from antisemitism. When my parents moved to the suburbs, the atmosphere changed.

Kids in the new neighborhood treated me differently, calling me names I'd never heard before. They said strange things like "Savior," "Jesus," and "You killed our Messiah," while throwing rocks and sticks and chasing me as I ran home from school.

I was shocked. I'd never killed anyone and surely didn't kill this Jesus guy! I didn't even know who Jesus was. I learned that the struggles of the Jewish people were those which most united us. Israel's struggle became the object of my attention.

My young adult years were a wild roller coaster ride, my own forty years of wandering in the desert. I sought fame, fortune, and the answer to the meaning of life. I crashed like a rock and lived in the streets, addicted to heroin for six years. Eventually, I became the president of the program that got me clean and worked in the Reagan White House. After forty years of wandering my self-proclaimed desert, God stopped it.

By God's divine appointment, my good friend, Franklin Graham, and I were traveling together. We had a free weekend between his preaching in Latvia and Lithuania. Knowing of my passion for Israel, Franklin asked, "What would you do first if you had a chance to visit Israel?"

I replied immediately, "I would get down on my hands and knees, praise the Lord, and kiss the ground!"

He looked at me with a big smile and said, "Well, you'd better pucker up because we have less than thirty minutes until we land in Tel Aviv."

I felt the same immense rush of emotions I'd felt only once before—holding my wife's hand after we'd finished praying the sinner's prayer, asking God to forgive my thousands of sins. I told God I wanted a personal relationship with His Son, Jesus. At that moment, I was born again.

Standing on the tarmac, I found myself in my ancient birthplace, the Land of Israel.

I was home.

Photo by Rebecca Kowalsky

Israel: A Place, a People, and the Firstborn of God Almighty

by

Pastor Mark Biltz

The Ramparts Walk inside the Old City

Israel is the only nation where the Creator of both heaven and earth decided their land would ever be before His eyes.

This Land has been set apart from every other land mass.

"But the land that you are going over to possess is a land of hills and valleys, which drinks water by the rain from heaven, a land that the LORD your God cares for. The eyes of the LORD your God are always upon it, from the beginning of the year to the end of the year" (Deut. 11:11–12).

"On that day, the LORD made a covenant with Abram, saying, 'To your offspring, I give this land, from the river of Egypt to the great river, the river Euphrates...'" (Gen. 15:18).

Jews are a distinct people group as well. They are set apart from all nations, being the only people group whose name of origin came directly from the Creator.

"And God said to him, 'Your name is Jacob; no longer shall your name be called Jacob, but Israel shall be your name.' So he called his name Israel. And God said to him, 'I am God Almighty: be fruitful and multiply. A nation and a company of nations shall come from you, and kings shall come from your own body. The land that I gave to Abraham and Isaac I will give to

you, and I will give the land to your offspring after you'" (Gen. 35:10–12).

All humans are God's children, yet Israel is designated as His firstborn.

"Then you shall say to Pharaoh, 'Thus says the LORD, Israel is my firstborn son'" (Exod. 4:22).

As the founder of El Shaddai Ministries, a ministry building bridges between Christians and Jews, I have led tours to Israel twenty times. I have found that everyone who comes for the first time is radically changed. Just as the Land of Israel has come alive as prophesied in the Bible, people who visit also become spiritually alive. The connection is real.

The prophets declared that one day Israel would return to their Land and a nation would be born in a day. We know that happened in 1948. I'm in awe that it was 1,948 years from the point of Creation to Abraham's birth. Abraham received the promise of the Land when he was seventy-five years old ... in the year 2023 A.D.

"I will take you from the nations and gather you from all the countries and bring you into your own land. I will sprinkle clean water on you, and you shall be clean from all your uncleanness, and from all your idols I will cleanse you" (Ezek. 36:25).

But then, we see that after God brings them into their land and cleanses them, God will give them a new heart, fill them with His Spirit, and they will follow God's laws!

"And I will give you a new heart, and a new spirit I will put within you. And I will remove the heart of stone from your flesh and give you a heart of flesh. And I will put my Spirit within you and cause you to walk in my statutes and be careful to obey my rules. You shall dwell in the land that I gave to your fathers, and you shall be my people, and I will be your God. And I will deliver you from all your uncleanness" (Ezek. 36:26–29a).

These are the times we are living in! Fasten your prophetic seat belts and hold on as this world enters the most prophetic times. The God of Israel is about to set up His throne in Jerusalem, and it will become the capital of the entire world without regard to what the nations wish!

Israel has always shined, and continues
to shine, as a bright light in this world
and as a true symbol of hope rooted in
God's goodness and faithfulness.

42

THE MENORAH AND THE MESSIAH: ISRAEL'S LIGHT AND HOPE FOR ALL

by
PASTOR BOYD BINGHAM

What an honor it is for me to have this opportunity to express my gratitude for Israel on this 75th celebration of the State of Israel. There are two thoughts that come to my mind when I think of Israel and the Jewish people.

First, the word *light*. Israel is truly a light in this world. When we think of light, we must think of the historical and spiritual significance of it in Israel's heritage.

The menorah—an instrument that is synonymous with Judaism—has great significance to the nation of Israel and is an instrument that God patterned to produce *light*.

The law of God that was given to Moses *illuminates* the heart of every man to the human condition and demonstrates that man is by his very nature a sinner.

The sacrificial system in the Old Testament *illuminates* man to the fact that one can receive forgiveness for breaking the law but only by the blood of a perfect sacrifice.

The prophets hold a blazing torch of certainty that *shines* bright in this world as they proclaim that God is not finished with His people and that the promises He made are still in effect.

The greatest and most luminescent light that Israel has ever given to this world was imparted two thousand years ago when Jesus was born in Bethlehem. Jesus' parents took Him to be circumcised in the Temple eight days after His birth, as was the custom of the law. Upon their arrival, they were met by Simeon, who gave a twofold prophecy concerning Jesus. The first stated that Jesus would be the *light* to lighten the gentiles. The second stated that Jesus would be the glory of His people. It is only by Jesus that gentiles, who sat in the darkness of idolatry and paganism, can say that they have seen a great *light* and are now welcomed into the family of God. It is only by Jesus that the full glory of God shined upon His people!

Second, Israel is the *hope* of the world. Hope has been perverted in the modern world to mean something that may or may not be a certainty. With this understanding, many people cling to anything as a form of hope—anything to give them a sense of rest, peace, and assurance.

This is contrary to what the Bible teaches. The hope that the Bible proclaims is unlike the world's hope, for it is sure, steadfast, and certain, providing *true* rest, peace, and assurance.

When I think of Israel, I think of this hope. Israel has her hope in the God of Israel and His mighty promises. He has always been, and will always remain, faithful to Israel! Yet, an even greater hope proceeded forth from Israel. It is through Israel that the true and "blessed hope" came, the fulfillment of hope for Israel, for gentiles such as I, and for the whole world: Jesus.

Israel has always shined, and continues to shine, as a bright light in this world and as a true symbol of hope rooted in God's goodness and faithfulness.

GOD'S CHOSEN WITNESSES

by

DR. BILLYE BRIM

When my husband (only forty-nine) passed away in 1986, I sought the Lord for His will for my life. His answer, so clearly impressed upon my spirit, surprised me. *Go to Israel and study Hebrew in the Land.*

Friends in Israel recommended the unique language school, *Ulpan Akiva,* in Netanya but warned that I would probably not be accepted. Its founder, Shulamith Katznelson, was appalled that Christian students had taken the ulpan's Hebrew for use in missionary activities. Against all odds, I was accepted.

Shulamith and I became close. I walked with her during two nominations for the Nobel Prize. I stood with her family at the funeral memorial for her brother, Shmuel Tamir, Minister of Justice. The two joint Prime Ministers, Peres and Shamir, passed before me as they paid their respects. This great lady introduced me to much more than national leaders: *Am Israel* (the people) and *Eretz Israel* (the Land).

I was thrilled on a field trip to Neot Kedumim, the Biblical Landscape Reserve, by their explanation of the early and later rains. I exclaimed to Shulamith, "Oh, I wish my Christian friends could see what I'm seeing."

She said, "Bring them."

And thus began our "seminar tours" in 1987. Shulamith arranged for us to eat and sleep in the homes of the Druzim, to be received by the Samaritan high priest, and to know pioneers in Judea and Samaria. We were the first foreign guests of the hotel Eschel HaShomron, in Ariel, the capital of Samaria.

We continued long after Shulamith's death. We experienced war, intifadas, and the return of Jews to their Promised Land. I worked in Soviet Russia from 1980 to 1991, where I knew the plight of the Russian Jewish refusniks. Then I was blessed to witness their miracle return from the north (Jer. 16:14–15; 23:7–8). Our friends in Ariel, from the youngest to the oldest, absorbed the Russian Jews so well. We enjoyed

the senior citizen Russian choir and the young dancers and singers.

Through the years, a few thousand have been enlightened to the miracle of Israel by the exceptional experiences of our seminar tours and will continue to do so as we build a place in Migdal in Galilee.

Israel's Calling

Immediately after the nations fell at the tower of Babel (Gen. 11), the Creator introduced Abram and the nation He separated to Himself for His purposes. Through these chosen people, God revealed Himself to the nations.

Plan A, I call it, was for Israel to live in their Promised Land at the crossroads of travel. Caravans and armies would pass through and see the people who worshiped the One Unseen God and the blessings that He bestowed upon them (Deut. 28:1–14).

Plan B was that if they strayed, He would scatter them to the earth's

four corners. But He would still preserve them as a nation. At the end of days, He would bring them back to their Promised Land—their gifts and callings still in effect, revealing God to the nations (Rom. 11:29).

The nations of this earth are to recognize His great sign—*the Miracle of Israel*, for it is a witness to the reality that God is alive and real and His Word is true.

Israel, the Jews, are God's witnesses on earth. Nations and men will give an account of how they appreciated or disdained His witness, whether they blessed or cursed God's chosen people.

"But now thus says the Lord, he who created you, O Jacob, he who formed you, O Israel: 'Fear not, for I have redeemed you; I have called you by name, you are mine…. You are my witnesses,' declares the Lord, 'and my servant whom I have chosen, that you may know and believe me and understand that I am he.'" (Isa. 43:1, 10).

TIKKUN OLAM
by
REV. REBECCA J. BRIMMER

A vineyard in Samaria

My love for Israel began before I was born. My father clearly remembered the day Israel became a nation. He'd heard the prophecies about the rebirth of Israel from an early age. On May 14, 1948, the news of Israel's rebirth was announced on the loudspeaker in his high school. It was electrifying. Every hair on his body stood straight up—God was real and proving Himself by fulfilling His promises to the Jewish people.

The Bible is full of the miracle-working power of God. The Exodus from Egypt, Jonah and the big fish, and Elijah calling down fire from heaven are just a few examples.

Modern-day Israel is one of the most compelling proofs that God is still active today. This tiny nation and its people are a powerful testimony to the character of God. He is faithful even when we are faithless. He is covenant-keeping, trustworthy, and a loving, merciful God.

There is a famous story in which the German Kaiser asked his chancellor, Otto von Bismarck, "Can you prove the existence of God?"

Von Bismarck replied, "The Jews, Your Majesty. The Jews."

On this small piece of oceanfront real estate, God is showing the world that He can be trusted to keep His word.

Israel's first Prime Minister, David Ben-Gurion, summarized the situation when he said that to be a realist in Israel, you must believe in miracles!

Improbable Miracles

Think of the statistical improbabilities of the miracles surrounding the birth of the State of Israel.

1. The ingathering of the Jewish people from over one hundred nations after a 1,900-year dispersion while keeping their identity is astonishing. Never has another people group who were dispersed worldwide for millennia come back to their ancient homeland.

2. Even though the Jewish people returned without a shared language, Hebrew—a nearly extinct language—was revived into a modern language. Today, it is a living, vibrant language of both the sacred and profane—another miracle.

3. Mark Twain visited the Land during the 1800s and described it as a "blistering, naked, treeless land." He called the villages "ugly, cramped, squalid, uncomfortable and filthy" (Twain, 1869). There were reportedly less than one thousand trees.

But the Jewish people returned, drained the swamps, irrigated the deserts, and planted millions of trees. Israel is the only nation that entered the twenty-first century with a net gain in its number of trees, made more remarkable that this was achieved in an area considered mainly desert. Today, the Land is a place of productive beauty. There is a special connection between the fruitfulness of the Land of Israel and the Jewish people, a direct result of God's special covenant with them.

In Genesis 12:3, God promised Abraham the world would be blessed through him. As a Christian, I appreciate that everything precious to our faith comes from the Jewish people: the Bible; the patriarchs; the prophets; the apostles; and Jesus.

Additionally, the Jewish people have blessed the whole world through technology, computers, medical advancements, and entertainment. Israel shows up to help whenever there is a disaster. The concept of *tikkun olam* (repairing the world) is a beautiful example of Israel showing the character of God to those in need.

As the leader of Bridges for Peace, I am often asked why I want to support Israel and bless the Jewish people. It's because I love the God of Israel and the Bible. There's no greater purpose in my life than to partner with the God of Israel as He shows the world His character through His actions in Israel. In the past seventy-five years, we have been chosen to witness and be part of the miracle of Israel.

Kayaking off the beaches of Tel Aviv

THE MIRACLE OF MODERN ISRAEL

by

DR. MICHAEL L. BROWN

Some years ago, when speaking to a group of high school students in a Christian school about the existence of God, I put forward this simple statement: "I think, therefore, God exists." In other words, the fact that we exist as sentient, feeling, rational, extraordinarily complex beings amid an extraordinarily complex universe is proof of God's existence. I see no other scientifically logical way to explain human existence and consciousness.

In the same way, as a committed believer in the God of the Scriptures, I see no way to explain the modern State of Israel other than the result of God's explicit will. How can I be so confident?

First, the Scriptures make it perfectly clear that Israel is to be the lasting homeland of the Jewish people.

God Himself promised this repeatedly in scores of different texts, most clearly in Psalm 105. In fact, in this passage alone, the theme is repeated so many different ways

that it's almost redundant. The Lord was making a point!

The psalm states,

"He remembers his covenant forever, the word that he commanded, for a thousand generations, the covenant that he made with Abraham, his sworn promise to Isaac, which he confirmed to Jacob as a statute, to Israel as an everlasting covenant, saying, 'To you, I will give the land of Canaan as your portion for an inheritance'" (105:8–11).

Notice the vocabulary used. This is God's covenant, His eternal covenant, the promise He made, His statute; this was something He swore and confirmed. It is eternal, for a thousand generations. Could He have made Himself any more clear?

It's true that under the law—the Sinai Covenant—God said He would exile His people from their homeland if they sinned and bring them back if they repented. But this does not annul His previous promises.

As Paul explained, *"This is what I mean: the law, which came 430 years afterward"*—meaning, 430 years after God gave His promise to Abraham—*"does not annul a covenant previously ratified by God, so as to make the promise void. For if the inheritance comes by the law, it no longer comes by promise; but God gave it to Abraham by a promise"* (Gal. 3:17–18).

That promise still stands.

Second, it's impossible to explain the existence of the Jewish people in their ancient homeland today without divine intervention. No other nation has been expelled from its homeland for hundreds of years only to return to its original homeland with its identity intact. Every other nation scattered from its homeland for centuries has ceased to exist as a nation, without exception—except for the Jewish people.

Jewish people survived as a nation despite centuries of terrible suffering, being expelled from country after country, herded together in ghettos, reduced to second-class citizenship, and sometimes even facing annihilation—most recently, under the Nazis. Yet the Jewish people live—as celebrated in Hebrew, *Am Yisrael Chai*—because God has preserved them.

As a Jew myself, I can say He has preserved us—not because of our faithfulness but because of *His* faithfulness, not because of our goodness but because of His goodness.

And think: the Nazis slaughtered six million Jews—two out of every three Jews in Europe—and yet today, more than six million Jews live in Israel. This could not have happened without the hand of God.

This is supported by Scripture, based on simple biblical logic. According to Scripture, when God blesses, no one can curse, and when He curses, no one can bless. When He opens a door, no one can close it; when He closes a door, no one can open it. When He smites, no one can heal; when He heals, no one can smite.

In the same way, when He gathers, no one can scatter, and when He scatters, no one can gather. And since the Bible tells us that God scattered the Jewish people in His anger, there's only one possible way they can be back in the Land today—God Himself regathered them!

To suggest that the Jewish people themselves, or the United Nations reestablished Israel, is to say that God's will was overthrown by human effort. Perish the thought!

This also explains why there is such extreme hostility towards the State of Israel, why so many radical groups want to wipe out the Jewish State, why the world's nations want to determine Israel's boundaries, and why these same nations refuse to recognize Jerusalem as Israel's capital.

It's the same pattern that has existed for millennia: the nations are hostile to the purposes of God, in particular, His purposes for Israel. This doesn't mean that everything Israel does is right or everything the Palestinians do is wrong. It doesn't mean that lovers of the God of the Bible should not pursue justice for all Middle Eastern peoples. But it does mean the State of Israel exists today because God decreed it. It is a modern miracle, indeed.

ENCOUNTERS WITH FORGIVENESS IN ISRAEL

by

STEVE BROWN

Christians have a murky history with the Jews. Many treated Jews horrifically in the name of Jesus. Several of us in Miami, where I pastored, held a dinner to ask forgiveness of Jews for the part Christians played in the antisemitic horrors throughout history. I said, "On behalf of my Christian brothers and sisters, I ask your forgiveness. I'm sorry and ashamed. There are many others who aren't here this evening who affirm the need for forgiveness."

Painting by Udi Merioz

An older Jewish man said, "Aren't you going to ask us to become Christians or to 'come to Jesus?' There's got to be a catch. You only want to ask for forgiveness?"

"Yes," I said. "That's all."

To my surprise, the man began to cry and said, "I don't know you, and you're asking me for forgiveness?" Then he told the dinner group his story.

As a schoolboy, gentile boys would wait for him under a bridge as he walked home. "Then, sometimes with clubs and sticks, they would chase me shouting, 'Christ killer!' I didn't kill Christ. I didn't even know who Christ was. As I got older and successful in business, I heard many antisemitic jokes from associates. I was humiliated. This is the first time I've heard any true remorse. Thank you."

Hatred is expected from those who have never experienced the unconditional love of God. But how in the world could Christians have so much hostility toward Jews? Since Judaism is our mother, most of our Scriptures are Jewish, our founder is Jewish, and our adopted heritage is Jewish, antisemitism is a major anomaly.

A few years after that dinner, I traveled to Israel to find answers to my questions. Few books had been written about antisemitism; most were so academic that only scholars read them. My research produced very few answers to my questions, questions I still have.

How could Martin Luther advocate the burning of synagogues, confiscating Jewish property, and destroying Jewish Talmudic writings? And it wasn't just Martin Luther. The list of Christians hating Jews is quite long. From Justin Martyr in the second century to Origen in the third century and Eusebius in the fourth century, Christian leaders made the spurious claim that Jews intended to kill Christians. Chrysostom, Cyril, Jerome, Augustine, and so many other Christian leaders said unconscionable things about Jews, things I can't even quote without wincing. When the Crusaders swept across Europe on their way to the Holy Land, they asked, "Why go to the Holy Land to kill the heathen,

when heathen live in our midst?" The torture and killing of Jews that followed were horrific. Then there are the pogroms, the national cleansing from Christian nations, and the persecution. The list goes on.

The picture, of course, isn't totally bleak. There have been many Christians like Corrie ten Boom and her family in Holland who helped Jewish people escape from the Nazis during Shoah, and themselves went to the death camps. The Sisters of Mary (a Lutheran Order of nuns started in Darmstadt, Germany) opened a guesthouse for Holocaust survivors in Jerusalem. An increasing number of Christians worldwide have recognized our "family connection" to Israel and rejoice in it.

But still, there is the stain of history. Even today, some Christians refuse to affirm God's love for Jerusalem, Israel, and His ancient people.

Then there are surprises. I visited the Avenue and Garden of the Righteous Among the Nations in Israel. I read over the long list of those who stood with Israel and Jews and heard the stories about gentiles who—often at great personal cost—stood with God's ancient people.

That those gentiles are honored isn't so much a surprise—but that I was encouraged by so many Israelis, welcomed into their homes, and supported in my Christian faith, is. Given our history, I was humbled.

Forgiveness always surprises me. We live in a "cancel culture" where there is little recognition of human frailty, and forgiveness is in short supply. How do you explain the forgiveness of those who have been horribly wronged? That's what I experienced from those friends at the dinner party and in Israel.

Israel really is a miracle for so many reasons. But Israel's willingness to forgive is also a miracle.

Photo by David Kiern

53

THE UNSTOPPABLE RESTORATION
by
DR. JUERGEN BUEHLER

Elon Moreh

As Israel marks the 75th anniversary of her rebirth as a nation, there is much for Christians to celebrate. We see in Israel's restoration clear evidence that God keeps His covenant promises, including physical and spiritual restoration. The prophetic fulfillment of these glorious promises has been happening before our eyes for more than seven decades.

Yet some Christians believe that the worst for Israel lies ahead during the Great Tribulation. However, the Word of God assures us that the people of Israel have already endured the worst through their exile, and although troubles may still lie ahead, Israel will be delivered from them all!

A Complete Turn-Around

In Zechariah, God declares, *"And as you have been a byword of cursing among the nations, O house of Judah and house of Israel, so will I save you, and you shall be a blessing. Fear not, but let your hands be strong" (8:13).*

After AD 70, when the Romans sacked Jerusalem and the Temple, Jewish history could be defined by destruction, desolation, dispersion, and persecution.

Today, however, Israel is best described as a Land of rebuilding, not destruction. Ancient ruins have been rebuilt into modern, vibrant cities. *"And they will say, 'This land that was desolate has become like the garden of Eden, and the waste and desolate and ruined cities are now fortified and*

The entrance to the City of David in Jerusalem

inhabited'" (Ezek. 36:35).

God has determined a new season for Israel (Isa. 43:19; 48:6).

It is no longer desolation but replenishment. Israel is the only country where the deserts are in retreat. Israeli flowers and fruits are exported around the world. *"...Jacob shall take root, Israel shall blossom and put forth shoots and fill the whole world with fruit" (Isa. 27:6).*

It is no longer dispersion and scattering, but ingathering. Almost half of world Jewry lives in the Land of Israel. *"I will take you from the nations and gather you from all the countries and bring you into your own land" (Ezek. 36:24).*

While Israelis still face hostility, they are supported by tens of millions of Christians. *"Foreigners shall build up your walls, and their kings shall minister to you; for in my wrath I struck you, but in my favor I have had mercy on you" (Isa. 60:10).* God's actions with Israel align with His prophetic Word. He has dramatically shifted from judgment and reproof to restoration and redemption.

Looking back over the past seventy-five years, the clear and defining trends are all positive, despite the wars and terrorism. Israel is on an upward trajectory, and it's because God's mercy and favor are upon her.

The New Paradigm of Favor

The Hebrew prophets indicate that nothing can stop God's restoration with Israel.

For instance, the prophet Isaiah starts his restoration chapters with the call to *"comfort my people ... and cry to her that her warfare is ended, that her iniquity is pardoned..." (Isa. 40:1–2).*

God has started an unwavering restoration process. This doesn't mean He'll never again correct Israel like a loving father does his son—it will be done "with measure," even as He humbles the other nations (Jer. 30:11).

The calling of the International Christian Embassy Jerusalem is to declare the season of God's mercy and favor upon Zion (Ps. 102:13; Isa. 40:1–2). It's a message of "comfort" to Israel and a challenge to the Church to join God in this great restoration process.

God is passionate about redeeming His family from the nations and restoring Israel. It's not a sideshow while His "real" work is among the gentiles.

Thus, there is much reason to rejoice as we mark seventy-five years of Israel's national restoration.

Painting "The Second Jewish Temple" by Alex Levin, Israel.

56

ISRAEL'S LONG JOURNEY:
FROM EXILE TO RESTORATION
by
SHIRLEY BURDICK

Ever since God told Pharaoh, "Let my son go, so he may worship me," Israel, God's firstborn son, has been on a long journey.

Like Abraham, generations of Israel have believed God's promises no matter how unbearable their lives have been, so they returned after an exile of more than 1,800 years with their belief, memory, and distinct identity intact.

In 2004, while in the Old City, my husband and I heard a group of American Jewish teenagers shout, "Let's hear from Josh's grandfather!"

A grandfather stood up to face the teens sitting on the steps of the Roman Cardo.

"What should we do with that golden dome over there?" Josh's grandfather pointed towards the Temple Mount.

"Negotiate."

"Pray."

"Blow it up!"

"America will take care of it!"

"Maybe the UN will do something?" The kids happily laughed and shouted out answers.

"Boys, we wait! Hashem promised that there would again be a Temple. We wait for Him to move, and we raise Jewish children to believe His promises. If I don't see it, Josh may see it. If Josh doesn't see it, his children and grandchildren may see it. The Jewish hope must be passed down. Look, we are already back! Mashiach will come. Hashem will do it because He already said He would."

Is that not faith?

This faith was not handed to them when they left Egypt to ensure a successful journey. It has developed through the journey. After their first major rebellion when they refused to enter the Promised Land, Moses said, *"And you shall remember the whole way that the Lord your God has led you these forty years in the wilderness, that he might humble you, testing you to know what was in your heart, whether you would keep his commandments or not"* (Deut. 8:2). Testing and hardship set the tone for Israel for the next three thousand-plus years.

The testing resulted in many failures, but God never ended their journey. When the tribes failed to drive out the nations as God commanded, He had a plan. *"Now these are the nations that the Lord left, to test Israel by them, that is, all in Israel who had not experienced all the wars in Canaan. It was only in order that the generations of the people of Israel might know war, to teach war to those who had not known it before"* (Judg. 3:1–2).

When Israel's sins were great, God was angry but continued with them. *"Therefore, thus says the Lord of hosts: 'Behold, I will refine them and test them, for what else can I do, because of my people?'"* (Jer. 9:7).

This journey of millennia has transformed Israel through testing and refining. We can see the transformation throughout Scripture.

In the Hebrew Scripture (Old Testament), Israel wouldn't give up idolatry. The first Temple was destroyed and the people went into exile because of idol worship. But later, in the Christian Scripture (New Testament), the subject of idol worship never comes up. Idol worship was no longer an issue in Jewish society in the Second Temple period. They transformed!

And, we know the last Jewish dynasty of the Second Temple period, the Hasmonean Dynasty, ruled its people with cruelty. According to traditional Jewish thought, the people again went into exile due to baseless hatred among each other. But now, Israeli society is like a big family. They feel each other's joy and pain; strangers laugh, dance, and mourn together. They are concerned with compassion and justice while observing God's commandments, even to the extent of Ultra-Orthodox men driving ambulances on the Sabbath. Again, they transformed and prevailed!

Where does this journey lead Israel? The Bible verse that inspired us to start the non-profit, Ten Gentiles, says, *"Thus, says the Lord of hosts: In those days ten men from the nations of every tongue shall take hold of the robe of a Jew, saying, 'Let us go with you, for we have heard that God is with you'"* (Zech. 8:23). Zechariah gave us the picture of Israel being the spiritual leader for the nations. When that time comes, Israel will be ready, and the nations will finally acknowledge and come alongside her.

Looking at Israel's journey, we are in awe of the people and of God. We fully believe in the glorious future that God Himself already ordained for Israel:

"'Behold, the days are coming,' declares the Lord, 'when I will make a new covenant with the house of Israel and with the house of Judah...'" (Jer. 31:31).

"I have already redeemed you" (Isa. 43:1; 44:22; 44:23; 48:20).

"I will redeem them from death" (Hos. 13:14).

"At that time I will bring you in, at the time when I gather you together; for I will make you renowned and praised among all the peoples of the earth, when I restore your fortunes before your eyes,' says the Lord" (Zeph. 3:20).

And many, many more.

We have already seen the start of Israel's restoration, and with God, Israel will accomplish it.

Happy 75th birthday, State of Israel! We rejoice with you!

Haifa port celebrating Israel's 75th anniversary

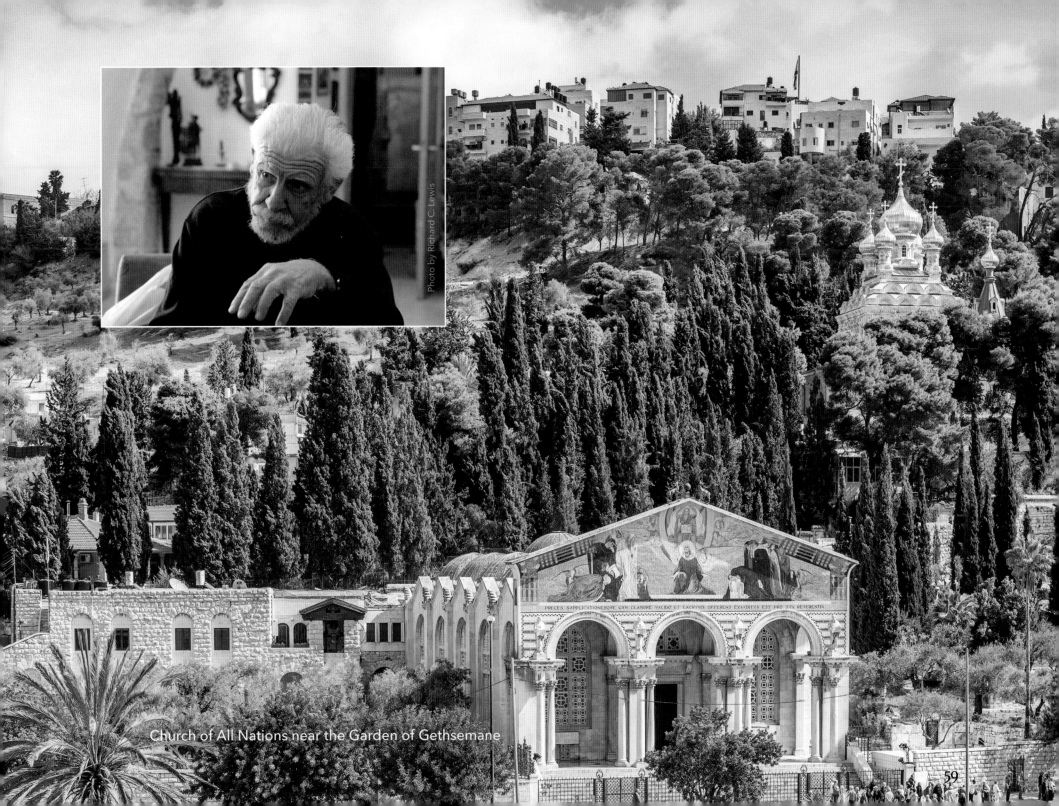

Photo by Richard C. Lewis

Church of All Nations near the Garden of Gethsemane

59

THE LAST QUESTION
by
NATHANIEL BUZOLIC

Seventy-five years ago, a nation was established in a day.

Seventy-five years ago, a dormant promise of God was brought back to life.

A nation that had been abruptly stamped out made an unexpected return to its ancestral homeland. *Am Yisrael Chai,* or "The People of Israel Live," was again boldly proclaimed by the physical descendants of Abraham, Isaac, and Jacob in the very Land God had sworn to their forefathers. The promise God confirmed throughout the books of the prophets has now become the physical proof of God's faithful character to His beloved.

However, 1,915 years before history would record Israel's stunning rebirth, a small group of Jewish men met on the Mount of Olives in Jerusalem. Former fishermen, ex-zealots, and retired tax collectors gathered around the man they believed was Israel's Messiah. In their midst was none other than their beloved Rabbi—Jesus of Nazareth. The rabbi who rose from the tomb. The prophet who called people back to God. The son of David who defeated our greatest enemy with a single strike of self-sacrificing love.

The second Temple still towered along the Jerusalem skyline, the Roman Empire still oppressed and controlled every aspect of Jewish life, and the disciples of this Bethlehem-born rabbi were still coming to grips with a risen Jesus who bore the scars of His fatal crucifixion.

The Gospels record the many questions these disciples asked Jesus over His three-and-a-half-year ministry. These historical accounts reveal the multitude of profound answers, statements, and commentaries Jesus gave them and others about the kingdom of God. But at this specific moment, there was only enough time to ask one final question. One last opportunity to get a clear answer from Jesus, their Messiah, before He would ascend on

Painting by Udi Merioz

a cloud to be at the right hand of the Ancient of Days, as both Psalm 110 and Daniel 7 so poetically outline.

So, what would the disciples ask? Would they seek further clarification on past events? Would they pursue a greater understanding of themselves? Would they ask about their next steps? Or their future ministry plans?

These men gathered in His presence and asked Jesus one simple yet revealing question:

"Lord, will you at this time restore the kingdom to Israel?" (Acts 1:6).

This was the last question from those who followed Jesus first, who witnessed His many signs and wonders, who would ultimately lay down their lives so that the Good News of God could be proclaimed to the ends of the earth. The disciples had a deep desire in their last moments with Jesus to know when they would see the kingdom of Israel fully restored.

This year, 2023, marks the 75th year of an event that saw a two thousand-year-old nation that had been previously wiped off the map reborn and re-energized.

Who could have predicted that those so profoundly pierced by the Holocaust could ever find a path to a new life in a distant land?

As a Christian who studies the Bible and reflects on God's covenant promises, I've realized that modern Israel is an ongoing miracle that many over the past two thousand years have longed to see but were unable to witness. What a privilege we have to be the generation who can say with confidence and undeniable evidence that the God of Israel keeps His promises.

I don't look at the rebirth of Israel as just a moment in history where an ethnic minority overcame impossible odds to regain their ancestral homeland. Nor do I see it as the simple formation of a Jewish State to regain its right of self-determination in the face of hostile enemies. From my point of view, Israel's official return is a divine event that allowed every nation, kingdom, empire, and individual who lived and breathed from 1948 onwards to witness the unbelievable resurrection power of a Living God.

The same Living God whom King David pursued.

The same Living God whom Abraham believed.

The same Living God whom the Jewish people have had a covenant relationship with since the giving of the Torah.

The same Living God who raised a dead nation back to life.

How did Jesus respond to the final question presented by His followers?

"*He said to them, 'It is not for you to know times or seasons that the Father has fixed by his own authority. But you will receive power when the Ruach ha-Kodesh [Holy Spirit] has come upon you, and you will be my witnesses in Jerusalem and in all Judea and Samaria, and to the end of the earth'*" (Acts 1:7–8).

To the Christian who reads these words—just as Israel returned as a nation, so too will its Promised King.

Let our hearts and minds be focused on this Land. Let our thoughts and prayers be for its first covenant people.

Painting by Udi Merioz

63

ISRAEL INDIVISIBLE:
THE 75TH ANNIVERSARY

by

LAURIE CARDOZA MOORE

I srael marks the 75th anniversary of its founding this year, honoring the remarkable story of its re-birth as a nation and its resilience to survive against all odds.

The ancient love story between the Jews and their homeland, the Land of Israel, dates back 3,500 years to the covenant God made with Abraham. Beyond revealing the Jews' deep roots in the Promised Land, the Bible records the unique nature of Jewish identity and God's everlasting commitment to them.

I had the honor of being the executive producer of Israel Indivisible, a long-form documentary recounting the story of Israel and the Jewish people as experienced by the people who lived and died to establish and hold God's Land. From Abraham and the promise to the fall of the Ottoman Empire, we took great pains to present the biblical, archeological, and historical evidence for the rightful Jewish ownership of ancient and modern Israel. From the early yearnings for Zion in the Diaspora to the search for peace today, the twists and turns of oppression and politics have made tiny Israel the most controversial nation, and the Jews who populate this small space of land the most persecuted of peoples.

At 4:00 p.m. on May 14, 1948, shortly before Sabbath, David Ben-Gurion read the Israeli Declaration of Independence in the Tel Aviv Museum of Art—today known as Independence Hall. Ben-Gurion affirmed the Jews' biblical roots in their Land—and their right to establish a state in their homeland. Launching this Jewish democracy,

Painting "Eyes of Life" by Alex Levin, Israel.

he offered "equality" to all the state's inhabitants. Even with equality, peace has alluded God's chosen. Israel has overcome legendary challenges to its right to exist.

Amidst their struggles, Zionism can toast seven miraculous achievements over the past seventy-five years.

1. After millennia of homelessness, the Jewish people re-established sovereignty over their ancient homeland. As promised by God, when the Jews returned, the Land bloomed and streams flowed in the desert, a modern miracle before our eyes!

2. Since 1948, Israel has integrated over three million immigrants—refugees fleeing persecution in the Arab lands, Ethiopia, and the former Soviet Union—coming home.

3. As the Jews have returned to their rightful place, sometimes facing complex dilemmas and persecutions from the global community, they're no longer victims.

4. Israel's Western-style democracy has maintained its unique Jewish heritage, expressed in the holidays, traditions, and Jewish national culture, while guaranteeing all citizens equal rights.

5. The model of the new Israel has balanced traditional values with trend-setting culture.

6. The once-dormant Hebrew language lives again throughout Israel!

7. For all its challenges, Israel has revolutionized and elevated the Jewish image worldwide.

Yet today, the world is seemingly divided into those who love Israel and support her people and those who abhor anything associated with Israel. As we observe this anniversary with our Jewish brethren, a new generation of antisemitism is sweeping the world. Europe is aflame with hatred of the Jews. American school children are fed antisemitic sentiments across a nation long credited with being Israel's greatest ally. Holocaust deniers abound on the dark internet while education on the most horrific event in history fades from hearts and minds just a short generation after humanity vowed: "Never again." Seeds of hatred are still tragically passed from one generation to the next—borne of long-held fear and ignorance and planted in the hearts of the innocent. We must vow to be the voice of change in support of Israel and our Jewish brethren.

God will have the last word over the affairs of man and His chosen Land! Psalm 121:4 tells us, *"Behold, he who keeps Israel will neither slumber nor sleep."*

As we celebrate Israel's Diamond Anniversary—we who love God and honor His commitment to Abraham must recommit ourselves to love, honor, and protect His chosen people and their eternal Land of Promise.

A view of Jerusalem's Hadassah Medical Center

VISITING ISRAEL AND LEAVING A NEW PERSON

by

DR. BEN CARSON

It was December 2014 and an experience I will never forget—my first journey to Israel. I was deeply considering a run for president of the United States. During that time, relations between the United States and Israel could be described as cold at best. As the only democracy in the Middle East and an unwavering ally to the United States, I felt it of utmost importance to travel to Israel to gain firsthand knowledge of what the people and policymakers face daily.

Upon arrival, I could not help but reflect on my Christian faith. My faith is the driving force of my life—to see the Holy Land in person and to reflect upon those beliefs at the various holy sites was moving. Of all the holy sites I visited, I felt the most profound impact at the Western Wall. The serene, peaceful feeling upon approaching the wall and placing my hand on it was truly an experience.

As I continued traveling throughout Israel, I could not have been more appreciative of the warm and hospitable reception of the Israeli people. I met with various religious leaders, military leaders, and medical professionals who provided valuable insight into the many problems facing the country and its people. The stories of tragedy, challenges, and triumphs that the people faced were moving and insightful. One of the more touching meetings conducted during my time in Israel was with members of the neurosurgery team at Jerusalem's Hadassah Medical Center. As a retired pediatric neurosurgeon, I know the amount of time and work that goes into the practice. Seeing that great work done halfway around the world was truly heartening.

I was able to tour Israel's borders to understand the security threats the country faces daily. The flying tour I received gave me a bird's eye view of the strategic challenges and threats on Israel's every side. The proximity of the danger Israel faces cannot be understood until you see it face to face. Surrounded by enemies who seek her demise, it's truly amazing that Israel has managed not only to survive but thrive.

As I wrapped up my trip to Israel, I regained fresh hope in the future relations between the United States and Israel. Although that relationship was strained then, the bond between Americans and Israelis is strong and cannot be broken over disagreements between policymakers and leaders.

There is no argument that Israel is a special place. The epicenter of many of the world's largest religions leaves a lasting impact on those who have the privilege of visiting. I will never forget my visit to Israel and the people I was blessed to meet. It is a truly inspiring and special place that will always hold a special place in my heart and the hearts of many.

THE LAND BETWEEN:
WHERE THE PAST AND PRESENT MEET TO DEEPEN YOUR FAITH

by

PASTOR DOUG CLAY

The Assemblies of God denomination believes you will understand the Bible and grow in your faith and love for God as you journey to and through Israel.

> Five gospels record the life of Jesus. Four you will find in books and the one you will find in the land they call Holy. Read the fifth gospel and the world of the four will open to you. (Jerome, AD 347–420)

If you want to learn all you can about a subject, visiting the origin of that subject is important. Jerome, in the third century AD, understood that the Land of Israel is the fifth gospel.

As you travel through the Land of Israel, you will survey the Old and New Testament, focusing on their culture, history, geography, and spiritual climate. The Land, the text, and the journey are always a transformational experience for you and your faith.

No longer will you simply read about biblical locations; now you will be able to picture them in your mind. You will recall the smells, the heat and cold, and the feel of the Land with its hills and canyons—all the while realizing how these elements played a part in the biblical narrative.

Understanding the brilliance of the placement of Israel as a strategic center for the spread of the gospel to all nations will humble you. It will become apparent to you that God placed people in certain locations to get His message out to the rest of the world. It's amazing to stand on ancient sites and roadways and discuss our predecessors of faith, like Abraham, who settled in Be'er-Sheva, located along the major roads that enabled the message of faith in the one true God to spread across the ancient world.

Israel is the "land between." To get anywhere in the East-West world of ancient times, people had to travel through Israel; it was the crossroad of the ancient world, connecting Asia and Africa. If you want to get a message out, spread it from the crossroads!

All aspects of Israel are important. As you walk through the Coastal Plain, the Central Hill Country, the Rift Valley, and the Transjordan, the ground you walk is the very place where obedience, faith, trust, hope, and redemption unfolded. And as you walk, it will continue to unfold for you as well.

HONORING OUR ROOTS:
WHY CHRISTIANS SHOULD STAND WITH ISRAEL
by
PASTOR TERRI COPELAND PEARSONS

What a wonderful time to celebrate seventy-five years of the modern Jewish State! It's an awakening for many to realize that this Jewish homeland is here to stay.

As Christians and leaders of a long-lived church and ministry, my family and I offer an enthusiastic "Hallelujah!"

Our support for Israel, both the Land and its people, has raised eyebrows among Christians and Jews. The big question is always, "Why do you stand with Israel?"

One answer is found in a basic tenet of Judaism: Honor!

My parents always taught us honor and respect. I remember my dad, Kenneth Copeland, pointing out a police officer, saying, "Kids, that man is your friend. If you need him, he will be there for you. But treat him with respect!"

The family rule is never to allow an officer, firefighter, or soldier to pay for their own meal when it is within our means to pay for it. My mother insisted we show respect to everyone. She didn't tolerate unkindness just because of someone's social or economic status or because they weren't part of the "popular crowd." I received a good scolding for not showing respect where respect was due.

But I have never seen honor taken to such a high degree as explained in the Chumash. I read the commentaries by Jewish sages and am in awe at the insights and depth to which honor is revealed. It is stunning.

No man is brilliant enough to originate a concept like honor. Honor could only come from God Himself. He is the One who first defined honor and exemplified it by crowning man with glory and honor (Ps. 8:5). A stand-out observation while reading through Torah commentaries is that honor is directed to the source or starting point. For example, we are commanded to honor our parents. Why? Because we are a product of a threefold cord: mother, father, and God. Honoring parents honors the God-and-man union—the source from which we came.

To follow that pattern, I must look at what is most precious to me and find the source of it. What is most dear to me? My relationship with the Lord. My Christian faith brought me to this marvelous walk with the King of the universe.

But where did my Christian faith come from? Its root is in the Word of God, which came through Jews.

Let's remember the patriarchs—Abraham, Isaac, and Jacob—were Jews.

Moses and all the prophets were Jews. The first family of Christianity, Joseph and Mary, were Jews. The twelve apostles were Jews. The apostle Paul was a Jew. Temple worship and the law, the foundation for civilized society, came through Jews.

Important to me is the fact that Jesus is Jewish. He never denied His Jewishness. He said, *"Truly, I say to you, as you did it to one of the least of these my brothers, you did it to me" (Matt. 25:40).* It wasn't gentiles He was calling His brethren. If the Jews were His brethren then, they are still His brethren now!

Judaism is the very root of Christianity. Judaism needs no explanation for its existence. Without Judaism, Christianity has no right to exist. We are a branch from that Jewish root. The branch cannot continue to live without the root, while the root goes on, with or without the branch.

When the New Testament speaks of a "New Covenant," the word "new" comes from a Greek word that does NOT mean "new" as in starting from scratch—like throwing out something old that is no longer needed and replacing it with something new. Rather, it means "new" as in "fresh," like a new branch on a bush or a new rosebud on an existing stem. Beautiful, isn't it?

Since Jews are a vital part of what Christians hold most dear, we must honor them, which is our privilege and delight! When we do what the Lord wants, the way He wants, there is such joyous reward!

Genesis 12:3 says, *"I will bless those who bless you, and him who dishonors you I will curse…."* Let's add to that the nature of God. Ezekiel 1:27 says God is a fire from the loins upward and a fire from the loins downward—burning with *chesed,* love that demands expression. God's love compels Him to confer blessing on mankind. Second Chronicles 16:9 says the eyes of the Lord search at a terrific pace throughout the whole earth just looking for someone to show Himself strong; to, someone to show the blessing of His love. Apparently, in ancient times so few would allow Him to show even a little of His extravagant kindness, until Abram.

Finally! A man who would believe all that God promised him and trust Him enough to obey completely. Although it was only one man, it was a start. But how could the Lord satisfy His great burning compassion through only one man? I have imagined their original conversation perhaps going something like this:

The Lord came to Abram and said,

"Look, Abram, I am the Almighty and I have great desire and full ability to bless you in every way there is to be blessed. Look at the stars. Look at how masterfully I placed them in the sky. I will teach you how the order and the wonders of the universe work. Look at their beauty. Did you know they sing? I will share with you My ability to create marvelous sights and sounds. Look at the sand, Abram. See how it holds back the water? I will show you how to hold back the ravages of sickness and disease, to prevent what can be prevented and to cure what can be cured. I will bless you beyond measure. But there are conditions to this enormous outpouring."

Abram: "Yes, Lord."

The Lord: "You must NEVER hold these things just for yourself. They are for all of humanity. For this is My will and My great passion—to bless humanity. Do you understand?"

Abram: "Well, yes, Lord. Except how can I do this all by myself? In all my lifetime, I couldn't reach all of humanity! I am only one man!"

The Lord: "Abram, I have a plan that covers that! First, look again at the stars in the sky. Can you count them? Look again at the grains of sand beneath your feet. Can you count them? I will multiply your seed into numbers beyond what you can see because your seed will last forever. And each of them will carry this same blessing if they will carry the same purpose—to help Me bless all men."

Abram: "Okay, Lord, okay. I'm starting to see the picture!"

The Lord: "But, Abram, that's not all. Even that is not enough to satisfy My compassions. This blessing of abundance in every scope of life that will be upon you to bless all the nations will also come on anyone who will help you to be that blessing."

Abram: "Oh, Lord! That is marvelous! I know! We could call this Abram, Av, Hammon, Goyim—Father of Many Nations and God Enterprises."

The Lord: "Abram, I have a much better idea. Let Me take the letter 'hay' from My name, Elohim, and just put it in the middle of your name. Easier to remember. Better marketing."

Abram: "All right, Lord! Abraham, it is!"

All lightheartedness aside, Jews account for 22 percent of all Nobel Prize winners and yet are only 0.2 percent of the global population. Jews have led the way for millennia in fields from science to the arts. Our world would be shocked to know how much is owed to the blessing that rests upon God's covenant people and their commitment to passing that blessing on to others.

This is why all of us: our family, the congregation of Eagle Mountain International Church, and the Partners of Kenneth Copeland Ministries, look for ways to show honor to the Jewish people for all they mean to us and to the world. It is our privilege to bless them as they continue building the Land of Israel, which is a testament to our covenant-keeping God.

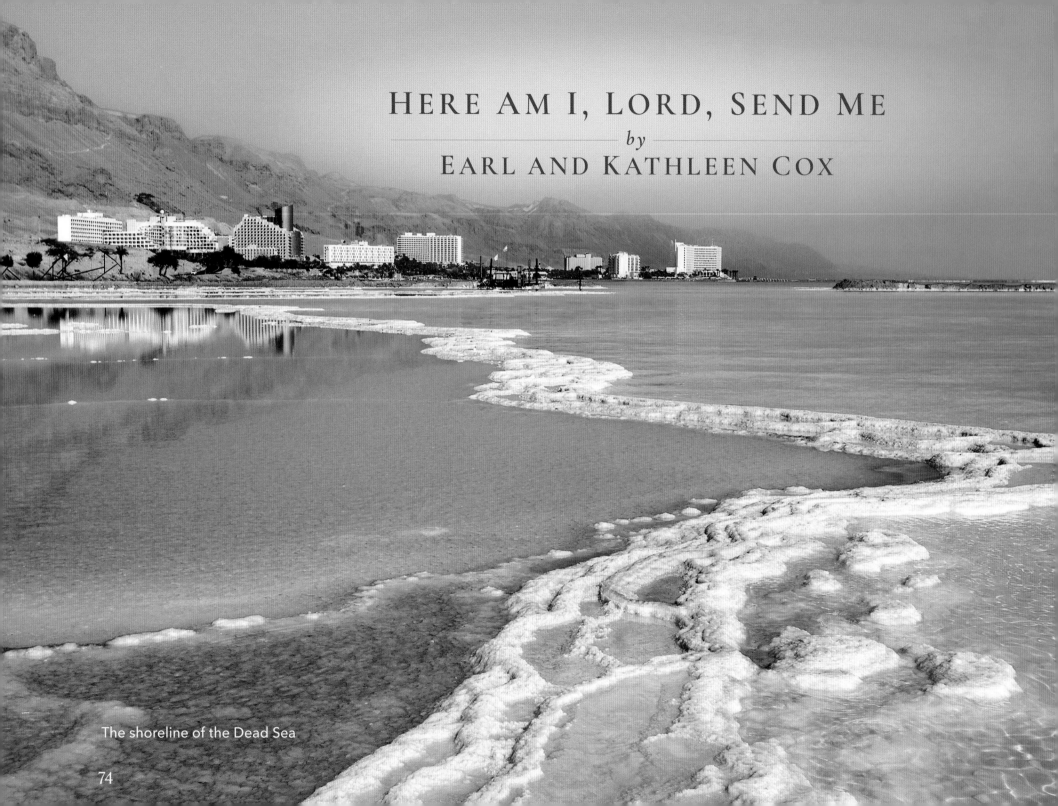

HERE AM I, LORD, SEND ME
by
EARL AND KATHLEEN COX

The shoreline of the Dead Sea

We've known the Lord most of our lives, however, He lived in our heads and not our hearts. The day the Lord called us to advocate for Israel and the Jewish people was transformational. Our faith in Jesus Christ moved from knowing about the Lord to knowing the Lord. At that time, we weren't remotely interested in Israel nor had any clear connection with Jewish people. We had to study a map to find Israel's exact location. God couldn't have picked less qualified people to advocate for Israel, Jews, and the Middle East. As a result, we made assumptions that seemed logical but were wrong.

First of all, we believed that Israelis and Jews would be thrilled to know that they have Christian friends to stand with them in adversity. Second, we believed that all Christians embrace Israel as God's special Land and the Jews as His chosen people. Third, we believed that all Jewish people were pro-Israel. Wrong, wrong, and wrong again.

During an early visit to the Holy Land, God revealed that our "Good News" was not necessarily good news for the Jews, and He used a petite, middle-aged women to bring us this enlightened message. This first lesson came from a daughter of Holocaust survivors. She shared her mothers' stories. One snowy, freezing evening in December, a song reached

the ears of the Jewish prisoners huddled in the camp. Her mother and the others were without heat, in threadbare clothes, burlap for blankets, covered in lice, dirty, starving, and many at death's door. From the barrack across the field, "Joy to the World" rang from the mouths of their savage Nazi tormentors. This is how many Jewish people were introduced to Christianity.

We were naive to think that we would immediately be welcomed as friends. Nothing we'd been taught in church prepared us for the historical truth of why Jewish people haven't accepted Christians. We were appalled to learn that much of Hitler's crimes were in the name of Christianity and that some of his Nazi thugs were church leaders and pastors who, after the Holocaust, went back to pastoring churches... Christian churches. Christian silence was deafening then, just as it is now. How can we possibly claim to love Jesus and not also love His family?

Each time Jewish people honor Holocaust victims, they repeat the words, "Never again!" These words must become ours, too. We must vow to never again be silent in the face of discrimination and anti-Israel propaganda. But vowing is not enough. We must support our promise with our actions.

Our second lesson came when we learned about "replacement theology" — a false teaching perpetrated within many mainstream Christian denominations which essentially states that God is done with the Jews, that the Church has replaced Israel, and that Christians have replaced the Jews as God's chosen people. "After all," many reasons, "aren't the Jews responsible for the death of Jesus?" Absolutely not! Our sins placed Him on that cross. No, Christians have not replaced Jews, and the Church has not replaced Israel.

The third lesson we learned changed our mistaken assumption that all Jews naturally support Israel and her right to exist as a Jewish State, which proved to be false for reasons too complicated to expound upon in this context. Israelis value life — all life — including the lives of Palestinians. Jews seem to have a collective heart to protect others from the sufferings they have endured throughout history. It matters not that the underdog status portrayed by the Palestinians and others may be a fabrication of the liberal media and the expert Palestinian PR machine. Israelis are all too ready to accept the blame.

Yet when confronted with evil acts of antisemitism and blatant injustice, it simply isn't part of their culture to protest loudly in their defense. This is what makes Christian support for Israel so crucial at this moment in time. Christians owe Jews a debt of gratitude.

God chose them to record, preserve, and protect His Word and pass it down from generation to generation, which they have faithfully accomplished.

Through Christ, we gentiles have been grafted into the natural olive tree, which is Israel. Through this grafting, God brought us into a new relationship with Him. If we truly love Jesus, we must also love His family. An attack on the Jews is an attack on all who love God. We must stand up and speak out in support and defense of Israel and the Jewish people. If not us, then who? If not now, then when? "Here we are! Send us," must be our response (Isa. 6:8).

We must stand up and speak out in support and defense of Israel and the Jewish people. If not us, then who? If not now, then when?

A CALL TO ENCOUNTER:
HOW A JOURNEY TO ISRAEL ALTERS LIVES
by
DR. TONY CRISP

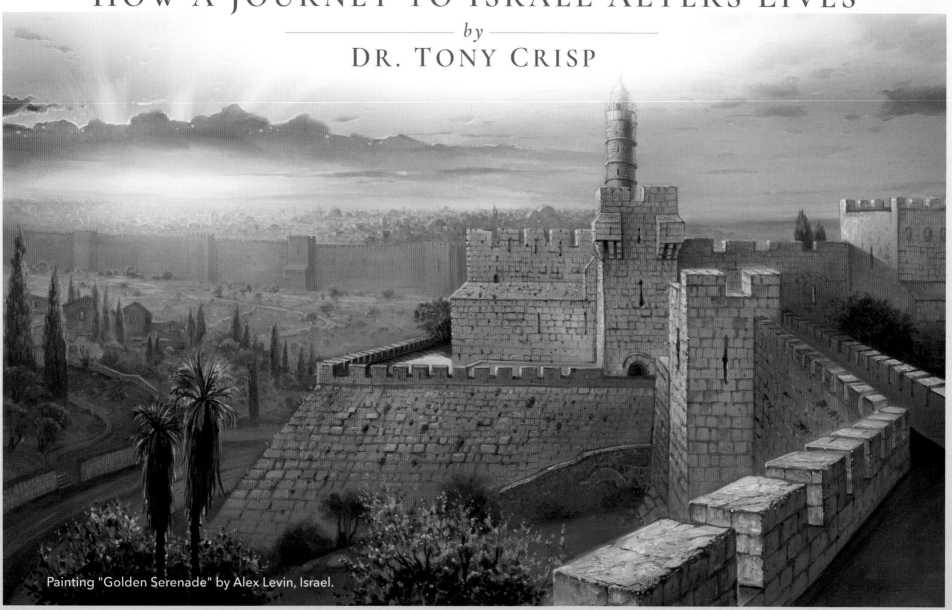

Painting "Golden Serenade" by Alex Levin, Israel.

In 1977, a twenty-one-year-old evangelical topped the mountains of Jordan and saw the Land of Israel all aglow. A stream of tears flowed as Bible stories coursed through his mind. As he came off the high eastern ridge of Jordan and the ancient Kings Highway down into the eastern Jordan valley, the biblical plains of Moab, his heart leaped.

Abandoned by his parents, he was raised by his grandmother, who taught him to read with the Bible. Taking in the great stories of Abraham, Isaac, Jacob, and Joseph, he learned of Jesus of Nazareth and became a devoted follower and a dedicated student of the Bible. The more he studied, the more he loved the Jewish people.

In the summer of 1967, the eleven-year-old boy sat with his grandmother and watched biblical prophecy fulfilled before their eyes. Scenes of men walking through an ancient gate and inside the walls of Jerusalem filled their screen. The grandmother turned to the boy and said, "The Jewish people are in control of Jerusalem. They will never let it go! Never forget this event all your days. The Jewish people are the apple of God's eye and are His people forever. He will be good to those who are good to the Jewish people, and He will curse those who try to harm them."

On his first trip to Israel, the young man was finishing a boat ride across the Sea of Galilee. As the boat approached the dock of Kibbutz Nof Ginosar, an older gentleman began sobbing. He looked toward heaven and said, "Why, Lord, did I wait so long to come to this blessed Land? It all seems so clear now!"

He turned to the young man and said, "Thank God you're here while you're young. Get as many people here to study as possible, son. You must!"

The young man lingered alone by the lake. His heart burned with the words of the older gentleman. A life-altering commitment was made there where the

Photo by Laura Ben-David

Yigal Alon Museum and the Jesus Boat Exhibit now stand. A commitment that would change the course of thousands of lives.

Since that first trip to Israel in 1977, I have taught thousands of evangelicals in the Land of Israel to love the Bible and Jewish people.

More than 90 percent of evangelicals never journey to Israel. Many do not understand how a trip to Israel aids in understanding the Bible. A trip with the proper guide will bring the Bible to life. The words of our sacred Scripture leap off the page and into three-dimensional reality.

The Bible is a Jewish book. It's written by Jews, to Jews, and primarily for Jews. The Bible is written from a Jewish, Middle Eastern perspective; it's not a Western book. Evangelicals greatly enhance their understanding of the Bible by touring and studying in Israel.

Every writer of the Bible assumed their readers understood the language, history, geography, and cultural context of the writer. The Bible is filled with assumptions. Yet Western evangelicals tend to read the Bible through Western eyes, not the proper perspective of the Jewish people. A trip to Israel answers questions that Western evangelicals don't even know to ask. Experiencing Israel aids the most erudite evangelical in better understanding the Bible.

Additionally, antisemitism is on the rise, and America and the West are no exceptions. Many Americans outside of major cities have never met a Jewish person. In many places, Jews are villainized. A trip to Israel often causes aberrations from truth to dissipate and opens relationships with real people.

Many church leaders talk about people they've never met and places they've never been, speaking a language they've never studied, about a culture as different as night and day to them. One trip to Israel can change a perspective—a life! It changed mine.

A bird's-eye view of the Sea of Galilee

ISRAEL MAKES THE BIBLE COME ALIVE

by
PASTOR RAFAEL CRUZ

I have had the privilege of visiting Israel on three occasions. Walking where Jesus walked makes the Bible come alive. It's revolutionized my Christian life.

I have been at the tomb, and it is empty! All of a sudden, the Bible becomes more than just a narrative. He is alive! He is risen!

One of the cities that impacted me was Capernaum, where Jesus conducted most of His ministry. There is a sixth-century synagogue there, built on top of Jairus' synagogue, where Jesus ministered on several occasions. It was here Jesus was asked to heal Jairus' daughter—and He did, by raising her from the dead.

On one boat ride on the Sea of Galilee, a storm came upon us. Even though we were drenched, it was an exhilarating experience! We imagined what the disciples felt when they encountered the storm with Jesus. Except instead of being scared we all rejoiced because, just as with the disciples, Jesus was in the boat with us! He will never leave you; He will never forsake you!

Then there is the city of Jerusalem. It's inspirational to see Jews worship God with such great devotion. All throughout the day, they pray at the Western Wall (the closest one can get to where the Holy of Holies was in the Temple). On the other side of that wall is the Temple Mount, where Herod's Temple was until it was destroyed by the Romans in AD 70. Jesus ministered there on multiple occasions, including turning the tables of the money changers and preaching to multitudes. It was the center of Jewish religious life.

You can also visit the City of David, the greatest of all Israeli kings, which has now been excavated and offers proof of the validity of the Bible. Archeological excavations like this corroborate the Bible. Forty authors and sixty-six books of the Bible, written over a span of about 1,400 years, create a cohesive story with no major contradictions that can only be explained as the supernatural work of Almighty God.

Another thing that shocks most people is how small Israel is. When the Philistines returned the Ark of the Covenant to the Israelis, it was left at Kirjath Jearim until King David brought it to Jerusalem. I assumed that Kirjath Jearim was hundreds of miles from Jerusalem but it's just a few miles from the City of David. Yet, this small country is the most important to Jews and Christians, and world history revolves around Jerusalem.

I was also impacted by Israeli patriotism. In spite of being surrounded by enemies and under nearly constant attack, Israelis are ready to fight to preserve their freedom fearlessly. I met two young girls in military uniform at the Western Wall who expressed great joy at being counted worthy to defend their beloved country.

The Jews eagerly wait for the first coming of Messiah, which Christians are convinced is His second coming. Then, the middle wall of partition between Jews and Christians will be broken down, and we will both be together in His presence forever and ever. Maranatha!

We need to embrace and love the Jewish people and, as Psalm 122:6 tells us:

"Pray for the peace of Jerusalem: May they prosper who love you."

THE STATE OF THE UNION
BETWEEN JEWS AND CHRISTIANS

by

CHRISTINE DARG

Jewish-Christian friendships have come a long way. Now, many Christians are friendly with Jewish people and many cutting-edge Jewish rabbis have dared to respond to new Christian overtures with a heart-warming re-evaluation and positive view of Christianity.

How did this breakthrough come about?

In 1965, the Second Vatican Council declared its stance on the relationship between the Catholic Church and Judaism through its document *Nostra aetate*, Latin for "In our time." This declaration condemned antisemitism and acknowledged the Christian history that failed to protect or respect our Jewish counterparts.

The *Nostra aetate* passed by a vote of 2,221 to 88 of the assembled bishops. A new day had finally dawned between Christians and Jews.

On the 50th anniversary of *Nostra aetate*, the "Church and Synagogue" sculpture at Saint Joseph's University in Philadelphia was dedicated to these sentiments, demonstrated through a pair of

bronze figures, side by side, personifying Christianity and Judaism. Both personifications wear crowns and hold their respective Scriptures, suggesting that we learn from one another. Indeed, Christians are enjoined in the New Testament to esteem the Jewish people as our elders in the faith!

In the past, two female figures representing Church and Synagogue often appeared sculpted on either side of a cathedral portal, as in the most famous example, the opposing statues of the Strasbourg Cathedral in France. The medieval figures reflect the erroneous belief that Judaism had been surpassed. Nothing could be more short-sighted! The Scriptures foretold that the nation of Israel would be regathered in the last days.

Having been brought up in an evangelical Protestant denomination, I watched with amazement as former Pope John Paul II further succeeded in fostering and deepening dialogue through his own compelling gestures. As the Polish pope, he famously visited the former concentration camp of Auschwitz-Birkenau to pray for

Photo by David Kiern

the victims of the Shoah, and he visited the Roman synagogue to express his solidarity with the Jewish community. In a historical pilgrimage to the Holy Land in 2000, John Paul was also the first pope to pray at the Western Wall, where he left a prayer.

The final text of *Nostra aetate* states that the Church "decries hatred, persecutions, displays of antisemitism, directed against Jews at any time and by anyone." Furthermore,

the statement says that all men are created in God's image and that the "Church reproves, as foreign to the mind of Christ, any discrimination against men or harassment of them because of their race, color, condition of life, or religion."

However, it was through our association with a Protestant organization, the Christian Broadcasting Network (CBN), that we learned first-hand of the movement of the Holy Spirit bringing Jews and

iStock.com/Rudy Balasko

Photo by David Kiern

Christians together. For many decades, Dr. Pat Robertson, CBN's founder, taught about the Levitical festivals of the Lord and the spiritual law of blessing Israel has embodied (Gen. 12:3). Then, by founding CBN's work in Jerusalem, my husband and I became close friends with many Israelis who today are bridge builders between Jewish and Christian communities.

Despite the bitter past, despite the long history of enmity between Christians and Jews, in 2015, the Center for Jewish–Christian Understanding and Cooperation in Israel published the statement: "To Do the Will of Our Father in Heaven: Toward a Partnership between Jews and Christians."

This Orthodox Rabbinic Statement is the first public Orthodox statement on Christianity since the Catholic Church changed its teachings toward the Jewish people in 1965. Citing rabbinic precedents, "To Do the Will of Our Father in Heaven" articulated a bold vision of appreciation of Christianity. More than one hundred Orthodox rabbis, teachers, professors, and communal leaders have signed the statement. Many of these Orthodox men are considered pariahs for having endorsed the statement, yet they believe they are doing the will of the Father in heaven by engaging in constructive dialogue for the good of humankind.

An Israeli clinical psychologist, along with Rabbi Dr. Josh Ahrens and other rabbis, commended the 2015 rabbinic declaration as "brave" and a "cause of rejoicing." He said,

> I'm grateful for the step and the crisis that this declaration is causing us; it means it will take us forward, God willing. This [movement] has to become mainstream. Jews are resistant to this relationship—it's very personal because our identity with history is our strength, but it's also a ball and chain. It will happen gradually, but we have to put our minds to furthering this cause.

Furthermore, the statement mentions Jesus as one of the Jewish people's own sages:

> …Jesus brought a double goodness to the world. On the one hand, he strengthened the Torah of Moses majestically … and not one of our Sages spoke out more emphatically concerning the immutability of the Torah.

Let that sink in!

After almost five decades of privileged and intimate involvement with Israel, I believe that "Doing the Will of Our Father in Heaven" is an ongoing end-time prophetic work of the Holy Spirit, and I'm humbled to be a part of this blessed stream.

The Negev Desert

LOOK AT THE TREES

by

PASTOR JERRY DIRMANN

An olive tree near the grounds of the Mar Elias Monastery

Modern Israel is arguably the most prominent sign that we are near the end of the age. The Bible contains many ancient prophecies about a revived nation of Israel, which, without divine intervention, are impossible to fulfill. Today, one such fulfillment requires only a flyover to verify: the trees.

The Jewish people experienced several waves of exile from their Promised Land. In the eighth century BC, the people of the northern kingdom of Israel were exiled to Assyria. Then, in the sixth century BC, the people of the southern kingdom of Judah were exiled to Babylon. Then finally, in the first century AD, the Jewish people were scattered all over the world. And during that two thousand-year period, much of the Land of Israel lay barren.

The Prophecy

Over 2,700 years ago the prophet Isaiah wrote:

"I will put [plant] in the wilderness the cedar, the acacia, the myrtle, and the olive. I will set in the desert the cypress, the plane and the pine together, that they may see and know, may consider and understand together, that the hand of the Lord has done this, the Holy One of Israel has created it" (Isa. 41:19–20).

This prophecy predicted that many trees would be planted in the Land of Israel. You may think, "So what's the big deal? People have been planting trees all over the world for millennia. How would we know if the prophecy was fulfilled?"

Let's look a little closer at the prophecy.

Verse 19 says, "I will plant." Considering that at least seven different kinds of trees are mentioned and that it says these trees would grow in unlikely places such as the wilderness and the desert, it seems obvious that the prophet Isaiah did not plant all those trees.

So, who was it?

If we back up a few lines in Isaiah's prophecy, the true author identifies Himself.

"When the poor and needy seek water, and there is none, and their tongue is parched with thirst, I the Lord will answer them; I the God of Israel will not forsake them. I will open rivers on the bare heights, and fountains in the midst of the valleys. I will make the wilderness a pool of water, and the dry land springs of water" (Isa. 41:17–18).

So there it is. The Lord God of Israel prophesied about the planted trees. God also explains who would water them. He would.

In verse 20, God revealed His reasons for planting all these trees. He said He would plant them so "that they may see and know, may consider and understand together, that the hand of the Lord has done this, the Holy One of Israel has created it." In other words, God wanted everyone to:

- *SEE* that He planted them.
- *KNOW* that He planted them.
- *CONSIDER* that He planted them.
- And *UNDERSTAND* that He planted them.

God sent a message. A message so obvious that everyone could *see* it. A message so extraordinary they would *know* it was a message. A message so astonishing they would have to stop to *consider* it. And a message so overwhelming they would know who it was from.

God sent an *obvious, extraordinary, astonishing,* and *overwhelming* message.

The Fulfillment

Remember, the nation of Israel is only about the size of New Jersey.

If I told you that in the past 120 years, over one million trees in Israel have been planted, would you believe it?

How about five million trees?

How about twenty-five million?

How about one hundred million?

Since 1901, over 250 million trees have been planted in the Land of Israel. Nothing like this has ever happened in the history of the world, and certainly not in a nation as small as Israel.

So what's the message?

Creator God is REAL!

Creator God is POWERFUL!

Creator God is FAITHFUL!

Creator God is a PROMISE KEEPER!

Creator God is the GOD OF ISRAEL!

And everything we read in the Bible—including things that seem impossible—is true.

Don't believe it? *Just look at the trees.*

FROM KINSHASA TO JERUSALEM:
THE SACRED TIES BETWEEN JEWS AND GENTILES
by
PASTOR RICHARD DIYOKA

I fell in love with Israel in June 1967 during the Six-Day War as a teenager. I followed the war on the radio. God was doing miraculous things in the Land of Israel, in Jerusalem specifically, and for the Jewish people. I had a great desire to see Israel win—and it happened! Hallelujah, glory to the Lord!

This began my desire to not only pray for Israel but to see and bless Israel. I applied for a visa in 1979, and although Israel had an embassy in Kinshasa, I was unsuccessful. This did not diminish my dream of seeing Israel.

I got in touch with the Messianic Jews of France and received their magazine and books to get news from Israel and on the relations between the Jews and the nations. It was a great pleasure and a blessing for me as a Christian.

After I got married, I read the Bible with fervor. The sacred ties between Jews and gentiles led me to read about Ruth's marriage to Boaz, and how the genealogy of David and Jesus came about through her. This cemented my passion to connect with the Jewish people so much that I gave my first son the name Obed, that he should be like the descendant of Ruth and Boaz, the patriarch of David.

My second son is Israel. My third child, my eldest daughter, is Shekinah (Shrina). And my fourth child, a daughter, is Naomie.

Through their names and their faith, my children know that we, as Christians, are inseparably tied to Israel and the Jewish people. That is the message that we need to give all our children.

In 1973, our former president, Mobutu, announced publicly from the United Nations that the D.R.C. (formerly Zaïre) broke its diplomatic relations with the State of Israel. This extremely sad news afflicted me deeply. The Bible declares of Israel, *"Blessed are those who bless you, and cursed are those who curse you" (Num. 24:9).*

Since that time, things have been very bad for our country. Despite that, my love for Israel never weakened. On the contrary, I continue to love Israel the same way Jonathan loved David in 1 Samuel 18:1–4: *"The soul of Jonathan was knit to the soul of David, and Jonathan loved him as his own soul."*

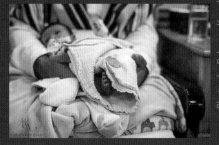

In 2008, I made my first trip to Israel. It was an unimaginable joy and blessing to walk the Promised Land, the Land of my ancestors Abraham, Isaac, and Jacob, the Land of my spiritual fathers, the prophets, the apostles, of Paul, the Land where the Almighty God sent His Son Jesus Christ to save me and redeem me by His Blood!

I visited many sites and was filled with joy! I have since visited Israel many times and made numerous friends. It was a joy to visit Israel with my son, and most recently, with my wife, Kyria Kapinga, during Israel's 70th anniversary. I witnessed the glorious opening of the American embassy in Jerusalem!

There are many examples of gentiles being intimately connected to the

Jewish people. Moses, the great prophet, married Zipporah who was referred to as an Ethiopian.

Joseph married Asenath, an Egyptian, and had two sons who are part of the twelve tribes of Israel.

Boaz married Ruth, the Moabite, and their son, Obed, was the ancestor of King David.

And from the House of David, whose matriarch was a gentile, come Mary and Joseph, through whom God gave us His Son, the Lord Jesus Christ. His death and resurrection saved us so that pagans and Jews might be brought together in the kingdom of God.

By the grace of God, and through love, God will achieve His plan for the gentiles. He continues to reveal Himself to His chosen people, according to the promises He made to their fathers Abraham, Isaac, and Jacob, and to the prophet Jeremiah.

May the Lord continue to bless the people of Israel with peace. Shalom.

iStock.com/FamVeld

89

A Jesus Freak Falling
in Love with Israel

by

Pastor Don Finto

Sea of Galilee

I came to a new understanding of Israel and the Jewish people during the Jesus Movement of the 70s and 80s. I was the pastor of a growing church on Music Row in Nashville when hippies were becoming "Jesus Freaks." Among them were an increasing number of young Jewish people who were a part of my "flock," but I had no grid for this.

For centuries, the Christian church had assumed that God was finished with the Jewish people, that the destruction of Jerusalem was a sign that God had broken covenant with Israel. But my new-found Jewish friends and I were finding clear biblical statements that God's covenant with Israel is everlasting, that as long as the sun is in the sky, Israel will remain a nation before God (Jer. 31:35–36), that even though they were scattered to the nations, He would one day bring them back to the Land of their inheritance and open their hearts to follow Him with all their hearts.

The prophets were sometimes very specific in what they saw. Isaiah declared, *"I will bring your offspring from the east, and from the west I will gather you. I will say to the north, Give up, and to the south, Do not withhold…"* (Isa. 43:5–6). We all know about the return from the south, Egypt, and the east, Babylon. But Isaiah also said from the north. In the 1980s, because of that prophecy, friends went to Moscow and marched around Red Square, speaking Isaiah's words over Russia: "Give them up! Give up the Russian Jews!" Less than ten years later, over one million Russian Jews had returned.

But what about the south? Oh, yes—the Ethiopian Jews. On May 24-25, 1991, thirty-five Israeli aircraft airlifted over fourteen thousand Ethiopian Jews to Israel. "To the south," Isaiah had said, "Do not hold them back." In those few hours, Isaiah's prophecy was coming to fulfillment.

But there's more! Jeremiah said that the Jewish return to their homeland would include *"expectant mothers and women in labor"* (Jer. 31:8). Two babies were born in one of the returning planes from Ethiopia.

This new understanding was so life-changing and overwhelming that I felt called, in the spirit of Daniel, to repent on behalf of the Church which so radically missed the Lord for all those centuries and had been the worst persecutor of the Jewish people. Daniel took upon himself the sins of his people, even though he was not personally responsible. I found his words perfect for my personal prayers. *"Lord … we have sinned and done wrong. We have been wicked and have rebelled; we have turned away from your commands and laws. We have not listened to your servants the prophets who spoke … to our ancestors"* (Dan. 9:4–6). Even though Daniel was not personally responsible for those sins, he carried the weight of the decisions of former generations. Even though I was not personally responsible for the persecution of the Jewish people, I felt the weight of the godlessness of my ancestors of faith.

Because of this life-changing revelation, I felt compelled to get the message out to as many people as possible. I never desired to write, but I felt compelled since I wasn't hearing any other Christian expressing what I was seeing. I chose the words of Ruth, a gentile of the past, who said to Naomi, her Jewish mother-in-law, *Your People Shall Be My People* as the title for my book, with another that soon followed, *God's Promise and the Future of Israel.*

God's covenant with Israel is everlasting, and the return of the Jewish people to their homeland is being fulfilled through biblical prophecies. Now, more than ever, we must confess, embrace, and intercede for the chosen people of God, aligning our prayers with God's plan.

WHICH WILL YOU BE?
A VOW TO STAND WITH ISRAEL

PRISCILLA FLORY

Yad Vashem- the World Holocaust
Remembrance Center

But Rut said,

"Don't press me to leave you

and stop following you;

for wherever you go, I will go;

and wherever you stay, I will stay.

Your people will be my people

and your God will be my God."

Ruth 1:16

(*The Complete Jewish Bible*)

November 2, 1979, was the first day of my first tour of the Holy Land. The trip started two years prior with my enthusiasm to visit the Land. My husband, Tom, asked me what I'd like for Christmas. My response? A trip to Israel! I asked and he gave! The trip was the first of many and established an eternal love for the Land and her people.

I remember that first day in the Land, praying that God would bring me back again, but not as a tourist. I wanted to live among the people. I wanted to go where they went; I wanted to do what they did and eat what they ate. I wanted to be immersed in the people.

Fast forward to January 1998, Tom and I were with our couples group, and I asked God what I should ask the folks to pray for me. When it was my turn to share, out of my mouth flew, "Pray that God will remove antisemitism from the Church!"

What on earth did that mean? Abba God taught me many things that year. The year was crowned with my second trip to the Land—I celebrated the Feast of Tabernacles in Jerusalem and then spent time as a civilian volunteer in the Israeli Defense Force.

I remembered my prayer on the first trip, to be immersed in the culture—never dreaming that it would be fulfilled as a civilian volunteer in the IDF. It was a priceless opportunity and one I repeated at age seventy-one.

I attended a seminar on that second trip on the Book of Ruth. Our Jewish teacher said that Naomi represents Israel, Ruth represents the church that sticks with Israel, and Orpah represents the church that turns her back on Israel. Which would I be?

When I visited the Western Wall, I had the strongest feeling I needed to get as close as possible. My body was pressed against it—I looked up and just above me was a dove. I began to weep, deep calling to deep, and all I could say was, "I will NOT turn my back!" The Wall was Israel to me—her God, her people, and her LAND. I vowed that I would NOT turn my back on her no matter what! I have been tested on that vow, but I am committed, and by God's grace, I will fulfill it.

After numerous trips to the Land, I have had the honor and privilege of getting to know and love precious people there. Although not blood-related, they are family to me, and I love them dearly. One gentleman even gave blood in honor of my seventieth birthday. We laughed when we realized that only two men had ever given their blood for me. He said, "And they were both Orthodox Jews!"

Sharing the Land and her people with family and friends is one of my greatest joys and privileges

in life! Tom and I took our two eldest granddaughters for a visit and studied the Book of Ruth with them. The Word came alive!

On another trip, each day God gave me a particular word. One day the word was HOPE. Hmm, how would hope show itself? At Yad Vashem, of all places! As I walked its hallowed spaces, I wondered, *Where is the hope?*

Nearing the end of my self-guided tour, I heard music; a familiar anthem was emanating from a video screen. HATIKVAH! Israel's national anthem, *HOPE!* Again, I wept. Out of the ashes of the Holocaust, God birthed the remarkable divinely destined nation, Israel!

She is seventy-five years young, and celebrating her is an honor! May her new year be filled with love, joy, peace, and yes, hope.

Israel, because she lives, her people will be my people, and her God will be my God! *L'Chaim, Israel!*

A poppy field in spring in Israel

REBUILDING BRIDGES:
ARGENTINA AND ISRAEL'S BLESSING

by

DIEGO FREYTES

The Bible reveals the key to the miracle of Israel in its relationship with the nations.

As early as 1895, Argentina was friendly towards the Jews. Many arrived in Argentina from the mid-nineteenth century until shortly after the creation of the State of Israel in 1948. Currently, around 80 percent of them live in Buenos Aires, constituting the largest Jewish community in the Spanish-speaking world, with about 180,000 Jews—the sixth largest in the Diaspora.

Around 2017, while studying God's Word, Genesis 12:3 touched my heart: *"I will bless those who bless you, and him who dishonors you I will curse, and in you, all the families of the earth shall be blessed."* A special love for the people of Israel grew in my heart. As a youth leader at the New Time Baptist Church in the city of Córdoba, I organized "Awakening Israel" in anticipation of the 70th anniversary of Israel. On May 12, 2018, around two hundred young people attended the event. It was beautiful to see a love for Israel born in some of them that remains to this day.

Curiosity grew in my heart and then turned into a desire to learn biblical Hebrew. God raised a brother in faith who donated the cost of my first biblical Hebrew module offered by Israel Biblical Studies, connected with the Hebrew University of Jerusalem. God's hand was in this miracle.

As a result of these studies, I discovered something significant I'd missed in Genesis 12:3:

"Blessed are those who serve you."

In Hebrew, the verb "to bless" is *levarech*. This is based on the BRK root which means "knee," implying a service rendered to someone by bending the knee towards them. God isn't suggesting we say nice words. The literal meaning of this verse is: "I will serve those who stand in solidarity with you by serving you."

I dug even deeper.

"A great curse to the one who despises you."

The opposite applies to those who curse Abraham. The first curse word, *mekalelcha*, comes from a root meaning "to look down on someone." The second word for curse, *aor,* means "to destroy completely." Therefore, the literal meaning is "whoever despises you, I will utterly destroy."

Now I understood these words given to Abraham and his descendants, the people of Israel. They contain a powerful blessing and a powerful destruction.

God began to speak to my heart about the history of my country. On July 12, 1938, "Notice 11" restricted the entry of Jews fleeing the Nazi regime to Argentina. The Nazis saw Argentina as a proud nation with a leadership capacity that they could reproduce. After the end of the Second World War, many war criminals convicted of crimes against humanity were received with "open arms" in Argentina, which not only ordered the processing of permits but also gave them housing and work. Argentina became a Nazi haven after the war.

Other shocking events could be mentioned, such as Argentina abstaining from the vote on the day the State of Israel was founded in 1948; the terrorist attack on the Israeli Embassy in Buenos Aires; the terrorist attack on the Jewish Mutual AMIA; or the death of a Jewish prosecutor in the framework of the inquiry for a treaty with Iran.

What happened to my nation? Argentina is in a deep economic, political, and social crisis that has lasted more than eighty years. Inflation grows at over 100 percent per year. There is only a memory of that dazzling nation.

Even so, the Word of God reveals that we can be part of the change from the curse to the blessing. That is why today, from our beloved nation Argentina, we ask God and the people of Israel for forgiveness. We begin to bless them, praying for the restoration of justice, knowing that God will keep His word and that Argentina will again be part of Israel's blessing.

Photo by Rebecca Kowalsky

Underwater view in Eilat, Israel

95

Jehovah Nissi: The Lord Our Miracle and Banner of Victory

by

Dr. Jim Garlow and Rev. Rosemary Schindler Garlow

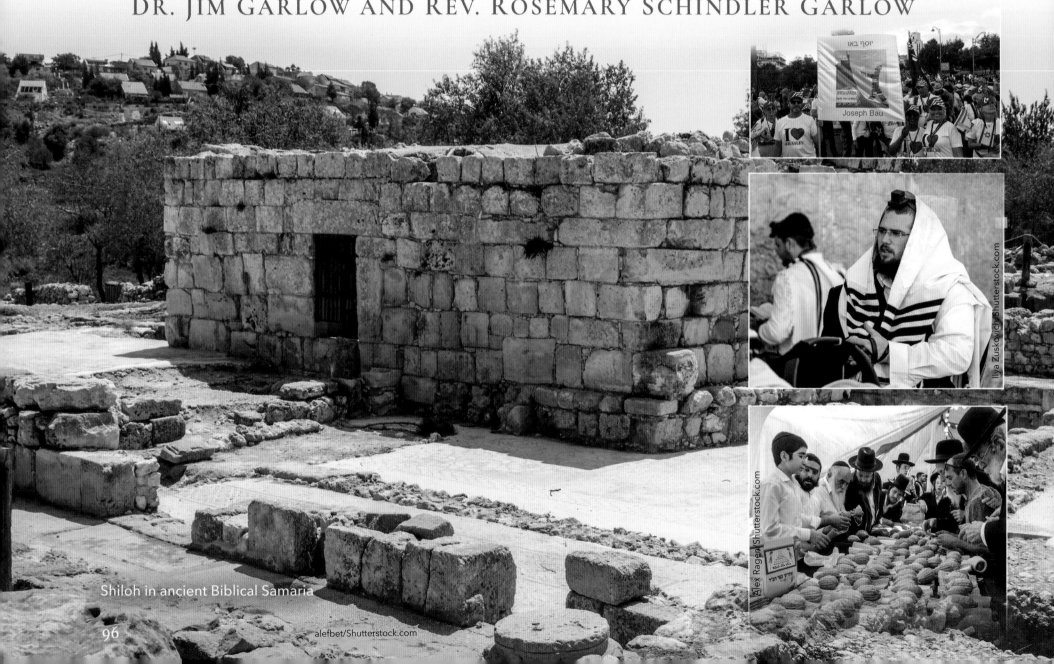

Shiloh in ancient Biblical Samaria

alefbet/Shutterstock.com

Whenever we hear the word "miracle," the God of Israel should come to our minds. He is Jehovah Nissi, the Lord our miracle, and our banner of victory, as His great name was revealed to Moses through victory over the Amalekites (Exod. 17:15).

Israel is the miracle, the signal to the nations of God's faithfulness to His covenant, to His Land, and His people. Israel is the ensign, the standard, the banner around which the nations shall gather. God says, *"Israel will be … a blessing in the midst of the earth"* (Isa. 19:24).

The Lord is bringing all the tribes of Israel from the corners of the earth back to His Land. *"He will raise a signal for the nations and will assemble the banished of Israel, and gather the dispersed of Judah from the four corners of the earth"* (Isa. 11:12).

A major shift has occurred. There are more Jewish people living in Israel than in the rest of the world. According to Danielle Mor, "2022 ended with triple the number of new immigrants than in 2021 and the highest in over twenty years!" It is imperative for us to help Jewish people make *Aliyah* to their homeland.

We host Covenant Land Bible Pilgrimages to Israel at least twice a year. The highlight is our stay in Jerusalem. The Bible mentions Jerusalem almost eight hundred times, more than any other location on earth.

Another favorite is ancient Shiloh, Israel's first capitol for 369 years, and the place where Hannah

Rosemary with Friends of the Israel Defense Forces and Women of Valor, Negev, 2015

Volunteers for Israel – Sar El Program serving the IDF near Tel Aviv, 2011.

prayed for a child, Israel's great prophet Samuel. There is a faithful Jewish community there, but tragically most of its citizens have experienced vicious attacks. David Rubin, the former mayor, was himself shot, along with his small son. They miraculously survived, and Mr. Rubin began "The Shiloh Israel Children's Fund" to help victims of terror in the biblical heartland.

Just as Jewish people have been the targets of hatred in the nations where they were scattered, so are the Bible-believing Jews in the heartland of Israel, the most persecuted and terrorized in the Holy Land. These areas are the "Jew-els" of the earth and its precious people His treasured remnant.

In 2005, I (Rosemary) hosted a Jewish and Christian solidarity tour to remember the victims of "Bus 19," a Jerusalem city bus blown up by a Muslim suicide bomber that murdered eleven people and injured over fifty. Tourism greatly decreased during the early 2000s, a tragic time

of terror attacks against the Jews. We never canceled a tour and Christians felt safe. We never had an injury; the "Miracle Banner" protected our passengers. As a statement of solidarity with the Jewish people, and to educate Americans, I (Rosemary) brought the remains of "Bus 19" to the San Francisco Bay Area, and I (Jim) brought it to my church in San Diego.

It is a miracle of modern transportation that you can be in Israel, from anywhere in the world, in less than a day. Tourism is revived.

Now is the time to come to Israel, the miracle nation, whose national flag is designed after the prayer shawl, the tallit, because the Jewish people declared that only through prayer and with God's help will Israel live.

Israel, the miracle nation, beckons all to come and witness God's faithfulness to His people, and to experience the rich history and vibrant culture of this Holy Land.

ISRAEL'S GLORIOUS FUTURE

by

REV. WILLEM J. J. GLASHOUWER

Photo by Richard C. Lewis

John Theodor/Shutterstock.com

Although the "birth pains" in the end times will be intense and painful, Jesus says the outcome will be glorious for Israel (Matt. 24). These "birth pains" ultimately lead to the birth of the baby: the kingdom of peace and righteousness on earth from Jerusalem, led by the King of kings and the Lord of lords, the Messiah of Israel. All the prophets of the Bible speak about it.

For example, Simeon in Luke 2:25–32:

"Now there was a man in Jerusalem, whose name was Simeon, and this man was righteous and devout, waiting for the consolation of Israel, and the Holy Spirit was upon him … when the parents brought in the child Jesus, to do for him according to the custom of the Law [Thora], he took him up in his arms and blessed God and said, 'Lord, now you are letting your servant depart in peace, according to your word; for my eyes have seen your salvation that you have prepared in the presence of all peoples a light for revelation to the Gentiles, and for glory to your people Israel.'" All is well that ends well.

In verses 36–38, we meet another Jewish person in the Temple:

"And there was a prophetess, Anna, the daughter of Phanuel, of the tribe of Asher. She was advanced in years, having lived with her husband seven years from when she was a virgin, and then as a widow, until she was eighty-four. She did not depart from the Temple, worshiping with fasting and prayer night and day. And coming up at that very hour she began to give thanks to God and to speak of him to all who were waiting for the redemption of Jerusalem."

The coming of Jesus the child fulfilled the prophecies that Israel cherished, hoping for the coming of the kingdom of the God of peace and righteousness from Jerusalem and throughout the world.

He fulfills the promise by the angel Gabriel, given to His mother Mary in Luke 1:32–33.

"He will be great and will be called the Son of the Most High. And the Lord God will give to him the throne of his father David, and he will reign over the house of Jacob forever, and of his kingdom there will be no end."

Revelation 11:15 triumphantly declares, when looking to the future in the prophetic past tense: *"The kingdom of the world has become the kingdom of our Lord and of his Christ [the Messiah], and he shall reign forever and ever."*

First, Jesus, the King Himself, demonstrated signs of the kingdom in Israel.

This was followed by signs of the kingdom in the world by the power of the Holy Spirit during the preaching of the gospel of the kingdom to all the nations of the earth (Matt. 24:14). These signs and wonders have occurred for two thousand years.

Finally, the kingdom of peace and righteousness will come worldwide when the Messiah King will again be among us to sit on the throne of His father David to rule over the House of Jacob. Peace will flow forth from Jerusalem into the whole world and the nations will train for war no more (Luke 1:31–33; Isa. 2:2–4).

Of His kingdom there shall be no end because He was resurrected from the dead and He lives forever. Israel will be no longer the tail of the nations but the head of the nations (Deut. 28:13).

Then all the covenants and promises that were made with Israel by God Almighty will be fulfilled in that kingdom to come.

All the promises made to Abraham will be fulfilled.

The Promised Land will have its promised borders.

The priesthood of Levi will function again in the final Temple.

The Kingship of the House of David will be established forever.

Jerusalem and the Temple will be the center of the world.

The New Covenant will be fully implemented in Israel.

The Covenant of Peace will be fully operational.

The wisdom of Torah will be the guiding light for all nations.

God will be all in all.

ISRAEL—LAND OF MIRACLES PAST, PRESENT, AND FUTURE

by
PASTOR TREY GRAHAM

God has performed unexplainable miracles throughout various cultures and centuries, but His miracle power has a focus on the Holy Land of Israel, the *"apple of His eye"* (Zech. 2:8). As the home of patriarchs like Jacob, prophets like Isaiah, and a Savior like Jesus, the Land of Israel is a *"land for which the Lord your God cares; the eyes of the Lord your God are always on it, from the beginning even to the end of the year"* (Deut. 11:12).

The God of Israel Is a God of Miracles in the Past

God called to Moses from a burning bush and assigned him the mission of teacher and deliverer (Exod. 3:2–10). God parted the Red Sea (Exod. 14:13–22) and later the Jordan River (Josh. 3:5–17), allowing His people to escape a past of slavery and begin a future of destiny. His miracle power caused the walls of Jericho to fall (Josh. 6:1–27), protected Daniel in a pit full of lions (Dan. 6:16–22), and his three friends from death in a furnace (Dan. 3:16–26). We remember the answered prayers of desperate mothers like Sarah, Rebekah, Rachel, and Hannah, who called out to the Lord when they needed a miracle.

The supernatural ability of our Heavenly King to hear the prayers of hurting people is a reality of the recent past as well. Ask military strategists how the State of Israel survived the War of Independence, the Six-Day War, or the Yom Kippur War. These thinkers may give answers about battle plans or courageous fighters, but in the end, there's only one answer that suffices—miracles.

The God of Israel Is a God of Miracles in the Present

God's commitment to Israel is not finished. From children playing in the streets of Jerusalem (Zech. 8:5) to Jewish immigrants moving to their ancestral homeland from the four corners of the earth (Ezek. 11:17) we see God's Word being actualized in our lifetimes. Modern diners who enjoy olives, pomegranates, almonds, and dates taste the miracle power of a God who can heal a barren land and cause the deserts to bloom (Isa. 35:1–2). Residents and tourists across Israel deal with unending traffic and construction as this modern nation continues to grow, to miraculously *"rebuild the ruined cities and inhabit them"* (Amos 9:14–15).

The God of Israel Will Be a God of Miracles in the Future

As the nations relentlessly demonize Israel and ignore the historical truth of Jewish heritage in the Land, believers can trust the miracle power of the Heavenly Judge who will *"restore the fortunes of Judah and Jerusalem"* (Joel 3:1–2). Bible students look forward by faith to the Temple being constructed on its rightful and historical spot, Mount Moriah in Jerusalem (Ezek. 37:28). Lovers of God look forward to visiting *"the House of Prayer for all peoples"* (Isa. 56:7) while experiencing the presence of the miracle-working God who *"will dwell in the midst of the people of Israel forever"* (Ezek. 43:7). Believers in Jesus as Messiah eagerly anticipate and longingly pray for His return to Jerusalem as King (specifically on the Mount of Olives), as the angels promised (Acts 1:9–12) and the prophets predicted (Zech. 14:4).

Israel is the Land of miracles. It is not the only place where God's presence is felt, but it is the only place where He declared that His name would dwell (Deut. 12:5; 16:2; Ezra 6:12; 2 Kings 21:4).

Israel holds a special place in the hearts of rabbis and pastors, kings and politicians, authors and teachers. Ultimately, however, Israel holds a special place in the heart of our Creator God, the King and Heavenly Father.

Painting "Sabbath Walk by David's Tower" by Alex Levin, Israel.

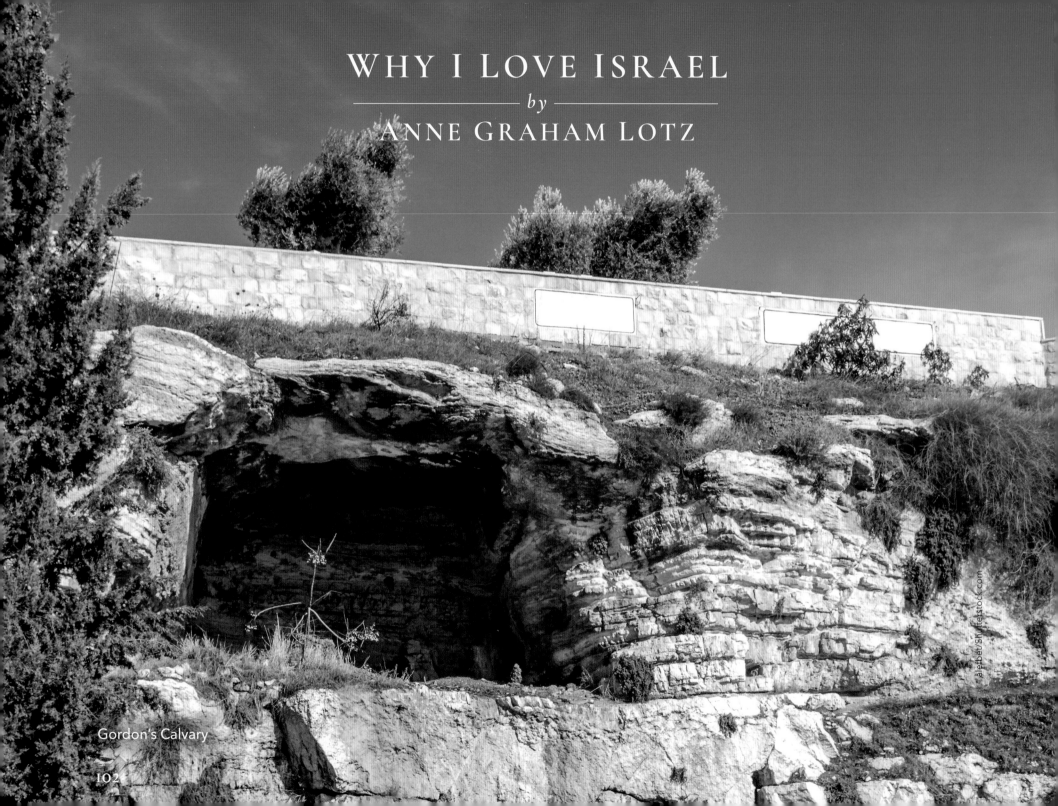

WHY I LOVE ISRAEL
by
ANNE GRAHAM LOTZ

Gordon's Calvary

I love Israel! Without a doubt, she is a miracle nation! Her very existence testifies to the reality of the God of Abraham, Isaac, and Jacob. Since I was a very young girl, Israel has been at the forefront of my heart and mind. The Bible tells us that God chose the Jewish people because He loves them (Deut. 7:7–9). He has put His name on Jerusalem (1 Kgs. 11:36). He has even done so literally in the topography of the city which is dissected by three valleys laid out in the shape of the Shin, the Hebrew name for God. Israel is where Jesus of Nazareth, God's Son, was born, where He lived and died and rose from the dead, then ascended into heaven with the promise that He would return.

I feel my life is intertwined with Israel because of something Jesus told His disciples in Matthew 24 when sitting on the Mount of Olives overlooking Jerusalem. When the disciples commented on the beautiful buildings, Jesus prophesied that Jerusalem would be destroyed. The disciples then asked Him two questions: When would this destruction occur, and *"What will be the sign of your coming and of the end of the age?" (Matt. 24:3).*

We know from history the answer to the first question. Jerusalem was destroyed by the Romans forty years after Jesus told His disciples it would be. As a result, the Jewish people were dispersed all over the world and Israel no longer existed as a nation.

Which brings us to the answer Jesus gave to them. While He listed many signs that included wars, famines, earthquakes, the persecution of His people, and signs in the heavens, He told a very intriguing parable.

"From the fig tree learn its lesson: as soon as its branch becomes tender and puts out its leaves, you know that summer is near. So also, when you see all these things, you know that he is near, at the very gates. Truly, I say to you, this generation will not pass away until all these things take place. Heaven and earth will pass away, but my words will not pass away" (Matt. 24:32–35).

Several days before this conversation with His disciples, Jesus used the fig tree to illustrate Israel (Mark 13:12–14; 20–21; 13:28–31). Like the fruitless fig tree, Israel was dormant and seemingly lifeless after her destruction for almost two thousand years. Then she began to show signs of life, culminating Friday, May 14, 1948, when she was again declared a nation. The United States was the first to recognize her legitimacy. The Jewish people began returning to their ancient Land from all over the world, speaking their ancient language, and even trading in their ancient monetary curren-

cy. It truly was a modern-day miracle! But there's more….

Jesus said the generation that witnesses this historic rebirth, experiencing the other signs He gave within that same generation, would be the generation that would signal His imminent return and the end of the age.

This is where it gets very personal for me. One week after Israel's rebirth as a nation, on Friday, May 21, 1948, I was born! Whatever Jesus meant by a generation could very well be my lifetime.

I believe Jesus, Yeshua, is the Messiah. Based on the signs He gave His disciples and the parable He told, I believe that if I live out my natural lifetime, I will see Him return to rule the world—from Jerusalem! Wars will cease. Love will triumph over hate. Right will triumph over wrong. Justice and righteousness will prevail. On that day, according to the prophet Zechariah, God declares, *"They will call on my name and I will answer them; I will say, 'They are my people,' and they will say, 'The Lord is my God….' And the Lord will be king over the whole earth" (Zech. 13:9; 14:9).*

A field outside of Bethlehem

Several years ago, I attended a special gathering at the Israeli Embassy in Washington, DC, celebrating the relationship between Israel and evangelical Christians. The message to all of us emphasized that Israel had a promising future due to three factors.

First, she would prosper because of her high-tech and medical breakthroughs.

Second, her military might and power were noted with pride.

Third, she would soar to be a world leader.

Following the address from the Israeli representative, I was invited to read an assigned passage of Scripture. I couldn't help but precede the reading with an affirmation that Israel had a more promising future than anyone could imagine! She would be more prosperous than anyone could dream, with everyone sitting at peace under their own vine and fig tree (Mic. 4:4). Her power will be so great that it will be supernatural because her God is God! And she won't just be a world leader, but the world leader because the Messiah will rule from Jerusalem. I summed up by saying I believe the Messiah—Yeshua, Jesus—will bring this about.

Israel's future is secured, and it is glorious! I was reminded of the prophet Daniel's vision in Daniel 7:13–14: *"I saw in the night visions, and behold, with the clouds of heaven there came one like a son of man, and he came to the Ancient of Days and was presented before him. And to him was given dominion and glory and a kingdom, that all peoples, nations, and languages should serve him; his dominion is an everlasting dominion, which shall not pass away, and his kingdom one that shall not be destroyed."*

As I stand in the shepherd's fields outside of Bethlehem, I can almost hear the echo of the angelic host proclaiming, *"Glory to God in the highest, and on earth peace to men."*

As I sit in a boat in Galilee, I remember the terror of the storm and marvel *"that even the wind and waves obey Him"* when Jesus commanded them to be still (Matt. 8:27).

When I wander through the ruins of Capernaum, I am amazed that He healed the sick, gave sight to the blind, and raised the dead.

As I pray in Gethsemane, walk through Antonio's Fortress, then look at the Place of the Skull, I am moved to tears as the words of Isaiah come to mind: *"Surely he has borne our griefs and carried our sorrows; yet we esteemed him stricken, smitten by God, and afflicted. But he was pierced for our transgressions; he was crushed for our iniquities; upon him was the chastisement that brought us peace, and with his wounds we are healed"* (Isa. 53:4–5).

My time in Israel has always ended at Gordon's Calvary, where I bow in worship—the tomb is still empty. Jesus has risen from the dead! He's alive! One day, He will return to the Mount of Olives, set up His worldwide rule from Jerusalem, and Israel will become all that she was intended to be—God's eternal home where He will live with all of us who have put our trust in Him (Rev. 21:1–3).

This is Israel's 75th birthday—and mine! Who knows? Could it be before this generation concludes in the next five years that we will see the Messiah come? If so, I look forward to seeing you in Jerusalem as we celebrate the miracle that is Israel!

Boat on the Sea of Galilee

Oleg Zaslavsky/Shutterstock.com

TOUCHDOWNS AND TESTIMONIES:
PRO ATHLETES EXPERIENCE ISRAEL
by
DARRIN GRAY

There are many complex layers to my ever-growing love for Israel and all that the Holy Land represents. I've served as a spiritual guide for forty NFL players, coaches, and alumni in the Holy Land over the last six years. These tours allow me to call men who played American football (NFL), loved God, and wanted to experience Him more fully by walking in Jesus' footsteps.

These pro-athlete tours allow me to express my spiritual gifts and to live out my specialized calling to guide faith movements via the influence of sports, media, and ministry.

Israel represents a master narrative of God's love for people expressed in Bible stories. The Bible comes to life by experiencing the Holy Land firsthand.

I am still in awe each time that I stand atop the Mount of the Beatitudes, visit Peter's home in Capernaum, take a boat on the Sea of Galilee, pray at the Western Wall, travel to Caesarea, or the contested places in Jerusalem where complete historical clarity is often hard to come by, places like Gethsemane, Golgotha, or the Garden Tomb.

Traveling Israel with the NFL cohorts, I experience the exhilaration of what once was and the expectancy of what it means as a Jesus follower. I earnestly pray for the hearts and minds of the players to be turned toward God so that they might be filled with the Spirit as we walk in the footsteps of Jesus. I want them to encounter God. To think about, read about, and talk about what they are experiencing. It's not just the experiences that count, but their reflection upon the experiences that reveal who Christ is to them!

Even as a professional sports media ministry executive, I still live vicariously through these men with their own measure of NFL fame as they become a cohesive band of brothers, shaped by the historical places and Bible verses that bring them to life.

I have a specialized calling to serve professional athletes so that they can, in turn, serve their families, teams, and communities. It unites my deep devotion to God with my passion for curating meaningful experiences.

I remember taking Ben Utecht, Super Bowl Champion with the Colts, to a chapel in

Photo by Richard C. Lewis

Bethlehem, where he spontaneously began to sing *Ave Maria*. Everyone stopped to listen. It was awe-inspiring.

I remember gathering atop the fortress at Masada with NFL alumni and US Special Forces as we encountered this symbol of resistance against the Romans in AD 73-74. We imagined what it would've been like to stand up for our convictions against the strongest empire in the world.

I remember group baptisms in the Jordan River with NFL players that led to moments of elation and celebration like the fist pump and a shout of joy from Miles Killebrew, Pittsburgh Steeler.

I spent time at the Western Wall, deep below the Old City in Jerusalem, and at the Jordan River

with twin brothers, Jacob (Las Vegas Raiders) and Cody Hollister (Tennessee Titans), and Jordan Kunaszyk, Cleveland Browns.

I shared epic stories about David and Goliath in the Elah Valley, reading 1 Samuel. I challenged the NFL players to go to the creek bed and choose five smooth stones. I reminded them that while David had several stones, he only needed one to slay the giant.

I asked them to consider which stone they needed, metaphorically, to slay a giant in their life, the obstacle that kept them far from God and disconnected from people. Many cried tears of joy and sorrow as they released that "giant" in their life.

That's what the Holy Land does…. It opens up hearts, minds, and souls, even tough athletes, so they can release what holds them back in life and claim that which will rescue them for a lifetime—a renewed relationship with Jesus.

Painting by Udi Merioz   107

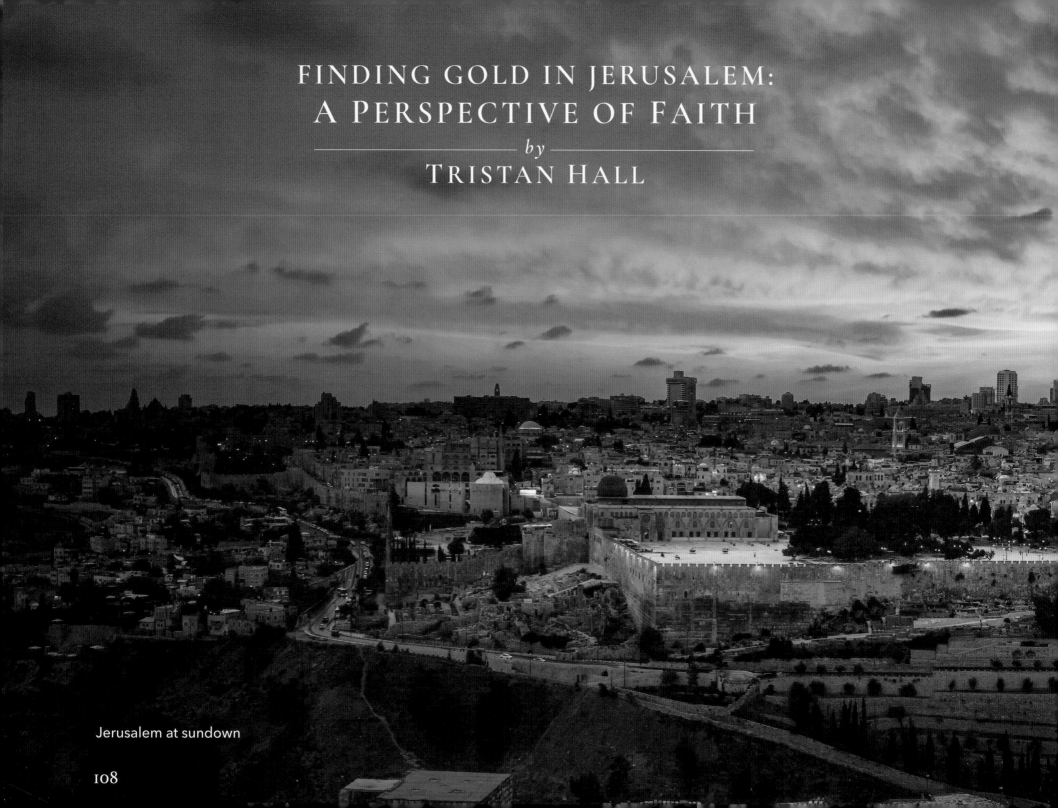

FINDING GOLD IN JERUSALEM:
A PERSPECTIVE OF FAITH
by
TRISTAN HALL

Jerusalem at sundown

I'll never forget the first time I glimpsed Jerusalem. Winding our way up the road from Tel Aviv by taxi, my anticipation levels rose. In the early morning slumber, the heavens suddenly opened like a treasure chest, and the gleaming gold of the first rays of amber dawn alighted upon the skyline of stone walls, as a curtain rising to reveal a most sumptuous stage.

In the dawning light, the stones appeared to glow with a golden luminance, redolent of songs and Scriptures that associate Jerusalem with the properties and substance of gold. After all, Jerusalem's destiny was always to be a city set apart, a city of royalty and holiness. A city unlike any other city.

Before I left for this journey, I happened to sing Psalm 122 for a congregation I visited. I knew this was my time to go up, to make my *Aliyah*, my ascent up the winding hills to Jerusalem, both physically and spiritually.

"I was glad when they said to me, 'Let us go into the house of the Lord!' Our feet have been standing within your gates, O Jerusalem!" (Ps. 122:1–2).

Psalms 120–134 are known as the Songs of Ascents, the fifteen songs traditionally sung by pilgrims coming up to Jerusalem to honor God at the appointed times of Pesach, Shavuot, and Succot.

For my visit, it was the cusp of Pesach. As I reflected, every word woven together was alive and imbibed with a rich tapestry of meaning. King David reflected, *"Jerusalem—built as a city that is bound firmly together" (Ps. 122:3).*

As my eyes rested upon the many gold-tinged tower blocks, the many modern apartments so characteristic of the newer parts of Jerusalem, I could concur with David's observation, even with the passage of some three thousand years.

"Where the tribes go up," David continued in the next verse, *"the tribes of the Lord."* What a privilege to traverse the ancient paths trodden by the twelve tribes of Israel of old, *"as was decreed for Israel, to give thanks to the name of the Lord" (Ps. 122:4).*

What a striking parallel we find in the pilgrimage of the tribes of Israel going up to worship God in Jerusalem, in the context of the broader pilgrimage of the tribes of the whole world to worship the Lord in Jerusalem, in the time to come spoken of by the prophet Zechariah:

"Then everyone who survives of all the nations that have come against Jerusalem shall go up year after year to worship the King, the Lord of Hosts, and to keep the Feast of Booths. And if any of the families of the earth do not go up to Jerusalem to worship the King, the Lord of Hosts, there will be no rain on them" (Zech. 14:16).

This Scripture speaks of truly earth-changing events and a glorious time to come for Jerusalem when not only the tribes of Israel but all humanity comes to Jerusalem to worship the King, the Lord of Hosts.

Yet, for many modern pilgrims to this city, it's sometimes hard to reconcile Jerusalem's future destiny with the city they experience today. They witness a modern, pulsating city, throbbing with all the same issues encountered in other cities worldwide. They see the traffic jams, hear the noise, and feel the tremors of the road diggers. The streets are not yet golden, and the inhabitants of Jerusalem, especially the new immigrants, face escalating challenges such as scarce housing and the rising cost of living in an already expensive country. Therefore, it is sometimes difficult for the new immigrant, the visitor, and the pilgrim to connect tomorrow's Jerusalem—the Jerusalem of biblical prophecy— with the Jerusalem of today.

Despite these challenges, I am reminded of the testimony of Caleb, son of Jephunneh, and

Joshua, son of Nun, when they entered Canaan to spy out the Land on behalf of the children of Israel before they came into possession of their Promised Land. Of the twelve spies despatched by Moses, only two gave a good report of what they saw. The other ten *"brought to the people of Israel a bad report of the land which they had spied out…" (Num. 13:32a)*. This begs the question: Why did Caleb and Joshua give a different report than the other ten? Surely they also saw and heard the same as the others, including those ominous or daunting things?

What do we of these modern times say of this Land, this City, when we enter it and spy it out? What testimony do we give to those within our worlds? Do we speak of the traffic, the noise, the terrorists, the giants—or do we laud the faithfulness of God?

Like the ten spies who gave a bad report, it is easy to focus on the challenges; to report simply what we see and experience in the here and now. Yet Joshua and Caleb pleased God because they looked at the Land through the eyes of faith, fitted and altogether framed by the promises of God.

The Lord said of Caleb, *"But my servant Caleb, because he has a different spirit and has followed me fully, I will bring into the land into which he went, and his descendants shall possess it" (Num. 14:24)*.

When we gaze upon Jerusalem, we too need to look through eyes of faith—faith in the promises and prophecies of God, to pan for the gold, not only in what Jerusalem is in our days now but to see beyond to what it *will be* in the future. We need to perceive Jerusalem's glorious destiny to come, when all the nations come up to worship the King, the Lord of Hosts, in Jerusalem.

As contemplated in so much midrashic literature since antiquity and as described in beautiful detail in Revelation 21, we need to speak of that golden time ahead when *Yerushalaim shel lamata*, earthly Jerusalem, will be touched, even eclipsed by and "closely compacted together" with the awe-inspiring and supernal *Yerushalayim shel lamala*, the heavenly Jerusalem. Can you see it coming?

III

THE PROMISE OF PEACE: ISRAEL'S ROLE IN A GLOBAL MIRACLE

by

PASTOR MALCOLM HEDDING

"When the Lord restored the fortunes of Zion, we were like those who dream. Then our mouth was filled with laughter, and our tongue with shouts of joy. Then they said among the nations, 'The Lord has done great things for them.' The Lord has done great things for us; we are glad" (Ps. 126:1–3).

Since 1948, we have witnessed breathtaking miracles emerging from this tiny nation. The Six-Day War of 1967 and the 1973 Yom Kippur War were great miracles of deliverance. These miracles not only helped to build the nation but have also enriched and blessed the world. In all spheres of endeavor, including that of *Aliyah* (the return of her people), agricultural, medical, digital, space exploration, defense, and technology of all types, Israel is a world leader and a light to the nations. It is thus wholly appropriate that we celebrate seventy-five years of Israel's modern-day existence, while also remembering that she is an ancient nation.

We, therefore, celebrate this amazing milestone with much joy because:

1. The God of Israel has been faithful.

God gave His word through an ancient Hebrew prophet that Israel would exist as a nation just as long as the sun, moon, and stars are in the sky. He has been faithful.

"If this fixed order departs from before me, declares the Lord, then shall the offspring of Israel cease from being a nation before me forever" (Jer. 31:36).

2. The God of Israel has been gracious.

Like us all, Israel does not deserve such kindness. God declares that He does not return Israel to statehood because of her merits; He has done this for His own name's sake, that He may be glorified, and that His works may be seen on earth. The miracles surrounding Israel's modern restoration are numerous and speak of God's great love and kindness.

"Therefore say to the house of Israel, 'Thus says the Lord God: It is not for your sake, O house of Israel, that I am about to act, but for the sake of my holy name, which you have profaned among the nations to which you came'" (Ezek. 36:22).

3. The God of Israel has vindicated the Bible.

Israel's restoration is validated in all of Scripture. Even Jesus spoke of Israel's dispersion and regathering. The Bible has been vindicated as the infallible Word of the Living God!

"Sanctify them in the truth. Your word is truth" (John 17:17).

4. The God of Israel's perspective.

Israel has a great future, but it will be won through conflict, difficulty, prayer, and more miracles. The future will see the exaltation of Jerusalem and peace flowing from it to the nations. The great Hebrew prophet Isaiah saw this coming and wrote:

"And many peoples shall come, and say, 'Come, let us go up to the mountain of the Lord, to the house of the God of Jacob, that he may teach us his ways, and that we may walk in his paths.' For out of Zion shall go forth the law, and the word of the Lord from Jerusalem" (Isa. 2:3).

Israel's modern restoration is the hope of the world. This is why we must be "Watchmen on the walls of Jerusalem," praying for her and seeking her good (Isa. 62:6–7). A day is coming wherein the gentile nations, even those who have hated and resisted her, will understand her miraculous existence and come up to Jerusalem to celebrate with her (Zech. 14:16–17). The beginning of this time has been witnessed in the recent signing of the Abrahamic Accords.

Painting "If I forget Thee"
by Alex Levin, Israel.

5. The God of Israel has given her friends.

The last seven decades have witnessed an unbelievable shift in history. Christians are helping to build up Zion! Though first greeted with skepticism because of the weight of Christian antisemitism through the centuries, Israel now knows that these Christians are sincere and fully dedicated to her. Israel's Prime Minister, Benjamin Netanyahu, stated that evangelical Christians are Israel's best friends in the world! Isaiah saw this remarkable day:

"Foreigners shall build up your walls, and their kings shall minister to you; for in my wrath I struck you, but in my favor I have had mercy on you" (Isa. 60:10).

That Christians, who once persecuted the Jews, are now blessing and serving Israel is evidence of God's mercy and kindness to the nation. Christians who love Israel are a prophetic sign to the Jewish people that a glorious future awaits them!

6. The God of Israel has made her a shining light to the nations.

Israel's democracy, stability, freedoms, and achievements are impressive. Sadly, she exists in a region that is in disarray and determined to destroy her. We are mindful of this and recognize that freedom is not free and must be defended. In the end, God will defend Israel and make her a greater source of blessing and light to the world. Moreover, God promises that He will build up Zion and then appear in His glory (Ps. 102:12–17). Through Israel and her Messiah, God will grant peace to the nations so that they dwell together in harmony. The United Nations was founded with the hope of bringing peace to the world; this is the longing of people everywhere. We are told this day will only come through the miracle of a fully restored Israel. Of this certainty, Isaiah the prophet also wrote:

"He shall judge between the nations, and shall decide disputes for many peoples; and they shall beat their swords into plowshares, and their spears into pruning hooks; nation shall not lift up sword against nation, neither shall they learn war anymore" (Isa. 2:4).

This is a future miracle that we can rejoice in as we celebrate Israel in her 75th year of statehood. God bless Israel and keep her.

iStock.com/Subodh Agnihotri

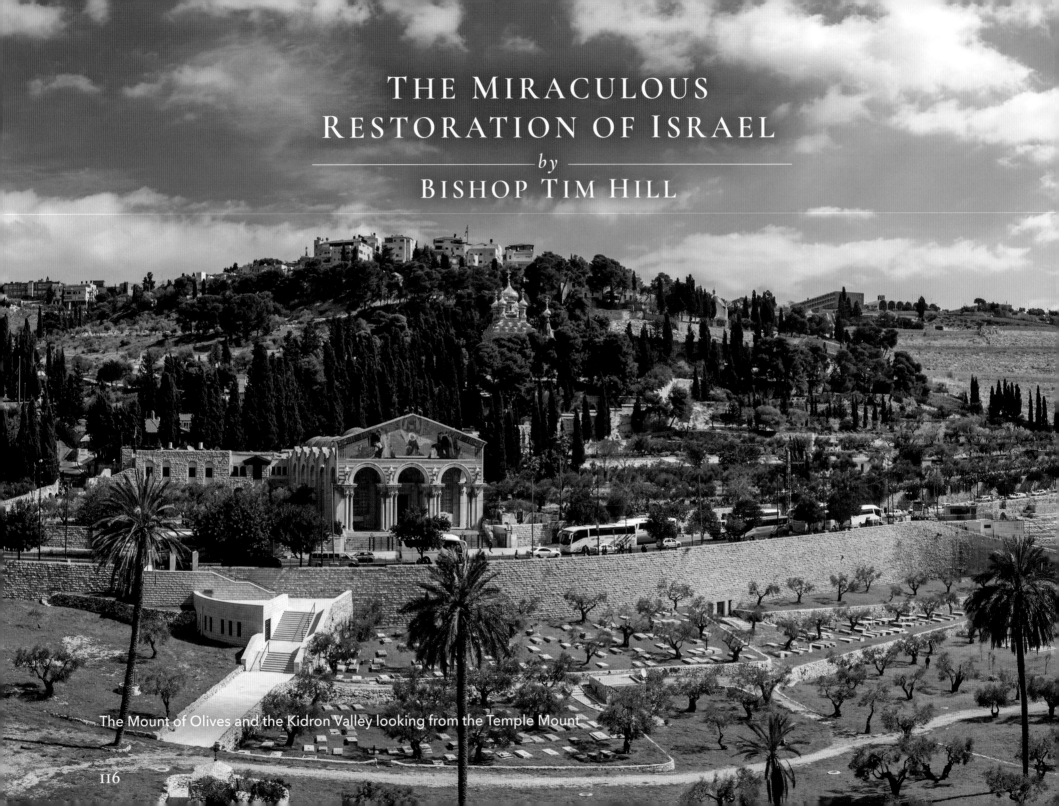

THE MIRACULOUS RESTORATION OF ISRAEL
by
BISHOP TIM HILL

The Mount of Olives and the Kidron Valley looking from the Temple Mount

Rostislav Ageev/Shutterstock.com

L uke, the writer of Acts, pens a marvelous story, just after the resurrection where Jesus supernaturally appears where the disciples are gathered. One can only imagine the excitement that must have filled that room as they gazed upon Him. In stark contrast, just a few days earlier, they witnessed His brutal death and subsequent burial. Now He stood before them in His glorified body.

In anticipation, the disciples asked, *"Will you at this time restore the kingdom to Israel?" (Acts 1:6)*. His response was not what they expected. They failed to comprehend what Jesus came to share—that they were on the verge of a world-changing paradigm shift, a time for the gentiles to be included in God's plan of redemption and the Jews to carry the message to the nations of the earth.

That was a mind-blowing concept. After all, Jews were forbidden to have anything to do with non-Jews. Now, they were commanded to introduce the Messiah of Israel to the gentiles.

The number of gentiles becoming believers increased rapidly, signaling the end of Jewish leadership and influence. At the Nicaean Council In 325 AD, there was a formal separation of the Church from the Jews.

Since then, we have been in the *time of the Gentiles*. As for the Jews, they were scattered throughout the world. Driven from their land, all hope of returning to their beloved Jerusalem was all but lost. Even the Hebrew language was relegated to prayer books. As a result, Christians erroneously assumed God was through with the Jews, and His promises to them were forfeited.

In recent times, however, an amazing string of events has occurred. We see the Christian Era slowly closing and the early signs of God's fulfilling promises made to Abraham four thousand years ago—a promise of land and of descendants to live in that land.

The first signs of this transition began in the late 1800s with an Austrian Jewish journalist, Theodor Herzl. His driving passion, and that of his followers, was the desire to restore a homeland for Jews. Five decades later, after a United Nations vote, that dream became a reality. On May 14, 1948, the Land of Israel was born, fulfilling Isaiah's prophecy.

That event, seventy-five years ago, was an indication to the world that the restoration of Israel was in full swing.

Furthermore, in the past seventy-five years, Jewish people have miraculously returned to the Land. In 1948, approximately 650,000 Jews lived in Israel. Today, over seven million Jews call Israel home, and they continue to come from all nations.

Another significant sign of the times is the involvement of Christians in the restoration

process. Over 2,700 years ago, Isaiah prophesied that gentile believers would be involved in the return of the Jews to their homeland (Isa. 49:22).

This prophecy's fulfillment is evident in ministries such as Ministry to Israel, Ezra International, Bridges for Peace, Ebenezer, Christian Friends of Israel, CUFI, and others involved in bringing Jews home from around the world, especially from the Former Soviet Union. In fact, for the past thirty-plus years, these ministries have assisted hundreds of thousands of Jewish people home to the Promised Land, just as the prophet said.

"Hear the word of the Lord, O nations, and declare it in the coastlands far away; say, 'He who scattered Israel will gather him, and will keep him as a shepherd keeps his flock" (Jer. 31:10).

Ezekiel gives us insight into the chronology of this restoration:

"I will take you from among the nations and gather you out of all countries and bring you into your own land. Then I will sprinkle clean water on you, and you shall be clean from all your uncleannesses, and from all your idols I will cleanse you. And I will give you a new heart, and a new spirit I will put within you. And I will remove the heart of stone from your flesh and give you a heart of flesh. And I will put my Spirit within you, and cause you to walk in my statutes, and be careful to obey my rules" (Ezek. 36:24–27).

It's as though Ezekiel wrote this yesterday!

God is restoring the Jews to their Land at this very moment. While many Jews are returning in less than righteous condition, the Lord makes it clear that He will cleanse them and eventually pour His Spirit on them, restoring them to the relationship they once had with the God of Israel.

What is so important about the Land and what is the purpose of the Jew?

The Land of Israel is the meeting place between heaven and earth. God chose Israel, particularly Jerusalem, as His dwelling place. The first and second Temples were built on the Temple Mount and He chose to abide with mankind on earth. When Jesus returns, His feet will touch down on the Mount of Olives, and He will enter Jerusalem, the place He proclaimed "the City of the great King." All of this points to God's passionate desire to dwell among us.

The purpose of the Jews is to be the revelation of God to mankind. It was on the Jews that God laid the mantle of priesthood. He stated in Exodus 19:6, "'...you shall be to me a kingdom of priests and a holy nation.' These are the words which you shall speak to the people of Israel." It was exclusively to the Jews that God gave the law on Mount Sinai, so they could eventually carry it to the nations of the earth.

At present, we are seeing the restoration of all things God has intended. We aren't there yet, but we are closer now than we have ever been before!

120

AGAINST ALL ODDS
by
DR. WAYNE HILSDEN

The Babylonians, Persians, Romans, and other great nations made their marks but they've disappeared. Most Jewish people were dispersed from their homeland for more than half of their history, but they are very much alive and making a remarkable comeback.

Mark Twain wrote,

> The Jew ought hardly to be heard of ... and his importance is extravagantly out of proportion to the smallness of his bulk. He has made a marvelous fight in this world in all ages and has done it with his hands tied behind him.... The Jew ... [is] exhibiting no decadence, no infirmities of age, no weakening of his parts, no slowing of his energies, no dulling of his alert but aggressive mind. All things are mortal but the Jews; all other forces pass, but he remains. What is the secret of his immortality?

The "secret of his immortality" is his divine calling to bless all nations. Throughout history, Jews have endured great hardship. From slavery in Egypt to near annihilation in Europe to existential threats from some of Israel's immediate neighbors, she has faced impossible odds. But Israel has only grown stronger instead of being wiped off the map.

Recently, US News and World Report named the State of Israel the fifth most powerful country in the world. Yet, the population of Israel is barely one percent of the world's population, with geographical dimensions minuscule compared to most other nations. Israel has been forced to fight numerous wars and is constantly threatened by terrorism within and outside her borders. This is a testament to the perseverance and ingenuity of the Jewish people, but also a testament to the almighty hand of Israel's God.

Israel has a divine mission to fulfill. God chose Israel to be a blessing and light to all nations. This calling was revealed to Abraham, Isaac, and Jacob. God promised that through them *"all the nations of the earth shall be blessed" (Gen. 18:18; 22:18; 26:4).*

Israel has already proven to be a blessing. The Jewish people revealed the one true God, a radical idea in ancient times when people believed in many gods, none of whom were omnipotent, omniscient, and omnipresent—the same yesterday, today, and forever like the God of Israel.

In addition to monotheism, Israel also revealed God's instructions for living a blessed life. The Ten Commandments continue to be the foundation of most legal systems around the world. Nations that have most honored God's laws have proven to be the most blessed.

The Knesset in session

John Adams, a former president of the United States, said: "I will insist that the Hebrews have done more to civilize men than any other nation." He then said that Israel has been an instrument to "proclaim and propagate to all mankind the doctrine of a supreme, intelligent, wise, almighty Sovereign of the universe, which I believe to be the great essential principle of all morality and consequently of all civilization."

Israel has also been a source of inspiration for music, art, and literature, producing some of the most creative works in the world.

We Christians are indebted to the people of Israel for the spiritual riches they have bestowed on us. *"They are Israelites, and to them belong the adoption, the glory, the covenants, the giving of the law, the worship, and the promises. To them belong the patriarchs, and from their race, according to the flesh, is the Christ, who is God over all, blessed forever. Amen"* (Rom. 9:4–5). This last gift is not the least but rather the greatest gift to Christians: Jesus the Jew, the promised Messiah.

Since Israel became a modern nation seventy-five years ago, it has been able to return to its legendary role as a blessing to the rest of the nations. We are witnesses to Israel's amazing humanitarian efforts inspired by her Hebrew Scriptures. Israel has played a crucial role in responding to disasters and crises, from floods in Mumbai and Houston to earthquakes in Haiti, Nepal, and Turkey. Modern Israel's amazing creativity in making medical and agricultural advances has saved innumerable lives around the world.

Against all odds, Israel has made tremendous progress in making peace in the Middle East. The Abraham Accords have shocked the world. From a position of strength, Israel has been able to make peace with many of her Arab neighbors.

Israel's providential preservation is not about to come to an end in the twenty-first century, nor any time in the future. Israel's covenant-keeping God makes this promise in Jeremiah 31:35–36: *"Thus says the Lord, who gives the sun for light by day, and the fixed order of the moon and the stars for light by night ... 'If this fixed order departs from me, declares the Lord, then shall the offspring of f Israel cease from being a nation before me forever.'"* I don't see the sun, moon, or stars disappearing any time soon. Israel will not either.

Against all odds, Israel will never disappear but will continue to "bless all the nations of the earth."

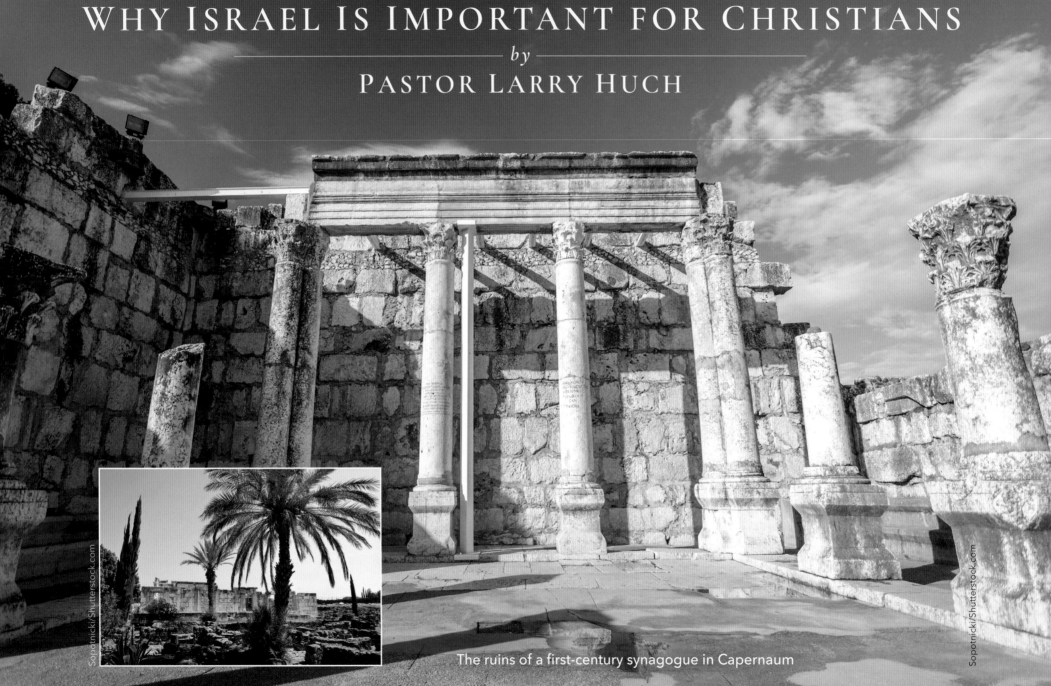

WHY ISRAEL IS IMPORTANT FOR CHRISTIANS

by

PASTOR LARRY HUCH

The ruins of a first-century synagogue in Capernaum

Israel's rebirth as a nation is the single greatest fulfillment of Bible prophecy we have seen in two thousand years. Throughout world history, doubters said that it could never happen. No people lacking land and a common language could possibly be reborn as a nation! Because it had never happened before, most of the world was convinced it would never happen. Yet the impossible did happen, exactly the way God said it would.

On May 14, 1948, the world witnessed the miracle the prophet Isaiah foretold: *"Who has heard such a thing? Who has seen such things? Shall a land be born in one day? Shall a nation be brought forth in one moment?" (Isa. 66:8).*

David Ben-Gurion, Israel's first Prime Minister, declared;

> The Land of Israel was the birthplace of the Jewish people. Here their spiritual, religious and political identity was shaped. Here they first attained to statehood, created cultural values of national and universal significance and gave to the world the eternal Book of Books. After being forcibly exiled from their land, the people kept faith with it throughout their Dispersion and never ceased to pray and hope for their return to it and for the restoration in it of their political freedom.

Against all odds, these hopes were officially realized seventy-five years ago. At that time there were only a few hundred thousand Jews living in Israel. Now today, because of God's prophetic plans to gather the Jewish people from around the world and bring them home, there are nearly eight million and growing. It's a modern-day fulfillment of ancient Bible prophecy.

The late Rabbi Jonathan Sacks who was Chief Rabbi of the United Hebrew Congregations of the Commonwealth once wrote:

> The day will come, when the story of Israel in modern times will speak not just to Jews, but to all who believe in the power of the human spirit as it reaches out to God, as an everlasting symbol of the victory of life over death, hope over despair. Israel has achieved great things. It has taken a barren land and made it bloom again. It's taken an ancient language, the Hebrew of the Bible, and made it speak again. It's taken the West's oldest faith and made it young again. Israel has taken a tattered, shattered nation and made it live again. Israel is the country whose national anthem, Hatikva, means hope. Israel is the home of hope.

The seeds of this hope began to grow in the late 1800s when Theodor Herzl, the modern-day founding father of Israel, was inspired to begin the Zionist movement. He saw the dangers of antisemitism and worked heroically to bring God's people back to their ancestral homeland—Israel. He said: "It is true that we aspire to our ancient land. But what we want in that ancient land is a new blossoming of the Jewish spirit."

Over these past seventy-five years, the world has witnessed the blossoming Jewish Spirit. The vision of so many Jewish leaders has come to pass. Israel has not only survived—it has thrived and has quickly developed into one of the most creative and innovative countries in the world. For example, although Jews are only 0.2 percent of the world's population, Jews have been awarded 24 percent of the Nobel Prizes in science and medicine.

As well, Israel remains at the center of God's prophetic plans. The eternal covenant He made with Abraham some four thousand years ago is still in effect. The Lord clearly promised, *"...I will bless those who bless you, and him who dishonors you I will curse, and in you all the families of the earth shall be blessed" (Gen. 12:3).*

This is the very first blessing (and the very first curse) God set in motion with Abraham. Even today, how an individual or a nation relates to Israel will have a profound effect on them. Until recently, most gentile believers haven't understood that we have become part of this phenomenal blessing. We (Christians) are "grafted into" this lineage and heritage. Israel's story is our story too. We are the "seed of Abraham." We are Judeo-Christians. This is what the apostle Paul teaches in Romans 11. Standing with Israel and being a blessing to the Jewish people is part of our Christian responsibility. It's a huge key to walking in the blessing of God—spiritually, physically, financially, and relationally.

Today, as we celebrate Israel's 75th anniversary, Jews from around the world continue to return to Israel, making *Aliyah*. God gave us numerous prophecies proclaiming this happening. The most stunning of them all is perhaps from the prophet Isaiah. The Lord showed him that in the last days, it would be gentiles who would respond to God's prophetic plans. We would play an important role in helping Jews who have been dispersed around the world to return to the Promised Land.

"Thus says the Lord God: 'Behold, I will lift up my hand to the nations, and raise my signal to the peoples; and they shall bring your sons in their arms, and your daughters shall be carried on their shoulders" (Isa. 49:22).

For nearly thirty years, our ministry, supported by multitudes of partners and friends from around the world, has continued to support Israel. We have built many phenomenal relationships and continue to fund many important charitable projects to be a blessing to the Jewish people.

It's been a fantastic and rewarding journey; one we invite all Christians to participate in.

My personal journey began with what can only be called a supernatural encounter with the Lord. It was on my very first trip to the Holy Land. One of the places we visited was Capernaum, the site where Jesus healed Peter's mother-in-law. There is an ancient synagogue there just inside the city gate. Going through the entrance, I happened to notice an inscription written in ancient Hebrew on the doorpost.

I was told it was a dedication plaque made by some of the descendants of the apostles. Puzzled, I asked our tour guide and dear friend Joseph: "Why would Christians support a Jewish synagogue? Weren't they followers of Jesus? Were they backslidden?"

His answer changed my life and the direction of our ministry forever. He said,

> The church and the synagogue were synonymous for three hundred and twenty-five years after the resurrection of the Lord. Jesus never intended for His followers to be separated from Israel, from God's people, or from the Torah. As Christians, we were to be grafted into Israel.

God showed me that day that He would teach me how to re-read the Bible through the eyes of a Jewish Jesus. Then I would teach these truths and revelations to the Church. This began a totally unexpected journey into discovering the Jewish roots of our Christian faith. It's a journey that has become a grassroots movement. Multitudes of Christians from around the world are now joining in.

iStock.com/DaliaOFF

So, on behalf of my family, my church, and my ministry partners around the world, we celebrate with Israel during this grand 75th anniversary year. I am immensely honored and humbled that God would allow us to become a leading voice and influence in standing with Israel and supporting the Jewish people. Seeing Christians and Jews come together according to God's Word in Malachi 4 and Ephesians 2 is amazing. It's an incredible fulfillment of Bible prophecy—and without a doubt, it's a revelation for "such a time as this."

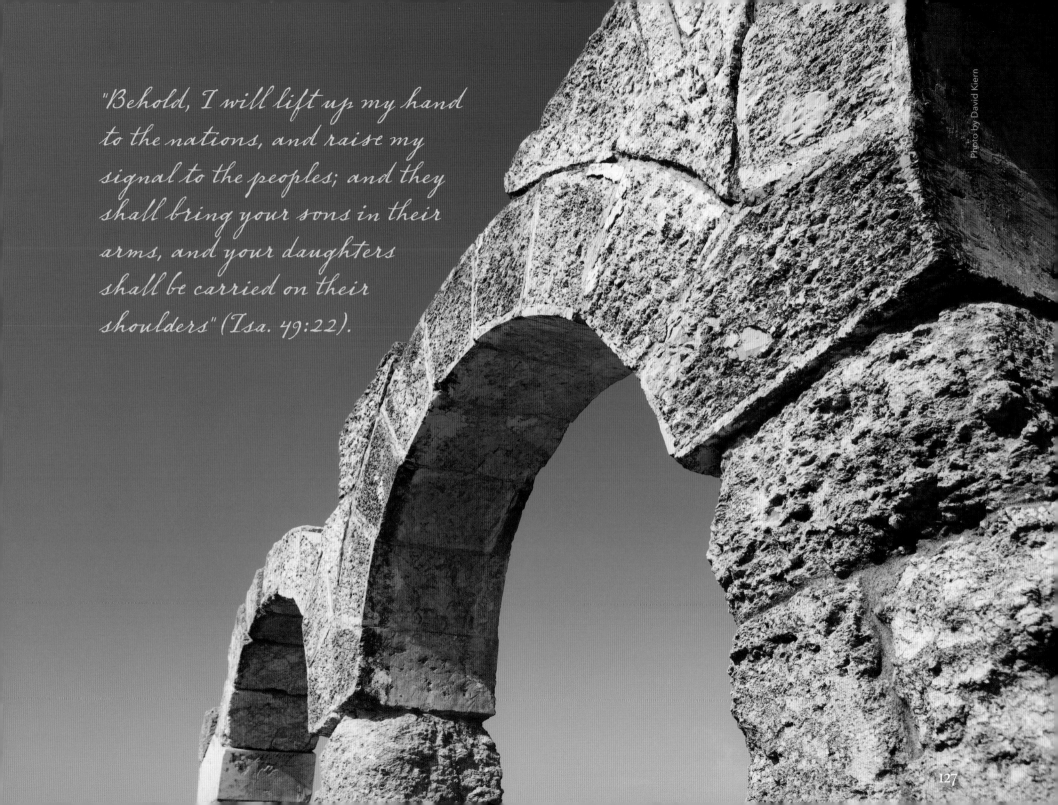

"Behold, I will lift up my hand to the nations, and raise my signal to the peoples; and they shall bring your sons in their arms, and your daughters shall be carried on their shoulders" (Isa. 49:22).

Photo by David Kiern

127

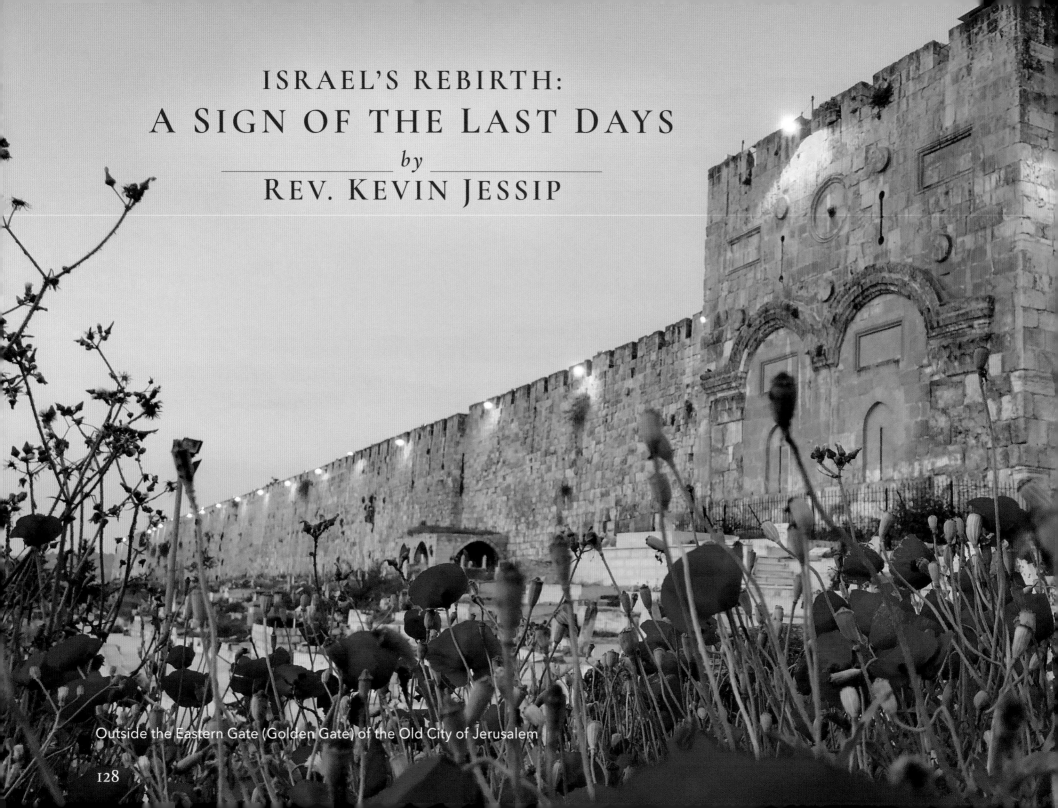

ISRAEL'S REBIRTH:
A SIGN OF THE LAST DAYS

by

REV. KEVIN JESSIP

Outside the Eastern Gate (Golden Gate) of the Old City of Jerusalem

John Theodor/Shutterstock.com

Overview of Bible Prophecy

The Holy Scriptures and Jewish scholars remind us that Messiah is coming. The age ends when the Tribulation (the "time of Jacob's trouble") begins, and the Messiah comes to earth to establish His one thousand-year kingdom after the Tribulation.

There will be seven years of Tribulation in which there will be judgment upon earth and a series of three trumpet judgments as described in Revelation. These judgments are the seal judgments (Rev. 6; 8–9) and the bowl judgments (Rev. 16). The persecution of Israel will continue (Rev. 12), and the multitudes will be saved (Rev. 7). During this period, the false messiah (known to Christians as the Antichrist) will rise and have dominion. No one knows who the false messiah is, and speculation is just that—speculation!

The Place of the Jewish Nation in Bible Prophecy

At age ninety-nine, nearly four thousand years ago, Abraham received promises from God to make him a nation, be his God, and give him a portion of land (Gen. 17:6–8). These promises are still being debated; however, to clearly understand the time we live in, one must understand some prophecies regarding Israel and the other nations.

Israel—the Key to Prophecy

In Scripture, God describes how the children of Israel eventually return to the Promised Land in the "last days" and rebuild Israel.

The prophecies found in Hosea 3:4–5 and Ezekiel 37:21, over twenty-five centuries ago, clearly state that someday, the children of Israel will return from the nations to their Land, Israel. The Balfour Declaration of November 1917, ratified by the League of Nations, signaled the beginning of the Jewish people returning to their Land after 1,847 years of wandering.

1948—Israel is Reborn

One of the greatest signs of our being in the "last days" was Israel becoming a nation on May 14, 1948.

Many New Settlements in Jerusalem on the Mountains of Israel

After 1,878 years, the State of Israel is once again a nation. *The Palestine Post* carried the great news, "STATE OF ISRAEL IS BORN!" Just as the prophet declared, Israel became a self-governing nation despite tremendous obstacles, including a massive Arab attack. Ezekiel 37:25 says that once the children of Israel return, they will dwell in the Land forever.

Israel to Build the Waste Cities and Never Be Removed Again

Another Hebrew prophet, Amos, described how Israel would build the waste cities and never lose their land again.

"'...they shall plant vineyards and drink their wine, and they shall make gardens and eat their fruit. I will plant them on their land, and they shall never again be up-

rooted out of the land that I have given them,' says the Lord your God" (Amos 9:14).

An Everlasting Covenant Was Made with Israel

In Psalm 89:3–4, God tells David that He made a covenant with the children of Israel and his seed forever.

Pray for the Peace of Jerusalem

"Pray for the peace of Jerusalem! May they be secure who love you!" (Ps. 122:6).

Why Pray for the Peace of Jerusalem?

Since Jerusalem became a city many years ago, it has had more wars and less peace than any other city on the earth. This special city in God's plan has been besieged over forty times.

Even so, we have a special command from God: *"Pray for the peace of Jerusalem…."* We pray because Israel's Messiah wants to live there and God has put His name there (1 Kgs. 11:36).

All Nations Are Coming to Jerusalem!

You and I are witnessing the final preparation for yet another (and final) siege against Jerusalem. Russia and its allies are building up massive armies for the great climatic battle that will soon be fought. Even though there is talk about peace in the Middle East, those who know the Bible know that there will be no lasting peace until Israel's Messiah comes back to defend and save her! Zechariah tells us what will happen when many nations come against Jerusalem:

"On that day shall the Lord will protect the inhabitants of Jerusalem … And on that day I will seek to destroy all the nations that come against Jerusalem" (Zech. 12:8–9).

Why is God going to bring all the world to Jerusalem? To show His glory (Ps. 102:16)!

Though many nations have scoffed at the most important spot on earth, they will be brought to Jerusalem to see the Lord magnified:

"So I will show my greatness and my holiness and make myself known in the eyes of many nations. Then they will know that I am the Lord" (Ezek. 38:23).

God Will Fight for Israel

Just as Israel is about to be totally defeated, the Lord will fight for Israel as He did so many times in the past, as he describes in Ezekiel 12:8–9 and Zechariah 14:3–4.

Israel's True Messiah Will Save Israel

Israel's true Messiah will be recognized when those left call on His name (Zech. 13:8–9). When Israel's true Messiah comes, instead of great rejoicing, there will be great mourning (Zech. 12:10–12).

One Thousand Years of Lasting Peace

When Israel's Messiah comes to Jerusalem at the end of the Tribulation, total peace will finally come to Israel and the entire world! This period will last

for a thousand years according to Scripture, and the Lord will be King over all the earth (Zech. 14:9).

God's Covenants Will Be Completed

This will be when God's covenants concerning Israel will be fulfilled. Israel's Land will be greatly expanded according to the Abrahamic Covenant (Gen. 13:14–15).

A New Covenant

The covenant the Lord made with Israel when He brought them out of Egypt will be changed, and a new covenant will be made with Israel (Jer. 31:31–33).

Messiah Will Rule from Jerusalem

The city of Jerusalem will now be where Israel's Messiah will rule, and His law will go forth out of Zion (Isa. 2:2–3)!

Photo by Rebecca Kowalsky

Tel Meggido National Park

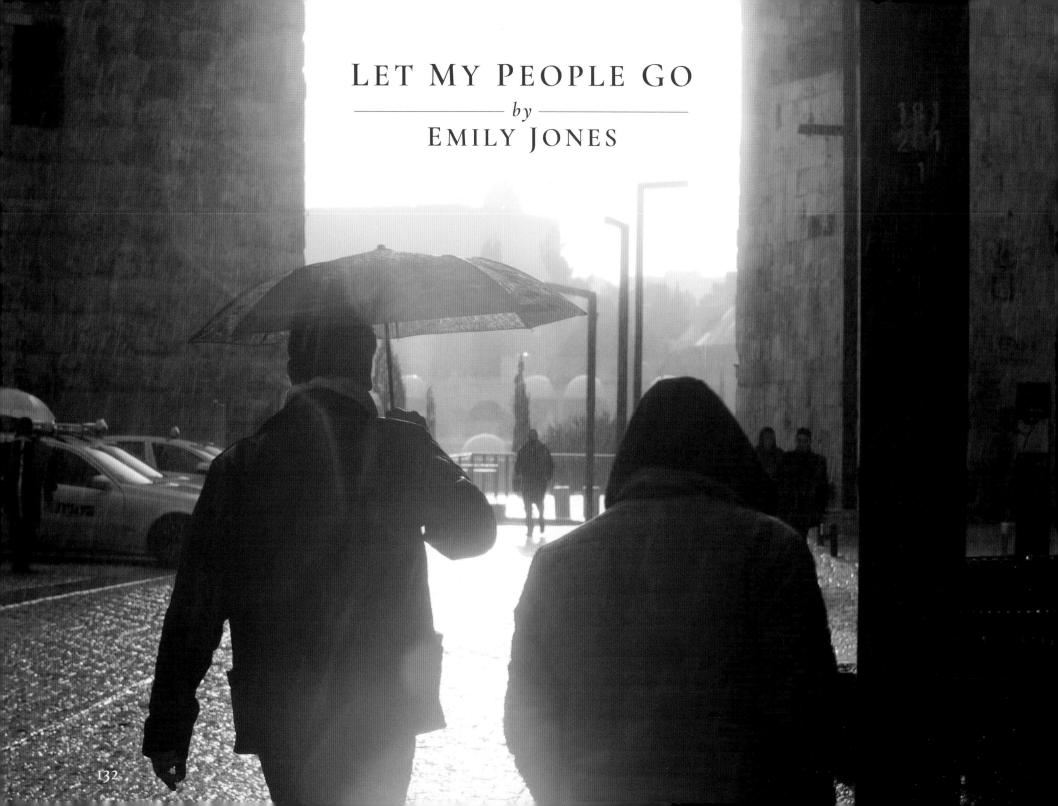

LET MY PEOPLE GO
by
EMILY JONES

As a devout Christian and African American woman, my faith and family legacy are deeply intertwined with Israel's. Israel is more than a place on the map; it's a dream, a promise, a fulfillment of prophecies, and where my faith was conceived long before I was born. As a journalist who has lived in the Land for several years, I am honored to play a role in telling modern Israel's story.

Israel's story is about hope, despair, celebration, conflict, grief, and deliverance. Despite all those characteristics, it's impossible to ignore God's fingerprints throughout Israel's past, present, and future. Israel's story is God's and a premier example of what it means to wrestle with a good God. The Jewish State is the physical representation of God's faithfulness—a witness to His character as a freer of slaves, a compassionate leader, and a just King.

Israel—"the Promised Land"—was the hope and dream of slaves whose backs bore the wounds of unspeakable cruelty. I'm not talking only about the Hebrew slaves whom their Egyptian taskmasters oppressed. I'm talking about my own family and countless other Black Americans. The story of God delivering the Jewish people with "a strong hand and an outstretched arm" inspired my ancestors while they were shackled to their brutal reality. Look no further than the well-known African American spiritual "Go Down Moses" taken from Exodus.

The Lord's words, "Let my people go," sang in my ancestors' minds when they poured out their sweat and blood in the fields.

They were the same words Harriet Tubman used to communicate with slaves on the Underground Railroad. They were the words Martin Luther King Jr. wrote in his 1963 letter from Birmingham Jail. The words were sung as a promise that if God could liberate Israel, He would liberate us too. And He did.

I see the dreams of Jews and African Americans—two people who were former slaves—come true. We both know God's character as a deliverer, restorer, and promise keeper. During Passover, when Israel stops to say, "We were slaves," my family says, "We were too." When Israel reflects on how God personally intervened to free the Jewish people, we say, "He's our chain-breaker too."

I see the continued realization of God's promises when I walk the streets of Jerusalem. His promise that Israel will be a Land flowing with milk and honey comes to life when I shop in the supermarket.

Abraham's numerous descendants are my friends and neighbors.

But strangely, I see God's character as a faithful leader and King the most clearly inside one of the darkest places in Israel—the Yad Vashem Holocaust remembrance center. Visitors who walk the cold, winding halls of Yad Vashem get a vision of hell on earth—a picture of how dark the human heart can be.

I wasn't necessarily shocked by the images of death and torture around me. My parents had

taught me from an early age about the horrors of the Holocaust. Instead, I was shocked to be greeted by a brilliant balcony overlooking the rolling hills of Jerusalem. I heard the Lord tell me, "Look at where you're standing. Evil men tried to wipe out my people; I bound up their wounds and restored them in the Land I gave their forefathers." At that moment, I truly grasped Isaiah 55:11, when God says His word will not return void and He will accomplish everything He intends to do. Israel's very existence against all odds demonstrates God's compassionate and trustworthy nature.

Israel means so much to me as a disciple of Jesus and the daughter of African slaves. It's a place of wonder, beauty, and complexity. It's a place where I've learned and grown, both as a journalist and a person of faith. It's where I've witnessed the power of prayer and the importance of hope. And most importantly, it's a place where I've personally seen God's character on full display—a memorial and reminder that He is faithful and true.

ISRAEL'S LONG JUMP:
PROPHECY FULFILLED AND MODERN DESTINY
by
PASTOR BECKY KEENAN

Israel's history could be written by gathering commentary from friends, lovers, and detractors. The fact that there is so much to say when it comes to Israel is in and of itself quite astounding, considering she is the size of El Salvador or New Jersey. Why do people care? Why such potent reactions throughout time?

I have my opinion. Israel emits a signal that produces polarizing effects in others. This signal is ethereal. Yet it's perceived by governments, religions, academics, artists, historians, and many others. This ethereal signal goes beyond the evident physical deeds of Israel. It's a powerful clarion call of sorts that seems to perturb the human spirit like nothing else. Some love it, others hate it, but all can't help but engage in it. This is extraordinary. Even those who say they do not care for Israel feel compelled not to ignore her and state their case clearly: "We don't care." Then why care so much not to care?

Choice has always been part of Israel's history. From her humble beginnings as a family to those who chose to join her, until now. God called Abraham to exit Ur of the Chaldeans, and his obedience created a testimony to those who knew him. Some chose to follow him; others did not. He was changed as a result of a choice, establishing a spiritual paradigm for the redemption of humanity. While we all have a capacity for choice, Israel is called to express to the world certain inspired principles, inviting other nations to join along.

The moment Abraham obeyed God, a spiritual portal was opened. He created a thread of faith that led to a God-given destiny. Abraham was not an exception. Neither are we. We must grow, mature, be trained, and respond correctly.

Israel has faced insurmountable challenges: slavery, conquest, exile, foreign domination, wars, harsh oppression, discrimination, killing campaigns, cruel religious persecutions, the Holocaust, antisemitism, modern lawfare, constant unprovoked missile attacks, and existential nuclear threat. Through all of this, Israel has grown strong and outstanding! In her amazing seventy-five years of modern existence, she has surpassed expectations in every area a modern country could. Her contributions to humanity are disproportionate. Her success has blessed millions, even as some choose to despise her. All should protect a country like her so she can continue to advance the world, yet Iran and its proxies seek her annihilation.

From the moment Ben-Gurion declared her the independent Jewish State of Israel, he propelled her forward from being the scattered people of a two thousand-year exile into everything God prophetically revealed in His Word. This has been the biggest long jump in history! Empires fell, walls were removed, and iron kingdoms were weakened for Israel to walk into her modern destiny. She, with Jerusalem as her eternal capital, is an open gateway for those who profess biblical faith.

From the invention of drip irrigation in the early days to the Iron Dome, David's Sling, and other defense systems, it is an irrefutable fact that Israel has prevailed. Isaiah 11:11–12 says God is waving a banner to all nations to understand His purposes with Israel and align with them. If the wars of 1948, 1967, and so many others are not enough to cause us to follow God's plan joyfully, nothing else will. If we think for one second that God's promises are not real, remember He has heard every prayer of every distressed and dispossessed Jew whose heart turned to Him for help. Israel is truly the homeland of miracles.

iStock.com/chameleonseye

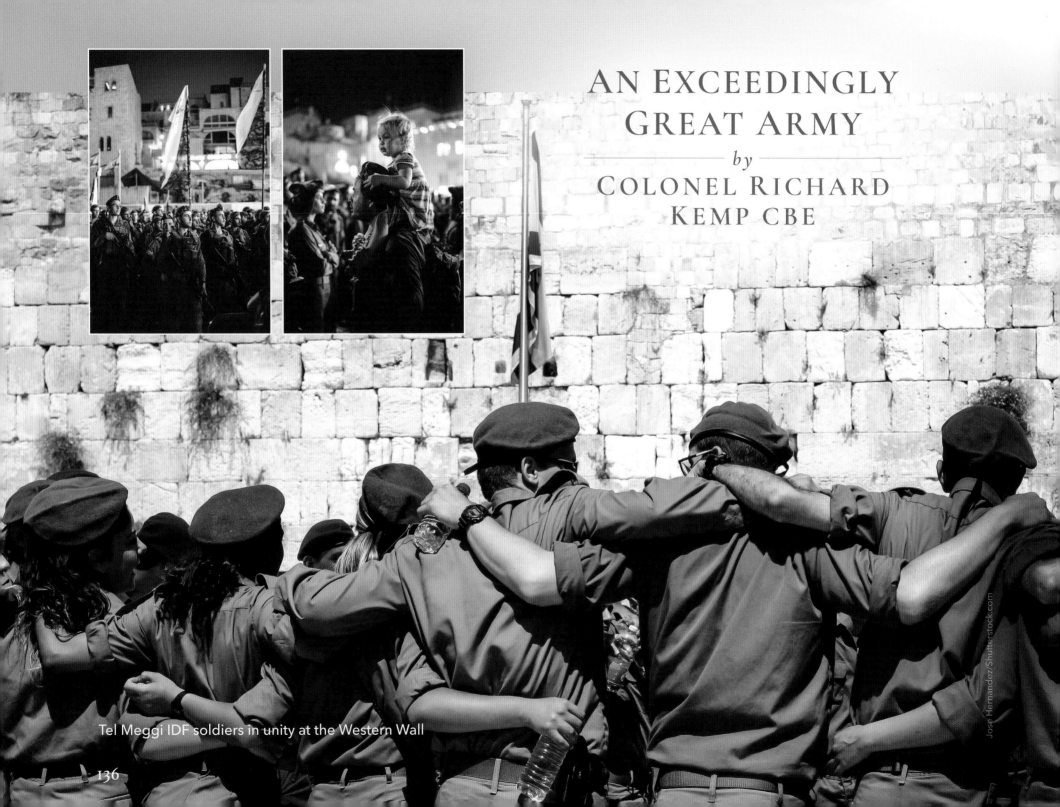

AN EXCEEDINGLY GREAT ARMY

by

COLONEL RICHARD KEMP CBE

Tel Meggi IDF soldiers in unity at the Western Wall

May 14, 1948, was one of the defining moments of the entire twentieth century—the nation of Israel was reborn in its eternal homeland against all odds. Many, especially Palestinians, call it the *Nakba*—or "catastrophe."

Conversely, many Christians and Jews believe that the rebirth of Israel was a modern-day miracle. The rebirth of Israel from the ashes of the Holocaust was prophesied in the Hebrew Tanakh, the Christian Old Testament.

The prophet Ezekiel had a vision about 2,500 years ago of a valley full of dried-out bones. With a thunderous rattling, the lifeless bones came together. Ezekiel was told to command life into them, which he did.

The prophet describes what happens next: *"Breath came into them, and they lived and stood upon their feet, an exceedingly great army"* (*Ezek. 37:10*). God told Ezekiel that this vision was about Israel, which could easily be a picture of the Holocaust.

A few years before Israel's rebirth,

Jews were herded into Nazi gas chambers. Six million perished—two-thirds of European Jewry. Today, the resurrected nation of Israel has one of the most powerful armies in the world, resulting from survival.

In May 1948, five surrounding Arab armies invaded the nascent state to snuff it out. Seriously outnumbered, and with an arms embargo imposed against it, the fledgling Israel Defense Forces (IDF), counting tens of thousands of Holocaust survivors among its ranks, prevailed in a year-long battle for the State of Israel. Had she been defeated, would there have been another genocide?

Nineteen years later, Egypt, Syria, and Jordan tried once again. The IDF was gravely outnumbered and out-gunned, but the Six-Day War of 1967 was one of the most remarkable defensive campaigns in military history. Many described it as a miracle. The IDF proved itself to be an exceedingly great army and remains so fifty-six years later.

Israel still needs that military might. The Iranian regime, on the verge of nuclear capability, con-

stantly pledges to wipe the Jewish State off the map. They are joined by the Hizballah and other groups to the north in Lebanon and Syria; Islamic Jihad in Gaza to the south with terrorist cells in Israel and Judea (branded "the West Bank" by the Jordanian invaders of 1948); and the Hamas in Gaza, also with cells in Judea. I can think of no other nation whose very existence is threatened like Israel; its exceedingly great army remains the shield and deterrent that stands in the path of aggressors.

The IDF's legacy began before statehood with the Haganah and the Palmach. British Army officers like Captain Orde Wingate, known as "The Friend," and Lieutenant Colonel John Henry Patterson, known as "Godfather to the IDF," influenced these Jewish militias.

My own support for Israel and the IDF originates working in British intelligence after 9/11 and while commanding troops in Afghanistan. I understood the immeasurable debt countries owe to Israel. Terrorist plots against many nations have been foiled directly due to Israeli intelligence, with many innocent lives saved. Israeli medi-

cal and military technology, as well as shared operational techniques, have not only saved the lives of numerous allied soldiers but enhanced their fighting capabilities.

I tire of the constant false accusations against Israel and the IDF—particularly bogus allegations of war crimes. I have been present on and near the front line in most of Israel's conflicts with Hamas, and I know that no other army in the history of warfare has taken greater or more effective steps than the IDF to prevent civilian casualties on the battlefield. The IDF fights with tremendous might and skill to defend its people but simultaneously adheres unbendingly to the laws of armed conflict. No army in the world, including those of Britain and America, has a higher standard of morality than the IDF.

The IDF is indeed an exceedingly great army—not just in its military achievements and prowess, but in its humanity and morality. It fights at the vanguard of the battle for Western civilization, and deserves our wholehearted support in its righteous struggle.

A TALE OF TWO MANUELS:
THE ROLE OF THE PHILIPPINES IN ISRAEL

by

PASTOR CONRADO LUMAHAN

In 1938, thanks to President Manuel L. Quezon's "open door" policy, 170,000 Jews from Germany and Austria were welcomed to the Philippines. Due to the Filipinos' hospitality, 1,300 were saved from the atrocities of the Nazi regime. During this dark period, six million Jews were murdered, of which 1.5 million were children.

On November 29, 1947, President Manuel A. Roxas instructed the Philippine Ambassador to the UN to vote in favor of the United Nations Resolution 181 to partition Palestine and establish the State of Israel—the only Asian nation to do so. That critical vote broke a tie in favor of the statehood of Israel.

Was it a coincidence or divine providence that the names of these two presidents were Manuel? Hebrew has no word for coincidence. "Manuel" is the shortest form of "Immanuel," which means "God with us." God was with His people when the Philippines opened its doors and when the Philippines voted for the creation of Israel.

Today, Israel remains isolated and threatened. Enemies think Israel has no right to exist as a nation or a people. Israel has been traumatized and terrorized, never knowing a single day of peace. They have been dehumanized and demonized. For this reason, God-loving people should stand in solidarity with the Jews. If God forever stands with them, why shouldn't we? There are many practical ways of biblically standing with God's covenant people.

First, we have to PRAY for the Jews. The Bible says, *"Pray for the peace of Jerusalem! May they be secure who love you"* (Ps. 122:6). This is a command.

We not only pray for the peace of Jerusalem but also for peace in Jerusalem. Going to Jerusalem is a memorable and life-transforming experience—the Bible comes to life. It is the city of the great King, chosen by Him in which to put His holy name forever and for His redemptive purposes.

Second, let us BRING THE JEWS HOME. Bringing the Jews home from exile, *Aliyah*, is God's promise. He says, *"I will rejoice in doing them good, and I will plant them in this land in faithfulness, with all my heart and all my soul"* (Jer. 32:41).

Third, let us FEED Holocaust survivors and the needy in Israel. Joseph, the son of Israel, provided food for all people during the seven years of great famine (Gen. 41:57). Had it not been for Joseph, few would have survived. Today, thousands of Holocaust survivors who miraculously escaped death are living out their final years in poverty and isolation.

Fourth, let us COLLECT MONEY to help them through services like the Genesis 123 Foundation. Paul says, *"For they were pleased to do it, and indeed they owe it to them. For if the Gentiles have come to share in their spiritual blessings, they ought also to be of service to them in material blessings"* (Rom. 15:27). Helping people in need is a righteous act. It is in giving that we are blessed.

Finally, let us PLANT TREES in Israel because Abraham (Gen. 21:33), his descendants, and God Himself planted trees in Israel. *"And out of the ground the Lord God made to spring up every tree that is pleasant to the sight and good for food"* (Gen. 2:9).

The Bible says, *"When you come into the land … plant any kind of tree for food"* (Lev. 19:23). Trees are a symbol of life, longevity, faith, rebirth, and righteousness. We can even plant a tree in Israel to remember a loved one. This is comforting and heart-warming to the grieving family.

These are some things Christians for Israel (C4I) is doing for the Jewish people. Wherever we go and whatever we do, we encourage Christians to love and comfort the Jewish people—touching hearts and moving hands to action.

REBECCA KOWALSKY

Prester John: The Untold Story of the Visionary of the Modern State of Israel

by

Dr. Robert Mawire

City of Ariel, Samaria, Israel

Prester John, a royal descendant of King Solomon and the Queen of Sheba, was the first to verbalize the idea of Israel's rebirth as a nation in her ancient homeland. He foretold the liberation of Palestine and the future rebirth of Israel as a Jewish homeland.

As a descendant of King Solomon and the Queen of Sheba, he was part of the longest-reigning Judean kingdom in Ethiopia, now known as Africa. They brought peace, security, and prosperity to the whole continent. They established unity with diversity, with many tribes living together in harmony until broken by colonialism.

In biblical times, Ethiopia was a blessing to the Jewish people. Centuries later, Prester John continued to bless them by funding their liberation with one thousand gold mines. The gold from his kingdom secured the Balfour Declaration.

It's not surprising that African gold helped in the rebirth of Israel.

The one thousand gold mines of the Prester John Dynasty were in Sofala, Zimbabwe. In biblical times, Sofala was known as Ophir and is referenced numerous times. For example, King David donated 110 tons of gold from Ophir to the Temple (1 Chron. 29:4–5). King Solomon and King Hiram of Tyre's fleet sailed to Ophir to bring back gold for the building of the Temple (1 Chron. 29:4–5; 1 Kgs. 9:27–28).

Prester John's letters offering his gold for the liberation of Palestine were translated into English, French, Italian, German, and Slavonic and were well-circulated in Europe for several centuries. They inspired worldwide exploration in search of his gold mines.

Cecil John Rhodes felt a divine calling as a vicar's son to fulfill Prester John's vision. He fought a bitter war against the Boers to stop the Dutch trekkers from accessing Prester John's land. Immediately after the war, he found the one thousand gold mines in Zimbabwe and shipped inestimable quantities to England. He kept the promise of Prester John: "I inform you that I give you full pledge (the gold from one thousand gold mines) to fight for the Holy Land."

Cecil espoused Prester John's vision to use the gold from Sofala to finance the rebirth of Israel. He invited Lord Balfour to join the Round Table and orchestrated obtaining the Balfour Declaration, which became the legal framework for creating the modern State of Israel. It read:

> His Majesty's Government view with favor the establishment in Palestine of a national homeland for the Jewish people, and will use their best endeavors to facilitate the achievement of this object, it being clearly understood that nothing shall be done, which may prejudice the civil and religious rights of existing non-Jewish communities in Palestine or the rights and political status enjoyed by Jews in any other country.

They set up a trust under the auspices of the Rothschild family to create the League of Nations and the United Nations to facilitate the creation of a homeland for the Jewish people in Palestine. Unsurprisingly, the League of Nations and the United Nations prioritized the creation of the modern State of Israel and enshrined it in both charters. They were created to fulfill Prester John's vision of a Jewish homeland in Israel to keep the ancient promise.

I'm filled with gratitude, mingled with awe, for my ancestor Prester John and his longing to see the rebirth of Israel in her ancient homeland, which Cecil John Rhodes fulfilled before passing away at the age of forty-eight.

As a result, Israel is a reality today. Though Prester John is unknown to most modern-day Israelis, his contribution remains as the Father of the modern State of Israel.

Prester John impassioned in me to gather the Jewish people back to Israel. Over the last forty years, I have worked with the late Mayor of Ariel, Ron Nachman, to build the leading Smart City in the world. I received a Lifetime Achievement Award from the World Jewish Congress and the Knesset. It really belongs to the forgotten, legendary visionary, His Imperial Majesty Prester John, King of Ethiopia, to whom we all owe a debt of gratitude.

How Israel's Story Unlocks Revival for the Nations

by

Pastor Tod McDowell

I was in a God-directed season of fasting and praying for the keys to global revival. On day thirty-five, I received a call from a trusted prophetic intercessor in Australia. She had just read some of my writings. She said, "Tod, I agree with your revelation on keys to global revival, but you are missing the Israel key." I was surprised and slightly offended. When I pressed her for specifics, she mentioned Don Finto's book, *Your People Shall Be My People.*

The president of Youth With A Mission (YWAM), John Dawson, had given me this book a few months earlier. I hadn't read it. I told her I would and thanked her for her boldness, though still slightly offended.

An hour later, I received a call from a school leader I oversaw. "Tod, I felt God telling me to ask if you want to meet with this week's speaker, Don Finto?" I was shocked. I had just agreed to read his book. Now God had my attention!

Two days later, I met Don. He seemed different than other Israel supporters I'd met. He didn't have a prayer shawl, a head covering, or a shofar. He didn't even have the Star of David around his neck or an Israeli flag anywhere. He looked scholarly and had warmth and love in his eyes, like a genuine pastor. He dove straight into Scripture. I felt reassured because he didn't take Scripture out of context. He began showing me how what God was doing in Israel today related to the nations.

He read Romans 11:12, *"Now if their trespass means riches for the world, and if their failure means riches for the gentiles, how much more will their full inclusion [greater riches] mean!"* The words "greater riches" jumped off the page. The Holy Spirit showed me that this was the key to the global revival that I'd been fasting and praying for. I interrupted Don and asked if he could pray for me. "I know this is a key to revival in my mind, but could you pray for an impartation into my heart?" As Don prayed for me, I felt God's love and pain for the Jewish people.

Soon I was facedown weeping. I heard God say, "You are married to the Jewish people." My mind couldn't grasp what that meant, and I wondered if my wife was Jewish. I now understand that God married the Jewish people when He covenanted with Abram in Genesis 15. As the book of Hosea shows, God is faithful, even when His wife is unfaithful. If God is married to the Jewish people, so am I.

How Is Israel a Key to World Revival?

Consider how the fulfillment of God's promises to the Jewish people of returning to the Land brings "greater riches" to the gentiles:

1. At the time of the first return of Jews to Israel in 1882, there also came a period of unusual evangelistic effort and success led by men like Dwight Moody and Charles Spurgeon.

2. The second return of Jews to Israel in 1904 brought about the Welsh Revival and the Azusa Street Revival in California.

3. Israel's independence in 1948 led to the Latter Rain Revival, evangelical awakening via Billy Graham, and the Healing Revival of Oral Roberts.

4. The Six-Day War, Israel's regaining of Jerusalem in 1967, started the Jesus Movement. Reinhard Bonnke started his ministry in Africa.

5. One day after the Vatican and Pope, the head of the universal church, established an Israeli embassy in Rome in 1994, the revival in Toronto began.

6. In September of 1999, Israeli and Palestinian leaders signed a memorandum renewing agreements made years earlier, including the release of Israeli prisoners, and fifteen days later, the International House of Prayer in Kansas City began their 24/7 prayer movement.

Supporting God's covenant with the Jewish people is a vital key to unlocking global revival. Let's bring global revival!

Painting by Udi Merioz

143

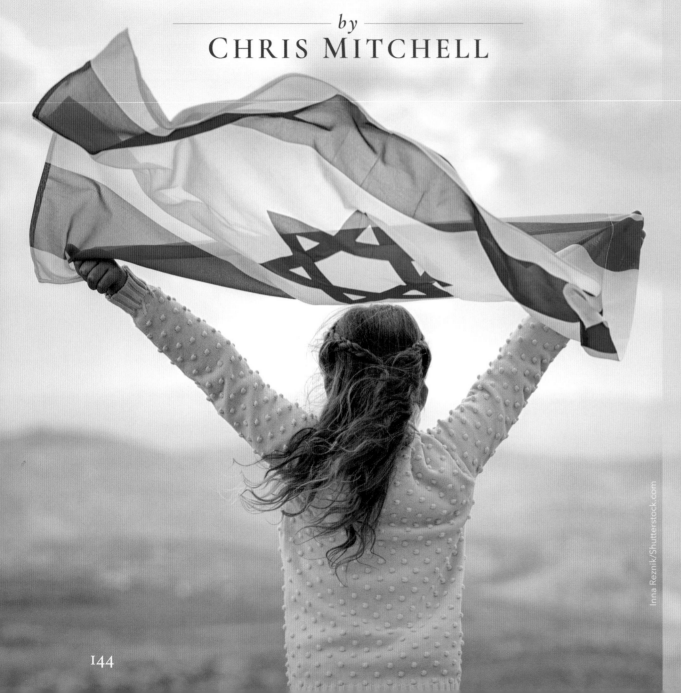

AGAINST ALL ODDS: THE MIRACLE OF ISRAEL

by

CHRIS MITCHELL

I srael's first Prime Minister, David Ben-Gurion, once reportedly said, "In Israel, to be a realist, you have to believe in miracles."

It's hard to describe modern-day Israel as anything other than a miracle. Never in human history has a nation been displaced and scattered to the four corners of the world and then regathered. After being dispersed to the winds during the Roman conquest of Israel two thousand years ago, the Jewish people hung tenaciously to their faith, customs, and culture. They cried, prayed, sang, and whispered, "Next year in Jerusalem."

While a small Jewish presence remained in the Holy Land for those two millennia, one day an even older prophecy began to unfold. Slowly as a trickle and sometimes as a torrent, the Jewish people returned to their Promised Land. Their return ebbed and flowed with the world's conditions. It gushed when the former Soviet Union collapsed. It slowed tragically when the British Empire dramatically restricted immigration before World War II, a policy many believe condemned thousands of Jews to the Nazi gas chambers. But like a phoenix rising out of the ashes, the Jews of the world came together to their homeland. To many, it signaled a divine migration and calling. They point to Ezekiel's prophecy in the valley of the dry bones and see a picture of modern Israel coming to life:

"The hand of the Lord was upon me, and he

brought me out in the Spirit of the Lord and set me down in the middle of the valley; it was full of bones. And he led me around among them, and behold, there were very many on the surface of the valley, and behold, they were very dry. And he said to me, 'Son of man, can these bones live?' And I answered, 'O Lord God, you know'"(Ezek. 37:1–3).

Now the Land of Israel teems with Jews from the ends of the earth—from Argentina, Morocco, Yemen, China, India, America, and beyond. For centuries, Israel was but a dream and a prayer. Despite overwhelming odds, pogroms, an Inquisition, the Crusades, persecution, and discrimination, Israel is now celebrating its 75th anniversary "against all odds." While the Jews survived, the nations that attacked them are no more. Mark Twain captured the essence of Jewish history when he wrote "Concerning the Jews" in 1899 for Harper's magazine:

> The Egyptian, the Babylonian, and the Persian rose, filled the planet with sound and splendor, then faded to dream-stuff and passed away; the Greek and the Roman followed; and made a vast noise, and they are gone; other people have sprung up and held their torch high for a time, but it burned out…. The Jew saw them all, beat them all, and is now what he always was, exhibiting no decadence, no infirmities of age, no weakening of his parts…. All things are mortal but the Jews; all other forces pass, but he remains. What is the secret of his immortality?

The prophet Jeremiah had answered Twain's query thousands of years earlier:

"Thus says the Lord, who gives the sun for light by day, and the fixed order of the moon and the stars for light by night, who stirs up the sea so that its waves roar—the Lord of hosts is his name: 'If this fixed order departs from before me,' declares the Lord, then shall the offspring of Israel cease from being a nation before me forever'" (Jer. 31:35–36).

Since August 2000, it's been my privilege as the Middle East Bureau Chief for CBN News to cover this miracle in the making—Israel. We've reported on how Israel has made the desert bloom as the prophet Israel declared. Revive an ancient and dead language like Zephaniah said. It has blessed the nations through the Jewish concept of *Tikkun Olam*, through Israeli volunteers reaching out during natural and man-made disasters. This tiny nation on the eastern shores of the Mediterranean has become a light to the nations through its technological prowess as the "Start-Up Nation." It's done this all

while battling terror inside its borders, existential threats outside, and the constant drumbeat of many nations clamoring for Israel's demise. Yet through it all, Ezekiel, Mark Twain, and Jeremiah testify: *Am Israel Chai!*—the People of Israel live!

FROM VILIFICATION TO VINDICATION: STANDING WITH ISRAEL IN THE FACE OF PERSECUTION AND INTOLERANCE

by

CHIEF JUSTICE MOGOENG MOGOENG

Abraham was seventy-five years old when God spoke to him concerning the birth of Isaac, whose descendants would multiply to become the nation of Israel—the same age as Jewish sovereignty in the Land of Israel this year.

The fulfillment of that promise to Abraham and the return of the Jews to the Land of Promise are not only milestones in the lives of the Jews and Christians but also prophetic. It deepens our conviction that He is the covenant-keeping God who fulfills His promises concerning our lives, families, and nations (Isa. 55:8–11; Num. 23:19).

Incidentally, the central Scripture of Abraham's story is also the one that ushered blessing into my life. In Genesis 12:3, God irreversibly declares:

"I will bless those who bless you, and him who dishonors you I will curse, and in you all the families of the earth shall be blessed."

This explains the blessings connected to the virtually inexplicable global influence, economic explosion, and unmatched technological innovations that the geographically "tiny" Land of Israel and the Jews, wheresoever they might be, swim in. This has been experienced by other individuals and nations who are unwavering in their support for the Jews and the Land of Israel.

I experienced faith-building per-

secution due to my refusal to express hatred for Israel and the Jews, as many in my nation, Anzaniah (South Africa), have no trouble doing. I believe there is a toxic yet growing intolerance for the Jews, and Israel in particular.

A massive and unrelenting smear campaign was launched against me for quoting Genesis 12:3 and Psalm 122:6 as the bases of my support for Israel and my commitment to pray for the peace of Jerusalem and, by extension, the peace of Israel.

It looked like the well-coordinated vilification strategy would work. But God ensured that I was effectively vindicated by the apex Court of Anzaniah on February 16, 2022. The court essentially said that my utterances on the Jerusalem Post Webinar were about my biblical beliefs, love, forgiveness, peace, and the need for mediation between Israel and Palestine. I believe that unmitigated shame fell upon those who cursed the Jews and the Land as they saw their plan nullified by the God whose word they had effectively risen against.

In October 2022, my wife and I had the enriching experience of visiting the Holy Land for the first time. The visit gave us a better perspective and gave a clearer meaning to the Bible in ways I never imagined possible.

Participating in the service with saints worldwide at the tomb of the risen Christ and sealing it with the Covenant Meal was a truly reviving experience.

I had life-changing breakthroughs and encounters with the Lord in Israel. I was honored with the Nehemia Award by the International Christian Embassy Jerusalem, which I understood to be an imposition of divine assignment on me to be a restorer of the destinies of nations.

The Lord also instructed me to atone for my nation's highly negative attitude towards Israel, which worsened by downgrading our Embassy. He also instructed me to covenant my country, Anzaniah, and the rest of my continent, Africa, with Israel, Palestine, and the rest of Asia according to Genesis 26:26–33. He also commanded me to establish, through prophetic action, the Isaiah 19:19–25 Highway between these nations and territories. This was done and sealed in Israel on October 16, 2022, exactly eight months after the Constitutional Court of Anzaniah vindicated me.

My faith was strengthened profoundly. And my resolve was heightened to obey God's Word, to love the Jews, the Land of Israel, the Palestinians and Palestine, and all other people in line with Matthew 5:44 and Matthew 22:35–40, no matter the consequences.

May this watershed moment—the celebration of Israel The Miracle—serve as a reassurance to the Jews and all true believers in Jesus Christ that ours is a covenant-keeping God who never changes nor forsakes His own.

iStock.com/Francis ODonohue

First century steps outside the House of Caiaphas

BEYOND SENTIMENTALITY:
THE CHRISTIAN RELATIONSHIP WITH ISRAEL

by

REV. JOHNNIE MOORE

One of my great blessings is my deep, rich friendships with Jews. A few years ago, I noticed that my older Christian and Jewish friends spoke the same way about the establishment of the modern State of Israel in 1948.

One of my eighty-year-old Christian friends speaks of his father pulling him to a radio to hear the announcement of Israel's independence. It was a formative part of his life. My Jewish friends speak similarly about that experience.

In both cases, the reconstitution of the State of Israel represented one of the only miracles they had ever actually witnessed. It was a transformative, spiritual experience, and it caused each person to embark upon their own journey with Israel.

For many Christians, that journey has also constituted a history lesson. Many evangelicals have been mortified to learn the history of Christian antisemitism.

As we celebrate Israel's 75th anniversary of independence, the Christian relationship with Israel needs to deepen beyond a sentimental relationship—but a substantive one, forged in a deep alliance but enjoyed because of genuine friendship.

There are plenty of opportunities for Jews and Christians to collaborate. Collaboration is stronger when we learn more about one another.

Christians, for instance, have to tell the stories of the generations of brave Christians who stood against antisemitism—but we also can't pretend that people who called themselves Christians didn't commit some of the most horrible crimes against the Jewish people.

We must celebrate the stories of famous Christian Zionists as heroes. When the founder of modern Zionism, Theodor Herzl, convened hundreds of Jewish leaders in the first Zionist Congress, serving as the symbolic parliament that would lay the groundwork for a Zionist movement around the world, Herzl also invited non-Jewish guests to attend, including ten prominent Christian leaders.

The term "Christian Zionists" came from Herzl himself as a way of describing his Christian friends. This is part of our Christian history and is celebrated as a legacy that we can be proud of.

We also must tell the other part of the story.

We must also tell our children about the Church's complicity with the Nazis. We must teach our children that history's greatest horror occurred in Christian Europe. We must tell them about the Wannsee Conference in January 1942, when fifteen Nazi leaders gathered outside of Berlin and voted unanimously to unleash the final solution on the Jewish people.

Each of those fifteen participants were professing Christians. All but four were Protestants.

This makes building relations between Jews and Christians all the more noteworthy. It also shows how our faith can be highjacked to wage a profane war of hate against even those whose faith and culture laid the foundation for our own.

We must also get to know the Jewish people.

Growing up in South Carolina, I loved Israel as a good Baptist, but I didn't meet a Jewish person until I was an adult. We can't truly *love* Israel and have no Jewish friends.

We can study the Hebrew Bible together as proud Jews and Christians. After all, it was the Hebrew

Bible before Christians started calling it the "Old Testament." Our Jewish friends have much to teach us about the texts they read first, wrote themselves, and read more than Christians do today.

We should spend more time in Israel experiencing Israel and her people. We should be role models for our children, taking them to Israel to get to know the Jewish people.

We must raise our voices against those who love to hate. When people say antisemitic things, we must speak quickly and clearly, especially if they are Christian.

To speak out requires paying attention and being informed. Knowing history, understanding nuance, and being brave and bold are our weapons, along with our faith.

As modern Israel celebrates seventy-five years, it's time for Christians to redouble their commitment to the State of Israel and the Jewish people. Our commitment needs to be stronger than feelings. Let's anchor in a friendship that can stand the test of time.

Why I Returned the Guatemalan Embassy in Israel to Jerusalem

by

President Jimmy Morales

In 2017, I returned the Guatemalan embassy in Israel to Jerusalem. It was a tough decision for me but very important as the president and a Christian.

Sixty years earlier, Guatemala voted in favor of the creation of a new Jewish State. We were the first country to open a commerce office with diplomatic representation in Jerusalem, giving Israel our full support. After this, along with fifteen other countries, Guatemala opened its embassy in Jerusalem. But, because of diplomatic pressure and security risks, all countries which had embassies in Jerusalem decided to move their embassies to Tel Aviv, Guatemala among them.

In 2017, the opportunity arose to restore the original relationship—to give total support to the new Jewish State, which encompassed recognizing her sovereignty. Why do I mention sovereignty? Because from a simple diplomatic and political perspective, it was the sovereign decision of a sovereign nation, so why should the international community violate her right to do so?

For this reason, as president of Guatemala, I decided to stand with Israel and return our embassy to Jerusalem. That decision constitutes a return to the beginning and the right path.

I am frequently asked why I did this. I made this decision because it was the right thing to do. That's very important, for in today's political environment, it often seems that doing the right thing may not be "good," whereas being "politically correct" isn't always determined by whether it is right or not.

I firmly believe that whoever is in a position of power must be brave to make the decisions that are the *right* decisions—no matter the criticism and the rejection from those loud minorities that threaten with violence and terror. As a Christian, my answer is biblical. I understand and embrace the promise found in Genesis concerning God blessing those who bless Israel.

I also realized that at that historic decision-making moment, God put me in a place to take action, like Esther, for such a time as this. I have always thought the right things must be done despite any consequences. From the day of my decision until now, I have been blessed and encouraged by the silent majority who thank me for having the courage to do the right thing.

Supporting Israel is not something I do for personal gain of any type nor any political endorsement from my people or anybody else. As a Christian believer, I don't think about giving or doing something to receive something in return. Our Christian message says that it is *"more blessed to give than to receive" (Acts 20:35).*

I am very proud of having done the right thing, showing the world that there are no small nations; there are only sovereign countries that shall manifest their will before the United Nations in defense of their rights and the rights of their partners, friends, and brothers.

These last words are significant, for this is how we see Israel, as a friend and a brother.

As the wise King Solomon said,

"A friend loves at all times, and a brother is born for adversity" (Prov. 17:17).

I pray that Guatemala and Israel will be friends forever.

Photo by David Kern

iStock.com/motimeiri

iStock.com/chaiyapruek2520

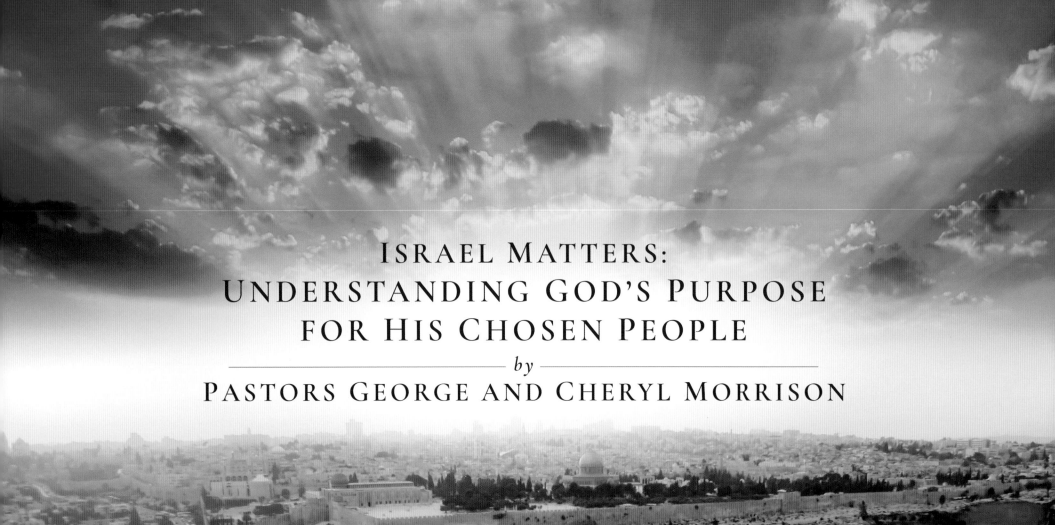

ISRAEL MATTERS:
UNDERSTANDING GOD'S PURPOSE
FOR HIS CHOSEN PEOPLE
by
PASTORS GEORGE AND CHERYL MORRISON

God is a promise-making, promise-keeping God.

God made a promise to a man (Abraham), which included a people (the Jews), a place (the Land of Israel), and a purpose (that the world would know God's faithfulness).

God's original promise to Abraham, the Jewish people, and the modern State of Israel demonstrates God's faithfulness.

The Promise

Throughout Scripture, we see God make promises and watch over those promises to bring them to pass.

The story of Israel begins with perhaps the most powerful promise in the Bible.

> Now the Lord said to Abram, "Go from your country and your kindred and your father's house to the land that I will show you. And I will make of you a great nation, and I will bless you and make your name great, so that you will be a blessing. I will bless those who bless you, and him who dishonors you I will curse, and in you all the families of the earth shall be blessed." (Gen. 12:1–3)

God's Promise Is a Place to a People with a Purpose.

God's promise is not a contract based on each party fulfilling their agreement with the other.

Photo by David Kiern

God's promise is a covenant. It is everlasting and unconditional. It is based on God's integrity and faithfulness to Israel, not Israel's faithfulness to God.

> "For when God made a promise to Abraham, since he had no one greater by whom to swear, he swore by himself" (Heb. 6:13).

If God is faithful to His promise to Israel, then He will be faithful to His promise to us.

The Place (Land of Israel)

"And nations shall come to your light, and kings to the brightness of your rising" (Isa. 60:3).

This was written to, and about, Israel. These persecuted people have become a mighty nation, standing out in the world with God's glory upon them.

We live in a unique time in history, the words of Ezekiel, Jeremiah, Daniel, Isaiah, and other prophets are coming to pass in our day.

One of the most dramatic examples is Ezekiel 36. This chapter is a prophecy to the Land of Israel.

Ezekiel 36:8 says, "But you, O mountains of Israel, shall shoot forth your branches and yield your fruit to my people Israel, for they will soon come home."

Since the time of Ezekiel, the Land of Israel has been conquered and re-conquered over twenty times. It has never been a homeland nor produced for any other people.

The People

God uses people to accomplish His work. In His sovereignty, He is determined to work in, among, and through people to fulfill His purpose.

"And I will make of you a great nation, and I will bless you and make your name great, so that you will be a blessing" (Gen. 12:2). God has used the Jewish people to be a blessing to all.

Israel has accomplished more in seventy-five years than any other country has achieved in centuries.

Israel leads the world in the number of scientists and technicians in the workforce.

The Jewish State is the third most educated country in the world.

Israel is ranked number two globally for funding start-ups, right behind the USA.

The cell phone was developed in Israel.

Israel developed the first ingestible video camera, so small that it fits inside a pill that can view the small intestine. (We have a friend who has had this procedure.) And so much more.

The Purpose

Some 3,500 years ago, God made an unconditional covenant with His chosen servant Abram (Abraham). The primary part of this covenant was that all the nations for all time would be blessed through Abraham's descendants.

Genesis 12:3 says, *"...in you all the families of the earth shall be blessed."*

God's Purpose for Israel: Summary

Through Israel came the Word of God (the Bible), inspired Scriptures of the Old and New Testament.

Through Israel's miracles of survival and restoration, we see evidence for God. Through Israel, we see God working in the world and making a name for Himself.

Israel matters.

iStock.com/Vladimir1965

iStock.com/chameleonseye

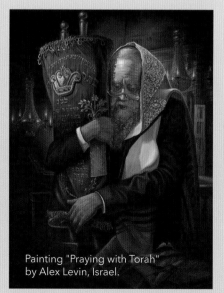

Painting "Praying with Torah" by Alex Levin, Israel.

155

THE DISCIPLINE OF REST:
INSIGHTS FROM LIVING THROUGH THE SECOND INTIFADA

by

SHELLEY NEESE

Painting by Udi Merioz

As young adults, my husband and I moved to Be'er Sheva, Israel, for three years of graduate school. Soon after moving into our apartment in 2000, two things happened. First, disgruntled Palestinians began blowing themselves up in shopping malls and bus stations to achieve "martyrdom." Second, our Jewish neighbors began inviting us over for Shabbat dinners. What I experienced at those Friday night dinners directly impacted how I managed to live through the Second Intifada. Israel taught me that rest is possible even where there is no peace.

I overheard Israelis discussing the devastating headlines and the war on terror six days a week. Hand-wringing over how Israel would survive was a national pastime. However, on Friday afternoon, the focus changed, and a different mood settled over the country. It was as if the entire country was preparing for a wedding reception with nothing to fear because there was so much to anticipate.

The woman at the post office, who was normally sharp-edged with my struggling Hebrew, would wish me a "Shabbat Shalom." My Israeli classmates who were stressed about drafting academic papers in English pushed away thoughts of schoolwork for twenty-four hours with no fear of falling behind. A cab driver, who heard we had no immediate family in Be'er Sheva, invited us to his family's Shabbat dinner. Children pushed grocery carts piled up with items so high that they couldn't see over the mound.

As a Christian, I have already experienced spiritual rest as promised in the Gospels. Jesus is spiritual rest personified. However, Israel taught me a different rest. I learned about the discipline of rest and the value of national rest. I saw Israelis as a collective choose to rest even when rest was far from their minds during the other six days of struggle. On those Shabbats, Israel transformed. I heard it in songs and clanging dishes on my neighborhood walk. I saw it in the carless streets and strolling families.

Before Israel, I thought rest had to be achieved when permitted in the academic calendar or with a planned vacation. Slowly, however, my husband and I learned that the discipline of Sabbath rest was also a divine gift. Israel was our teacher.

On Sabbath, we stopped studying even though we were in the hardest programs. We started walking to church even though it took almost an hour. Because everything was closed, there was no temptation to run errands. We ate, played games, and visited friends at the park. Invitations to Shabbat dinners came in every week. As guests, we learned that our secular Jewish friends still had Shabbat dinner, perhaps minus the liturgy but not the joy. Our more religious friends' ceremonies often went past midnight.

Shabbat conversations did not deny or ignore the current realities of Israel's difficulties. Rest never equaled denial. On more than one occasion, Shabbats were interrupted by news of bombings. I will never forget when news trickled through our Shabbat meals of twenty-one Israelis who died after a terrorist bombed a discotheque in Tel Aviv. After studying Jewish history, I learned that the Second Intifada was not unique. Persecution is a common thread in the long Jewish story. The will to rest, the obedience to observe rest, always continued, despite the external threats to that rest.

Israel taught my husband and me the discipline of rest. Rest is a choice, not a reward. National peace is not a prerequisite for national rest. I am forever grateful that Israel opened her heart and homes to us, even amid her uncertainty and pain, to teach that important lesson. Even though I have been back in the United States for two decades, I continue the tradition of a weekly "wedding reception" in my home. And just as my Israeli neighbors opened their doors to resident aliens in the form of southern Christian newlyweds, I insist on applying that same principle around our own dinner table.

Shabbat Shalom, Israel.

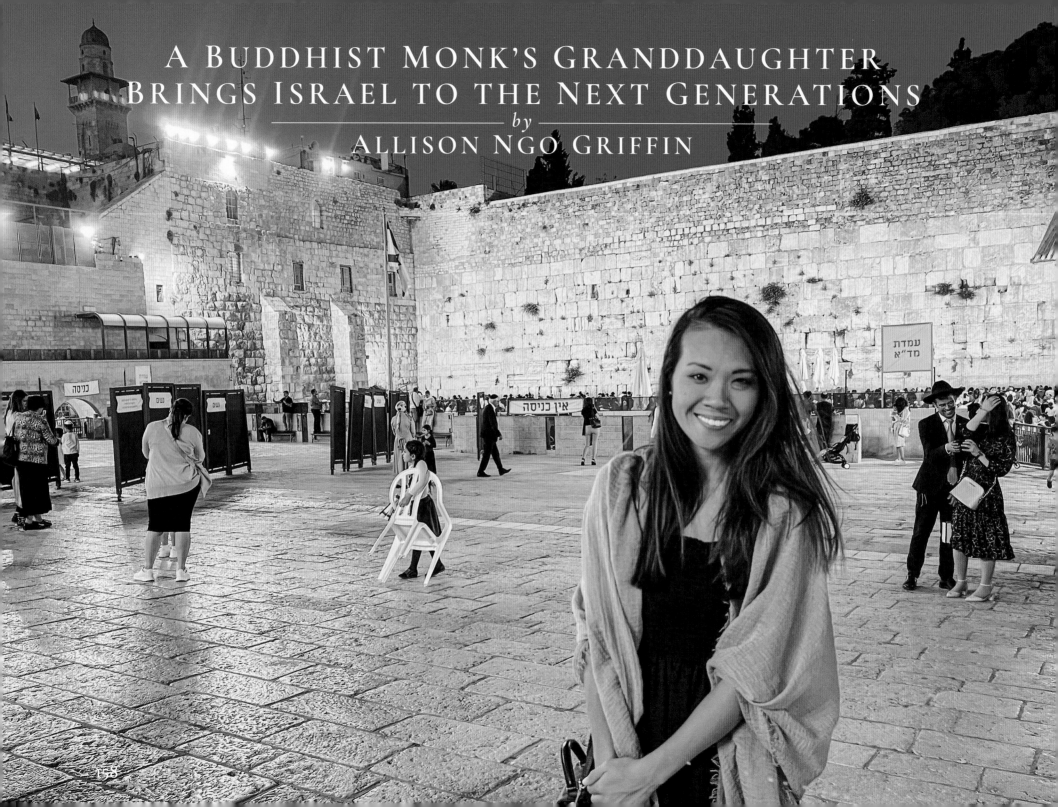

A Buddhist Monk's Granddaughter Brings Israel to the Next Generations

by

Allison Ngo Griffin

I grew up in a devout Buddhist family in Texas, where my grandparents ran a Temple as Buddhist monks. I was drawn to the Jewish community in college and asked some of my closest friends, "Why are the Jews such a tight-knit community?" "Throughout history, we've been persecuted; it seems everyone around the world wants to kill us. So we have to stay close together," one said. It broke my heart.

When I gave my life to Jesus at the age of twenty-three, I didn't understand the significance of Israel and the Jewish people. The first church I attended led me astray with replacement theology. This was my mindset for years until I started studying Scripture in depth in Bible school. This is when I learned that Jesus was Jewish, all of His disciples were Jewish, that He kept the Jewish feasts, and that His genealogy was Jewish. To fully grasp Jesus' life, death, resurrection, and call here on earth, I believe you must understand the Jewish storyline.

In 2019, the Lord clearly spoke to me and confirmed through others that I was to quit Bible school and take a trip to Israel. I was invited to the Jerusalem Prayer Breakfast. While praying for peace in Jerusalem, I met Peter Griffin, another American attendee. We were engaged four months later and married in March 2020, proudly displaying the Israeli flag on our wedding cake. Our marriage is a walking testimony of Genesis 12:3, which says, *"I will bless those who bless you."*

The younger generation is told that Israel is an apartheid and oppressive state. We're told to boycott Israel for defending herself. If only we, as the body of Yeshua, could heed Paul's warning: *"Do not be arrogant toward the branches. If you are, remember it is not you who support the root, but the root that supports you"* (Rom. 11:18).

I am now an event coordinator for events that involve Jews and Christians coming together under one God and around a mutual love for Israel. I hope that through unity between Christians and Jews, the younger generation will catch what I didn't early in my faith: to understand that the God of Israel is a faithful, covenant-keeping God.

Who in the Church will rise and defend our Jewish brothers and sisters as antisemitism arises? Who will bring comfort and speak up for Israel like Corrie ten Boom and Dietrich Bonhoeffer? Who will be her most loyal friend when the international news outlets and the UN try to delegitimize the Jewish people's right to their historic and God-given homeland? While millennials and Gen Z weren't fortunate to witness the large displays of God's power, love, and faithfulness to the Jewish people in the 40s and 60s, we can share these testimonies with the younger generation as we celebrate Israel's 75th anniversary.

May He enlighten the hearts of my generation and inspire in them a love for Israel and the Jewish people as He has done in mine. This is my heart's desire and will be the Griffin family's mission for generations to come.

ISRAEL'S NEXT 40 YEARS:
A FUTURE BEYOND OUR IMAGINATION

by
BOB O'DELL

Seventy-five years have passed since the re-establishment of Israel in 1948. Some years later, a theory made rounds in Christian circles that Jesus was returning by 1988. Millions of books were sold based on a misunderstanding of Luke 21:32. When 1988 came and went without tumult, Christians were forced to acknowledge that a forty-year Israel was too short.

Now we sit at Israel's seventy-five-year mark. What else are we underappreciating, if not completely missing? Let's look at two massive changes in Israel right now: one secular and one spiritual.

The Secular Change

For a nation's population to remain stable without immigration, the birth rate must have 2.1 children born for every woman in a nation. *Israel has the highest birth rate of any Western nation.*

The birth rate within the religious community is over four births per woman. In contrast, the birth rate within the Jewish non-Orthodox community averages around two births per woman. And since the Orthodox community is more conservative than secular, the

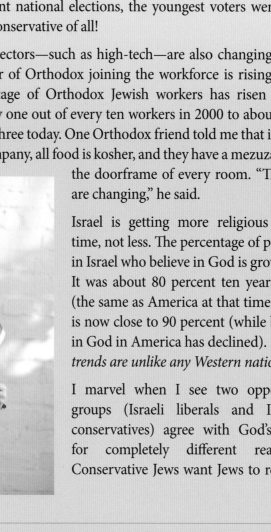

nation of Israel is getting more conservative over time!

In recent national elections, the youngest voters were the most conservative of all!

Work sectors—such as high-tech—are also changing. The number of Orthodox joining the workforce is rising. The percentage of Orthodox Jewish workers has risen from roughly one out of every ten workers in 2000 to about one out of three today. One Orthodox friend told me that inside his company, all food is kosher, and they have a mezuzah on the doorframe of every room. "Things are changing," he said.

Israel is getting more religious over time, not less. The percentage of people in Israel who believe in God is growing. It was about 80 percent ten years ago (the same as America at that time), but is now close to 90 percent (while belief in God in America has declined). *These trends are unlike any Western nation!*

I marvel when I see two opposing groups (Israeli liberals and Israeli conservatives) agree with God's will for completely different reasons. Conservative Jews want Jews to return

Israel, is unlike any other Western nation. Its conservative population is growing, and the strength of its base is in its younger generation.

because of prophecy and because "it's the right thing to do." Liberal Jews want more Jewish immigration to keep the conservative leanings of their country in check!

Future Israel is more God-fearing than we realize—an Israel that will come into better alignment with the Bible, the Torah, and a righteous worldview.

The Spiritual Change

During my recent visits to Israel, I've noticed that Judaism is changing.

While Judaism is steeped in tradition and deeply respects past practices, there is one wildcard that overturns everything else.

That wildcard is the Land of Israel!

Since the destruction of the Temple in AD 70, Judaism has developed around the exile. With the Temple destroyed, the power shifted away from the centralized authority of the Sanhedrin and shifted to the local rabbi. That rabbi had to exert more authority within the Jewish communities or the Jews would have drifted away from their practice of Judaism.

This Is Called Rabbinic Judaism.

The focus of Rabbinic Judaism was on things universal to Jews, things that could keep them distinctive as a people. It was a matter of survival.

But as Jews return to Israel, the commandments associated with the Land (and there are many of them) will rise in importance. Hundreds of additional commands would activate if a Temple were built. The Jews of Israel will have to consult the Torah and come together to fulfill such matters. The focus will swing away from the local rabbi and towards the Torah itself! Not that rabbis will be demoted, but such decisions cannot be made at the rabbinical level; they have to be made at a national level.

The Future of Israel

Israel is unlike any other Western nation. Its conservative population is growing, and the strength of its base is in its younger generation.

Spiritually, Israel is transitioning from Rabbinic Judaism to Torah-based Judaism, driven by the return of Jews to the Land of Israel.

If this world had ended in 1988, a very different Israel would have limped into the millennium. Less than forty years since, Israel has seen many profound changes, with more coming.

The future of Israel is much bigger than could have been envisioned forty years ago. And suppose the Messiah tarries another forty years? What will Israel look like in forty years?

I suggest that Israel's future is again incomparable to the future we envision today.

I suspect it will always be that way because our God of Wonder wouldn't dream of having it any other way.

FROM FAMILY ESTATE TO CULTURAL DIPLOMACY:
THE LEGACY OF VILLA MELCHETT
by
LORD SIMON READING

Photo by David Kiern

I had carefully camouflaged my Jewish heritage although two of my grandfathers are among the founding fathers of modern-day Israel.

My grandmother, Eva Marchioness of Reading, lived there on and off from the early 1930s to the late 1960s. She hosted influential guests in a private villa on the western shore of the Sea of Galilee. Looking eastward across the water to the then Syrian-controlled Golan Heights, she showed them the best of Israel, essential parts of biblical Israel, and the significant political geography of modern Israel.

My great-grandfather, Lord Melchett, built the villa in 1929. Another great-grandfather, Rufus Isaacs, was the first Marquess of Reading. He received the highest honor ever granted to a Jew by Britain (a Marquessate) and was Chairman of the Palestinian Electric Corp, now the Israeli Electric Corporation.

My family history embodied in this century-old villa was inseparably connected to Israel's modern and biblical history. I realized I must embrace my birthright and connection to the Land and the people. It could no longer remain private.

I discovered our family museum in Tel Mond, a small town in Galilee. I learned that former Israeli President Ezer Weizman's father was Sir Alfred Mond's (later Lord Melchett) plantation manager at Tel Mond. President Weizman invited us to meet him and asked why it took fifty years to visit Israel.

After leading several trips to Israel, it became clear that Villa Melchett was not only a former family estate giving me a foundation in the Land, but that it was ideal for hosting foreign dignitaries, out of the spotlight, to share how the biblical and modern history of Israel are intertwined, and to help them understand how their countries must support Israel, to eradicate replacement theology and rampant antisemitism. I call this "Cultural Diplomacy."

In the past two decades alone, we have hosted representatives from some forty nations. The fruit of these efforts is creating new models of support for Israel at the UN and throughout the nations.

We also host students and other groups, bringing the idea of Cultural Diplomacy to the next generation. And these days, when Israel is fraught with domestic strife, Villa Melchett is also a venue to bring people together to dialogue and create understanding. The peaceful scenery surrounding this precious site is infused with civility, underscoring Israel caring one for another, something that took me too long to embrace from my own family's past but now which drives me.

Today Villa Melchett has hosted dignitaries from forty nations along with the European Coalition for Israel, the International Coalition for Israel, and founding Chair, Tomas Sandell, whose work continues to make a vast impact on the world stage.

Coming from the UK, it's important to remind Great Britain and the United States of their historic commitment to the Land and people of Israel. I call it a three-legged stool of support, starting with British Restorationists in the nineteenth century, the unequivocal British support for establishing the State of Israel in the 1917 Balfour Declaration, and Britain, the US, and world powers reiterating this at the San Remo in 1920.

We must remind the British and American governments that the reasons for the agreements they supported (including the 1947 UN vote to establish a Jewish State) are no less valid. President Truman was the first to recognize the newly reborn Jewish State in 1948 and the underlying reasons have not changed.

Where Villa Melchett can be a catalyst for creating a groundswell of support for Israel in the UK, the US, and around the world, as a service to the Land, people, and State of Israel, and with the deep pride and connection to my family history intertwined within, the doors are open. I pray that it will be a source of continued blessing.

CONNECTED BY BLOOD, BOUND BY FAITH: ISRAEL, MY HOME

by

JOHN RILEY

Long before I was given the opportunity to host the Middle East Report, I was connected to Israel. It was in my blood.

The fact that my mother was Jewish planted something deep inside me. She was one of twenty children born into a Jewish family in Morocco, half of whom moved to Israel. I grew up a Christian but was connected to the Jewish people by blood. My family roots and Christian faith gave me a deep love for Israel and the Jewish people. It's part of my DNA physically but also spiritually.

Being in Israel is simply being home.

When I am in Israel, I see Jewish history, biblical history, unfold before my eyes. When there's a significant archeological find, it connects me to my Jewish roots. My Christian faith is rooted in the history of the Jewish people, and that's unavoidable. That's something every Christian needs to know and affirm.

From the Golan and Galilee to Beit Shean and Beit Shemesh, through the valleys and up the hills, you see the Bible come to life at every turn. Every stone, every biblical site, must be understood from a Jewish context—historically, geographically, and sociologically. Without that, you really can't understand the Bible.

Christians need to do a deep dive into this biblical truth. A visit to Israel brings that home and brings you home, even if you don't have a Jewish mother.

Walking the trails, swimming in the seas and rivers, driving through the Land, and skiing the Golan slopes are how families connect with the Land, which also gives us Christians a deeper connection as well.

We owe a great debt to the Jewish people for the laws and the core of morality, and for preserving these over thousands of years, despite persecution and suffering for maintaining their faith. We don't need to rewrite the Bible; we need to understand it from this perspective. There's nothing like being in Israel and reading the Word of God in the Land of the Bible, among His covenanted chosen people.

To inform, equip, educate, and motivate people to make this connection is not just my job; it's my calling. We need to make a difference in our communities. But we also need to be sure that, as Christians, we are bound to Israel as family. This is rooted in the Truth, which is rooted in love for Israel and the Bible.

When you come to the Land, you see that Israel is a beacon of hope.

Its national anthem is *Hatikvah*, the Hope. As the Jewish people have realized the hope of coming home, Israel fulfills its role as a hope, an inspiration to us all.

Yes, I am connected to Israel through the blood of my family. I have cousins in Israel, and when I see them, I am home.

But I am also related to Israel through the blood of Jesus. All Christians are. We know what this means for our faith and salvation. But we cannot forget that Jesus was a Jew. The Jewish people today are His brethren. Just as we have a personal relationship with Jesus, if we have a relationship with Him, we must have a relationship with His family. We must never forget that we are grafted into all of Israel.

As Israel celebrates seventy-five years of miraculous and inspiring independence, we see Israel being light and hope to this world. As their brethren, we must also adopt this responsibility.

Israel is family, and in Israel, we are home.

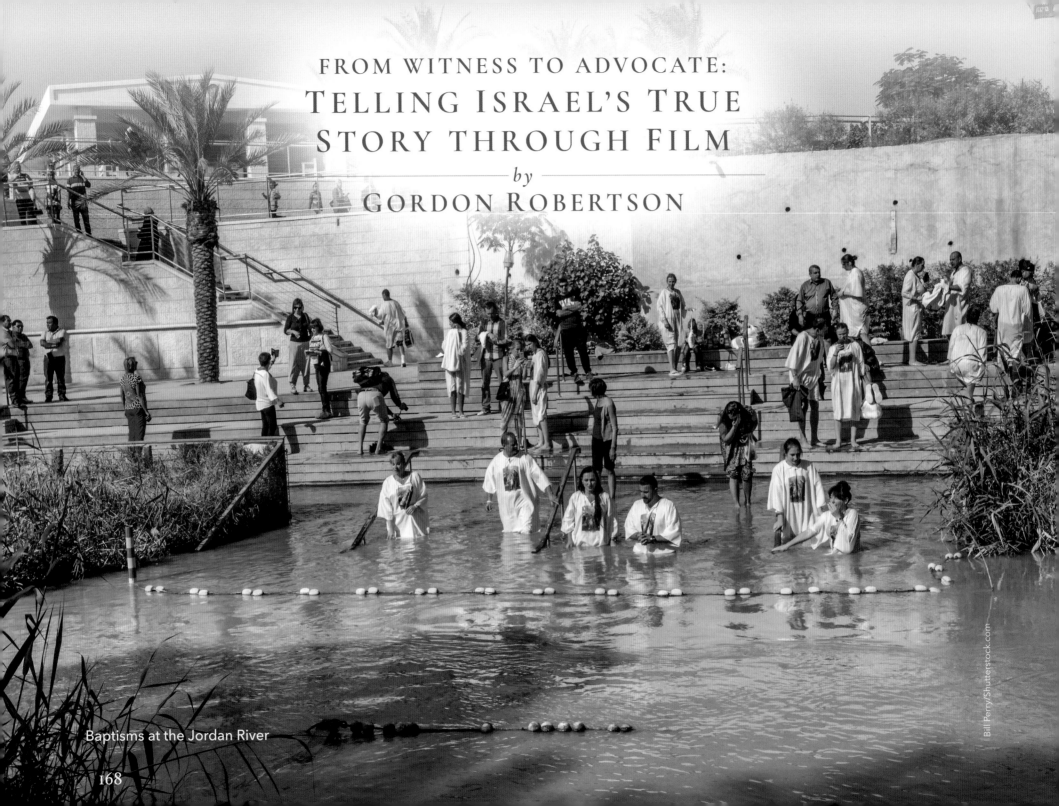

FROM WITNESS TO ADVOCATE:
TELLING ISRAEL'S TRUE STORY THROUGH FILM
by
GORDON ROBERTSON

Baptisms at the Jordan River

In 1969, when I was just eleven years old, my father, Dr. Pat Robertson, took me along on his first trip to the Holy Land. What I saw changed me forever.

We went to the Western Wall, where we saw rabbis dancing with Torah scrolls. This was just two years after the Six-Day War, which finally opened the way for Jewish people to worship at their most sacred place. We witnessed the jubilation of those rabbis—rejoicing that they were restored to their homeland, that the words of the prophets had become true, that they could celebrate God's Word and pray at the place He had designated in Jerusalem, the city He had chosen.

I couldn't understand a word they were saying, but the jubilation they expressed was infectious, and I was changed.

It changed me so much that I wanted to make sure each one of my children had the same experience. So, in a sort of Christian bar mitzvah, I took each of my children to Israel when they were twelve. They were baptized in the Jordan River, and together we visited the Western Wall and prayed. As my son and I were leaving that experience, he turned to me and said, "Dad, I can't explain this, but I feel like I'm at home."

That was obviously an emotional moment, but so much more so because it was generational: for my father to love Israel, for that to be transmitted to me at age eleven, and then for that love to be passed on to my children.

The tie is more than intellectual; it's more than just what we read in the prophets in the Bible. It's profound and very personal.

Years later, I met with Israel's then Consul General in New York, Ido Aharoni. He told me that Israel had a public relations problem because her true story wasn't being told. It dawned on me that the Christian Broadcasting Network had the means to do something about it, so that's when CBN started this journey.

It's my goal to correct the narrative about Israel, particularly of the Boycott, Divestment, and Sanctions movement, and show the truth about Israel and her people. We have been doing this for the past two decades through the reporting of CBN News, which has a bureau in Jerusalem. Then God opened the door for us to produce films.

Our first project was *Made in Israel,* revealing why the Jewish State is often called "the start-up nation." It features some of the wonderfully inventive things coming from its people, such as devising ways to grow more food with less water, creating technology behind the electronic devices we rely upon, and developing new ways to treat cancer, diabetes, and even blindness.

Second was *The Hope: The Rebirth of Israel,*

Photo by David Kiern

exploring the half-century before the founding of modern-day Israel as described by its founders and visionaries, including Theodor Herzl, Chaim Weizmann, David Ben-Gurion, and Golda Meir.

The third film, *Whose Land Is It?,* is the most political of the series, carefully examining the claims of both the Palestinians and the Jews to Israel.

Next, we produced *In Our Hands: The Battle for Jerusalem,* the story of the Six-Day War, which debuted in movie theaters worldwide. Shot entirely on location in Israel, it tells the story of the battle for Jerusalem through the eyes of Israel's 55th Paratrooper Brigade. This film combines dramatic reenactments with archival footage, interviews with war veterans, and commentary from former Israeli Ambassador to the United States, Michael Oren.

To help document the iron-clad connection of modern-day Jews to the land of their forefathers, CBN Films produced the four-part series, *Written in Stone*. Each episode focuses on a particular period of the Bible: *House of David, Kings and Prophets, Secrets of the Temple,* and *Jesus of Nazareth*.

We also produced *Treasures of the Second Temple* to trace the historical path of Judaism's most sacred treasures after Rome sacked and looted Jerusalem in 70 CE.

For Israel's 70th anniversary, we filmed *To Life: How Israeli Volunteers Are Changing the World*. This is particularly close to my heart because when CBN's humanitarian arm, Operation Blessing, worked with Israeli teams after an earthquake in Haiti, I saw firsthand what IsraAID and the IDF can do in a disaster. I wanted to show the untold story of how a small country like Israel is providing incredibly outsized humanitarian aid to the world's nations and those who consider Israel an enemy, such as the Syrians and Palestinians.

In the film, we asked the Jewish volunteers, "Why do you do this?" It gripped my soul to hear them repeatedly say that they don't serve out of obligation or guilt—they simply do it because it's who they are.

In Isaiah 49:6, when God speaks of the restoration of Israel, He says, *"I will make you as a light for the nations."* How interesting to note that in Genesis 1:3, when God said, *"Let there be light,"* the light simply needed to do what it was created to do. And so when God says to Israel, "I will make you a light to the nations," they only have to be who they are. They are indeed a light to the nations.

We need to tell this story because this is what God is doing today.

Photo by David Kiern

iStock.com/Rudy Balasko

Photo by David Klein

172

INHALING PURPOSE, EXHALING GOODNESS: DISCOVERING THE SOUL IN ISRAEL
by
CURTIS ROBINSON

I celebrated my 75th year with my beautiful wife, Sheila, in Israel. At age seventy-five, God called Abraham to go to Canaan (Gen. 12:1–3). Now, I was in the Land God promised to Abraham and his descendants, at the same age he was when he was called.

I always dreamed of going to the Holy Land. As a child, my mama taught me the Bible. When she took us to church, I tried hard to imagine the great men and women of the Old and New Testaments. What did they look like? What was it like during Bible times?

Part of me wanted more proof that these stories were true. Were they myths to scare us into believing or attending church? Or were there men named Abraham, Jacob, Moses, David, and Jesus—born with nothing in a manger in Bethlehem?

At seventy-five years, my questions were answered when my wife and I met author, speaker, professional coach, and facilitator Pastor Dr. Joel Freeman of the Freeman Institute. Joel led a small group on a fantastic journey to Israel for ten days. Our experience was transformational.

Indescribable feelings swept over me when we arrived at the Sea of Galilee. I pictured how a divine and human man could walk on water after a storm in which His disciples were afraid.

We went places to ingest the atmosphere, learn, share, change, and bond. However, nothing impacted our lives more than when we decided to get baptized in the Jordan River, where Jesus was baptized by John the Baptist.

Painting by Udi Merioz

To be baptized is to be reborn. Baptism allowed us to repent and ask God to forgive our sins, to become anew in the flesh, but mainly in the heart.

That chilly sunny morning, we all said a prayer. Donned in unique garbs, my wife got baptized first. When it was my turn, I looked at the water and marveled. The water felt cold, comfortable, and reassuring.

The minister asked if I wanted to say anything before my body was dipped into the Jordan. All I could say was, "I hope God will forgive me for my sins and pray He has mercy on my soul."

If the heavens declared His glory at that moment, we felt it as five couples who dedicated our lives to goodness, God, and humanity.

We felt a lifetime of burden lift and cast into the Jordan River. I remembered the Old Negro Spiritual we sang at church, finally understanding what it meant when the song says, "Roll, Jordan, roll"—a spiritual sung by enslaved Africans working on plantations in the Americas in the 1800s in resistance to their enslavement and cruel treatment. "Wade in the water" for freedom was the baptism from oppression.

Harriet Tubman had our ancestors wade in the water to throw off the scent for the dogs coming to recapture those running for freedom. As my people had a spiritual heritage of being enslaved, our ancient Hebrew brothers and sisters had a spiritual heritage of their enslavement. The oppression of the Jews from biblical times to the Holocaust to the present is synergistic to Black people, Middle Passage, and slavery in the present.

I felt a duty to help those less fortunate to live for the soul—*Neshama*. "Neshama" means "breath": *"Then the Lord God formed man of the dust from the ground and breathed into his nostrils the breath [Neshama] of life, and man became a living creature [soul]" (Gen. 2:7).* Our breath of life is our soul. Being baptized in water freed us to inhale purpose and exhale goodness to others.

Living for the soul with obedience and faith in goodness could not have come together without our trip to Israel.

As the State of Israel commemorates its 75th birthday, may her *Neshama* breathe its breath of life to its people and ALL the world in *Ahava* (love), truth, and certainty (Amen).

iStock.com/Jacek_Sopotnicki

GOD'S FAITHFULNESS TO ISRAEL AND THE CHURCH

by

BISHOP JOSE RODRÍGUEZ AND DR. VILMA RODRÍGUEZ

Why do Christians love, honor, and bless Israel?

First, God chose to send us the Savior of the world, our beloved Jesus Christ, through Israel. According to the prophet Micah, the Messiah was to be born in Bethlehem of Judah, the homeland of King David (Mic. 5:2).

"For to us a child is born, to us a son is given; and the government shall be upon his shoulder, and his name shall be called Wonderful Counselor, Mighty God, Everlasting Father, Prince of Peace" (Isa. 9:6).

This prophecy was fulfilled in every detail when God the Father introduced His Son, Jesus, to the world.

Second, the Word of God tells us that salvation comes from the Jews.

"You worship what you do not know; we worship what we know; for salvation is from the Jews" (John 4:22).

Third, God told Abraham that in Him all the families of the earth would be blessed.

"I will bless those who bless you, and him who dishonors you I will curse, and in you all the families of the earth shall be blessed" (Gen. 12:3).

Fourth, because it is a command from our God.

"Pray for the peace of Jerusalem! 'May they be secure who love you! Peace be within your walls and security within your towers!' For my brothers and companions' sake I will say, 'Peace be within you!' For the sake of the house of the Lord our God, I will seek your good" (Ps. 122:6–9).

Fifth, we are God's people and spiritual Israel. God has grafted us to the good olive tree (Rom. 11:16–18; 24). The apostle Paul explains:

"But it is not as though the word of God has failed. For not all who are descended from Israel belong to Israel, and not all are children of Abraham because they are his offspring, but 'Through Isaac shall your offspring be named'" (Rom. 9:6–7).

Paul speaks of this in Romans 10:20: *"I have been found by those who did not seek me; I have shown myself to those who did not ask for me."*

Where does this leave the Jews, who were promised great salvation in the covenant God made with Abraham? Paul asks this same question in Romans 11:1: *"I ask, then, has God rejected his people?"* In other words, has Israel been cast off?

Paul's response is very blunt: *"By no means! For I myself am an Israelite, a descendant of Abraham, a member of the tribe of Benjamin. God has not rejected his people whom he foreknew"* (Rom. 11:1–2a).

Finally, Paul says, *"Therefore welcome one another as Christ has welcomed you, for the glory of God. For I tell you that Christ became a servant to the circumcised to show God's truthfulness, in order to confirm the promises given to the patriarchs, and in order that the Gentiles might glorify God for his mercy. As it is written, 'Therefore I will praise you among the Gentiles, and sing to your name'"* (Rom. 15:7–9).

God has fulfilled and continues to fulfill His word with Israel. We know that the God of Israel will also fulfill His promises to us, His Church.

MODERN ISRAEL IS A FULFILLMENT OF BIBLE PROPHECY

by

JOEL C. ROSENBERG

Long before any of it happened, Bible prophecy foretold the destruction of Jerusalem and the Holy Temple in AD 70 and the miraculous rebirth of the sovereign State of Israel that came to pass on May 14, 1948.

It's a dramatic, astonishing story and not one that everyone knows.

Let's begin with the bad news.

In the year AD 70, tragedy struck the Jewish people—*my* people.

The Roman army—led by Titus, a future emperor—besieged and sacked Jerusalem. They destroyed the Temple, burned most of the city to the ground, and carried the Temple treasures back to Rome. It was a grisly end to what became known as the First Jewish Revolt.

Then came AD 135 and the Second Jewish Revolt. This one was led by Simeon Bar Kokhba, who many Jews hoped was their messiah. But that rebellion, too, was crushed by the Romans, who slaughtered more than one million Jews.

Most of the rest of the Jewish people quickly fled the Land of Israel—which the Romans called "Palestine"—and were dispersed worldwide. And there we lived in exile for the next 1,900 years.

As painful as these events were, they fulfilled biblical prophecy.

In Matthew 24:1–2, we read this: *"Jesus left the Temple and was going away, when his disciples came to point out to him the buildings of the Temple. But he answered them, 'You see all these, do you not? Truly, I say to you, there will not be left here one stone upon another that will not be thrown down.'"*

This was not guesswork; this was prophecy. And it all came to pass, just as Jesus—whom we call "Yeshua" in Hebrew—foretold.

But Yeshua and the Hebrew prophets did not just prophesy judgment and destruction.

Here's the good news.

They also spoke of God's great mercy towards the Jewish people. Isaiah, Jeremiah, Ezekiel, and other prophets of God told us that one day the Lord would regather the Jewish people from exile, bring us back to the Promised Land, help us rebuild our country, our capital—Jerusalem—and miraculously resurrect the sovereign State of Israel out of the ashes.

Among the most famous and detailed of these dramatic and encouraging prophecies are those found in the Book of Ezekiel.

Ezekiel was a Hebrew prophet who lived in exile in Babylon—modern-day Iraq—more than 2,500 years ago.

In the first chapters of Ezekiel, and again in chapter 33, we learn that the Lord appointed Ezekiel to be a "watchman on the wall"—that is, to carefully listen to the Lord's voice, carefully watch geopolitical and spiritual events and trends, and faithfully warn the nation of Israel when there was trouble or danger ahead.

But the Lord also gave Ezekiel visions of an exciting future in which the geopolitical State of Israel would be raised from the dead.

Sadly, very few Church Fathers throughout history took these prophecies literally. Sure, they loved God, His Word, and His Son, the Lord Jesus Christ. But they could not conceive of God bringing back millions of Jewish people to the Land of Israel, planting us back in our ancestral homeland, helping us rebuild the ancient ruins, making the deserts bloom, and establishing a sovereign state.

But that's what's so beautiful about prophecy. Just because people don't understand what God is saying, or don't take His Word literally, God will not be stopped from bringing it to pass.

The most famous of these prophecies about the rebirth of Israel is found in Ezekiel 37, in a passage known as the "Valley of the Dry Bones."

It describes a gradual process in which God takes a people who feel dead and buried and have little or no hope of redemption, much less resurrection, and fashions us into a great nation once again.

From the massacres of Czarist Russia, known as the pogroms; to the death camps of Auschwitz and the Holocaust, and the murder of six million Jews; to the murder and impoverishment of Jews throughout the evil empire of the Soviet Union; the prospects of the Jewish people could not have been bleaker in the twentieth century.

Yet when all hope seemed lost, God kept His word. The prophecies came true. God opened our graves and brought our people out, many of them just skin and bones. But He brought them out of Europe. He brought us out of exile. And He brought us back here to the Land of our forefathers.

Against all odds, David Ben-Gurion declared our independence on May 14, 1948.

Against the onslaught of five Arab armies, we prevailed against those who sought to annihilate us again.

And today, the Jewish people and the Jewish State of Israel live.

Am Israel Chai!

My family and I are among the millions of Jews who've returned from exile to settle here, become citizens, and stand shoulder to shoulder with our people as God does a miraculous work.

Seventy-five years ago this year, Ezekiel's vision came to pass.

The prophetic rebuilding of Israel is not over. Not every element of these prophecies has yet been fulfilled; there's much more to come. Just think how extraordinary this is.

These powerful end-times prophecies have come to pass in our lifetime.

Indeed, the very fact that Israel exists and that the Jews have come up out of our graves and back to the Holy Land after centuries of exile is the single greatest proof of the existence of God, the reliability of Scripture, and the power of Bible prophecy.

The Bible is the only book ever that told us for over two thousand years that all this would happen. And it did.

Was it a guess?

No, it was *God.*

That is the purpose and power of Bible prophecy.

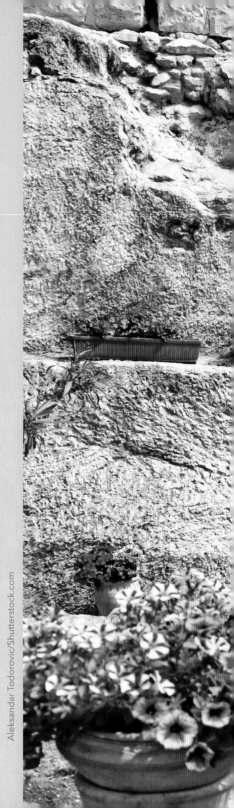

The Garden Tomb

THE CENTER OF THE UNIVERSE

by

SHARON SANDERS

"*At that time Jerusalem shall be called the throne of the Lord, and all nations shall gather to it, to the presence of the Lord in Jerusalem…*" *(Jer. 3:17).*

This year celebrates Israel's 75th birthday. We applaud Jerusalem—the reconstruction of this city is a marvel to behold. So many marvelous excavations are uncovering the original stones and appearance. Jerusalem has risen from the ashes of AD 70 to show herself to the world. Israel is your caretaker—God is your Maker and Beloved King.

There are no words adequate to describe her mystical beauty and character—alleyways and hidden treasure troves of history, whether in the Old City or newer Jerusalem, are a journey of discovery. Her stones talk, crying out with the loss of her people. But one can also hear the stones rejoicing at their return. The train of nations is coming … the miracle of the past becomes the miracle of the future.

According to Micah 4:1, the House of God will be built on top of the highest mountain in Jerusalem. The nations will flock to see it. Here will be where Messiah comes and reads the Torah (Isa. 2:3) to all peoples. Jerusalem will be a place of judgment for the nations (Matt. 25:32–33), on how Israel and the chosen people were treated.

The entire universe points directly at earth. The Temple Mount and the Holy of Holies are the center of the earth, so the universe points at Jerusalem! This city will be a royal diadem in God's hand (Isa. 62:3). God watches over this city (Deut. 11:12). It is a "focal point" from which all directions are orientated, all four corners of the earth (Ezek. 5:5; Job 38:4–7).

A pastor in Singapore reminded me that in the latter days, the nations will go up to Jerusalem and worship in the rebuilt Temple.

The building up of Jerusalem is part of the "*restitution of all things*" *(Act 3:20–21).* The former glory of this marvelous city will be surpassed to even greater glory at Messiah's appearing (Jer. 3:17) and it indeed will become the "throne of the Lord."

The awakening of Jerusalem heralds the coming Redeemer. During His reign, the earth will be "*full of His knowledge*" *(Isa. 11:9),* and He will be King over all of the earth—from Jerusalem. A descendant of Judah will hold the scepter (Gen. 49:10) and sit on God's Holy Hill. His dominion will be from sea to sea and to the ends of the earth (Ps. 72:8). All nations will say, "*Let us go up to the mountain of the Lord, to the house of the God of Jacob [Jerusalem]*" *(Mic. 4:2).* Hearts will rejoice; bones will flourish with health (Isa. 66:14). God will comfort Jerusalem as a mother comforts her child (Isa. 66:13) and will extend His peace to her.

Lift your hands, stand and praise

Photo by David Kiern

God with joy as we watch God fulfill all of His promises. The city of Jerusalem welcomes her people who have longed to see her.

As Jews and Christians pray to God, "Thy kingdom come," we declare the spiritual significance of the greatest city on earth, Jerusalem, the City of God. Come and visit the City of the Great King who will one day crown her with His Glory—the greatest milestone yet to come.

Shepherd's Field:
A Portal of Faith

by

Dr. Victoria Sarvadi

Painting by Udi Merioz

My husband and I provide annual study tours to the Holy Land but we don't always visit typical tourist locations. Instead, we focus more on ancient caves, underground tunnels, ruins of synagogues and fortresses, and archeological sites. We introduce our groups to the Land of Israel past, present, and future and the Shepherd's Field is always a must.

Located five miles south of Jerusalem on the outskirts of Bethlehem lies Bethlehem Efrat. There you will find an obscure and craggy plot of land, full of rocks and ruins that contains no inspiring memorial or beautiful garden but instead is a profound place of prophetic discourse and historical significance.

According to Genesis 35, as Jacob and his family journeyed from Bethel, Rachel began to give birth with grave difficulty. As she lay dying in the land of Efrat, Rachel named her newborn baby "My Son of Sorrow," as Jacob named the child "Son of My Right Arm." Some 1,500 years later, another baby is born in the same place. *Yeshua*, a Son of Sorrows who carries all our pain and now sits at the right hand of the Father!

Rachel, whose name means Ewe, was laid to rest in this place. Her tomb can still be visited in Efrat not far from the field.

We read that Jacob pitched his tent beyond Migdal Eder which is Hebrew for the "Tower of the Flock." This tower was located in Shepherd's Field, the very same field where young David watched over his sheep and was anointed king some five hundred years later.

No, this was not an ordinary sheep field. It was a sacred place reserved for sheep that were born for Temple sacrifice. The Mishna states that the five-mile perimeter around Jerusalem is considered holy, as were all animals within it. Being a Sabbath's walk from the Temple Mount, the priests went to this field daily to find suitable lambs for Temple offerings. The High Priest trekked every Passover to choose the Passover Lamb, then brought the lamb destined to die through the Eastern Gate four days before Passover as families waved palm branches upon his entry, shouting, "Hosanna!"

The shepherds of Shepherd's Field were not your everyday vocational shepherds but rather priestly-trained and Temple-assigned men of skill. They were taught to deliver and determine the lambs without blemish and meticulously care for them for a holy purpose.

The lower floor of the Tower of the Flock held a nursery for ewes in labor. It was a sterile area where babies were born in safety. It was customary for newborn lambs to be immediately swaddled to prevent any thrashing resulting in a cut or bruise from their little hooves, disqualifying them from sacrifice. The babies were delivered, wrapped, and placed in a hewed-out stone while they settled and calmed down.

The prophecies of Micah 4:8 and 5:2 concerning the birth of Messiah are determined to be in Bethlehem Efrat and specifically at the Tower of the Flock.

Imagine the scenario: the Temple-trained Jewish shepherds, educated in the Torah as it pertains to sacrifice and prophecy, watching over their flocks while Joseph and Mary (who was in labor) are shown to this emergency place of shelter in the same field.

The book of Luke clues us in on the location of the birth as it was a place in Bethlehem (which was known for the birth of sheep) and where there was plenty of swaddling and a feeding trough (Luke 2:6–7). Upon hearing the harkening of angels, the priestly-trained shepherds, skilled in the delivery of lambs, ran to the only place they knew baby lambs were born and swaddled and placed in mangers —the Tower of the Flock.

This beautiful story plays out vividly in the imaginations of all who gaze upon this field. A pasture of profound history and a sacred portal where heaven announced the One who split time in two and changed the lives of billions of people worldwide. *Yeshua*, the Lamb of God, has become our salvation!

THE FRIENDS OF ISRAEL:
BRINGING COMFORT AND HOPE TO GOD'S PEOPLE
by
DR. JIM SHOWERS

I grew up in a Christian home where my father taught me to love and appreciate the Jewish people and support the nation of Israel. He impressed on me that Israel is the apple of God's eye (Deut. 32:10) and, if God loves them with an everlasting love (Jer. 31:3), we should love them too.

Under his mentoring, I understood that the Bible teaches that the Jewish people were chosen by God to be His special nation to bless the world. No other nation can claim such a divine

Photo by Richard C. Lewis

selection. God chose Israel to be the conduit through which He would give His Word and Messiah to the world. Through the descendants of Abraham, Isaac, and Jacob, God promised to bless all the nations and bring salvation to mankind. My Savior, Jesus, was a Jewish man.

As I grew older, I became aware that some people in the Middle East hated Israel enough to go to war against the nation. My father told me about Israel's decisive victories over her Arab neighbors each time she was attacked. In 1967 I was amazed at how the undermanned and under-equipped nation of Israel defeated her enemies. The only explanation for Israel's overwhelming victory in six days that made sense was that God was on her side.

Little did I know as a child that I would eventually lead a historic Christian ministry to Jewish people, The Friends of Israel Gospel Ministry. But that is often how the Lord works, redirecting our paths to take us to places we could never have envisioned.

The Friends of Israel began in 1938 in Philadelphia as Christians gathered to pray for the Jewish people in Nazi Germany. They were dedicated to becoming a voice of hope and comfort to Jewish people fleeing the horrors of the Holocaust. Following Kristallnacht in 1938, The Friends of Israel Refugee Relief Committee was launched.

The founders chose "The Friends of Israel" because they believed God would faithfully honor His promise to resurrect the nation of Israel. Their belief in Scripture led them to name us ten years before modern Israel was born.

"Refugee Relief Committee" reflected the pressing need for Jewish refugees to flee Germany. But it was driven by God's promise to Abram in Genesis 12:3 that He would "*bless those who bless you.*" In Isaiah 40:1, the Lord says, "'*Comfort, comfort my people,' says your God.*" It is God's heart that the Jewish people be comforted, and we Christians can comfort them.

Four years after our founding, we began a magazine, *Israel My Glory,* to communicate biblical truth about Israel and the Messiah to the Church. We teach each generation of Christians what the Lord says about Israel and His Messiah, lest they lose their understanding of Israel and Christian Zionism.

Today, The Friends of Israel Gospel Ministry has grown to 125 employees ministering to the Jewish community in fifteen countries. We continue the work started by our founders eighty-five years ago to bring comfort to Israel and communicate biblical truth.

We salute Israel on her 75th birthday as a modern nation. Israel is a miracle of God and is living proof that the Lord does what He says He will do. There is no other way to explain the existence of Israel than the hand of God at work—returning Jewish people to the Land, reforming the people into a nation, reviving their ancient language, and protecting them from their enemies. No other nation in history has ever been exiled and returned to be reborn except Israel. We are privileged to live at a time when we can witness the miracle of God—Israel!

THE TRUMPETING PLACE:
STANDING WITH ISRAEL AS MUSICIANS
by
RICKY AND SHARON SKAGGS

Photo by David Kiern

186

As musicians, we look at Israel differently. We see how God set apart the Levites, whose role was to sing and play music in the Temple. Incredible. God had His own backup band. While Levites have not been able to perform their Temple duties since the destruction of the second Temple nearly two thousand years ago, some signs and markers prove their sacred role still exists today.

When you stand beneath the southwest corner of the Temple Mount in Jerusalem, there's a large stone that was thrown down when the Romans destroyed Jerusalem in the year AD 70. The stone is inscribed with two words that mean "To the Trumpeting Place."

While the trumpeting wasn't for worship purposes, the stone is a sign of the location where the priests blew a trumpet announcing the beginning and end of Shabbat, the Sabbath, during the Second Temple period. While we know this is valid biblically, the rock is a proof text to a passage in the historian Josephus's book, *The Jewish War*. He describes part of the Temple as "the point where it was custom for one of the priests to stand and to give notice, by sound of trumpet, in the afternoon of the approach, and on the following evening of the close, of every seventh day."

Hallelujah. We love it when historians document and prove things that we know are true biblically.

As Christians and musicians, we've taken up our trumpets (and other musical instruments) to stand with Israel, to provide a mighty sound that affirms biblical truth, and our special role and relationship regarding Israel and the Jewish people.

As Israel celebrates her 75th year of independence, we see her being discriminated against throughout the world in sports, diplomacy, fake news and moral relativism, and even among musicians. As Christians who love and support Israel, it's paramount to stand with Israel as a pillar of our faith. The foundation of Christianity is in Israel and with the Jewish people. Israel is not just God's people but Jesus' brethren. When Jesus speaks about "the least of these, my brethren," He's speaking about His people, God's chosen people, the Jewish people. How can we not stand with them?

Of course, Israel is the only democracy in the Middle East, an ally of the US and the West, and against Islamic extremism—it makes sense to stand with Israel.

It strategically makes sense to stand with Israel. But as a matter of faith, it's imperative. God is calling Christians to bless Israel. In so doing, we will see God's blessing for us and our countries.

Despite the blessing of the Abraham Accords and Arab and Islamic countries establishing diplomatic, trade, and even strategic military relations with Israel, there are many Israel haters among us. Jews in Israel live daily with the threat of terrorism, and our Jewish brothers and sisters face a surge in hateful and violent antisemitic acts that cause them to live in fear worldwide.

Now, more than ever, it's vital that we, as Christians, stand in solidarity with our Jewish neighbors.

On the occasion of Israel's 75th anniversary, we offer a simple prayer for Israel and the Jewish people. It's connected to Aaron and the Levites and is still timeless and relevant.

"The Lord bless you and keep you; the Lord make his face to shine upon you and be gracious to you; the Lord lift up his countenance upon you and give you peace" (Num. 6:24–26).

THE BLESSING:
INSPIRING THE NEXT GENERATION
TO LOVE ISRAEL AND THE JEWISH PEOPLE

by

ANN STACY

I was born the same year as Israel into a home that revered the Jewish people and the Land and State of Israel. My great-grandfather was born during the Civil War. He died twenty years before the State of Israel was born, but he left our family a legacy of knowing the Jewish people were not only God's chosen people but also "God's Time Clock." Since the Jewish people had been in exile for almost two thousand years, I still marvel at his understanding that they would return one day, which would be the beginning of The Redemption and The End of Days.

Today, that's a message I seek to impart to everyone, especially Christians, and especially my grandchildren and their generation.

As a teen, the Adolf Eichmann trial impacted me greatly. I had one persistent thought that remains with me today: *Why didn't more people help the Jews?* In college, I saw that Scripture had become historical fact. Today, I worry that my grandchildren's generation will not have even a basic understanding from which my love for Israel—and all of ours should be—is derived.

Over the years, I have developed a passion for collecting Holocaust stories. I felt they might someday disappear from the shelves, erasing the memory of the six million Jews murdered, those who survived, and the reality of the horrors committed against them. I have bought used Holocaust books from cities, schools, universities, and even church libraries stamped "DISCARD," praying I am wrong, but with hundreds in my collection to bear witness.

The evil Nazis made Jew-hatred acceptable, the foundation for the genocide they perpetrated. But that did not die with Hitler and Eichmann. I witnessed this personally on one of the saddest days of my life, September 11, 2001. My husband and I were on a business trip. That night, just hours after learning of the catastrophe, we headed to a prearranged dinner. Still shaken, I commented that "This is all about Israel."

A man started ranting about the Jews, telling everyone the Jews were interlopers in the land of the Palestinians! At my husband's nudging, I answered him directly, "The Jews are God's chosen people; God gave them the deed to the Land in the Bible, and gentiles are to be a blessing to the Jews."

While I stood my ground and defended the Jewish people and my faith, I swore I would never be in that position again without an arsenal of facts behind me. I needed to get to Israel to see for myself. The following month, I did. Because of the intifada, it felt as if we were the only tour group in Israel. Our tour guides were Orthodox Jews living in Judea and Samaria. Bombings occurred in restaurants, bars, hotels, buses, etc. Amidst all this, we met true heroes basing their lives and the lives of their families on their belief in the promises of God to restore them to the Land, Eretz Israel. Their knowledge of Hebrew Scripture stunned us. It was as if they had just stepped out of the Bible.

A decade later, the horrific murder of the Fogel family shook me to the core. Two generations were wiped out in what should have been a peaceful Friday night, the Sabbath. I prayed and knew I had to go to Itamar, the town in Samaria where they lived. I joined Americans for a Safe Israel, knowing that if there were ever a group that would take me there, it was them. I didn't realize that AFSI was 99 percent Jewish. If I had known that, I might not have gone, erroneously thinking I wouldn't be wanted. But it was just the opposite. They welcomed me graciously, drawing me to go to Israel with them again and again.

Back in Texas, when we first began hosting Israelis in our home, which we call "The Blessing," we knew no Jews in the area. Almost all the Christians we knew had never interacted with Jewish people without missionizing them, if at all.

Today, it's not such an anomaly for serious Jews and Christians to agree over the Sabbath, Torah, the Temple Mount, Festivals, Eretz Israel, etc.

In some ways, our home has become like Longfellow's *Tales of the Wayside Inn*. The difference is that just about all our guests are Jewish, from esteemed government officials to zealous pioneers to everyone in between. It's

not always by necessity that they stop by here, but we hope they still come for rest and refreshment to tell their stories to our growing group of Texas Zionists.

My great-grandfather would be overjoyed to see prophecies of the Time of Redemption coming to pass and, in part, in his great-granddaughter's home.

Photo by Richard C. Lewis

iStock.com/irisphoto2

189

JERUSALEM: MEASURING LINE FOR THE NATIONS

by
BISHOP ROBERT STEARNS

As we celebrate the 75th anniversary of Israel as a reborn nation, there is one city within her borders that best demonstrates the biblical and historical significance of this restored nation—the eternal capital of Israel, the "City of Gold"—Jerusalem.

Jerusalem is of enormous significance, historic depth, and messianic hope for Jews and Christians. Jerusalem is the geographic center of the entire biblical narrative. As such, it holds a place in the Judeo-Christian value system that no other city can fill.

From the days of Abraham who traveled to Mount Moriah some four thousand years ago to the conquest of Jerusalem by King David to the miraculous, triumphant reunification of the city in 1967 to its status as the governing seat of the Knesset today, the city of Jerusalem has played a central role in world events and in the uniting of God's people. Referred to in the Bible as "Zion" or the "City of the Great King" (Ps. 48:2), Jerusalem has weathered hundreds of conflicts and battles. Still, it has remained an unshakable testimony to God's covenant faithfulness.

Although the city appears daily in headlines, it's not journalists and politicians who've placed Jerusalem at the world's center. This was initiated in the heart of God Himself.

World events have demonstrated that Jerusalem is God's sacred measuring line for His dealings with humanity. As we encounter the permanence of God's covenant in that city, we are faced with a question that affects our whole lives.

What will we do with Jerusalem?

Many nations have tried to conquer Jerusalem and wipe out any vestige of Jewish history.

Many have tried to change Jerusalem to be more "palatable," more flexible, less confrontational, less absolute.

World leaders have tried to rewrite Jerusalem's history to avoid the declaration of truth that proceeds from it.

All have failed.

Jerusalem is not to be tinkered with to suit one's liking. God has reserved choice words of judgment for those who would destroy Jerusalem.

If we desire to be on the side of history where God's covenant lives, we must protect the true identity of His Holy City.

On the surface, it may appear that subscribing to the biblical definition of Jerusalem is too narrow in one's thinking and too exclusive against other viewpoints that would define the city by other means. Valuing Jerusalem truthfully opens our thinking to a multi-dimensional understanding of world history and current events, thus blessing all nations.

As a follower of the rabbi Jesus from Nazareth, my devotion to the God of Israel increases with my appreciation for the culture and heritage of nations worldwide. As a result, I experience new facets of my faith.

Jerusalem is a standard of truth and an open invitation to all people. It is an expression of the ancient *and* a declaration of what is yet to come. It is an established city and an unfolding prophecy of international, universal proportions.

Nations now stream up to Jerusalem in fulfillment of the words found in Isaiah 2 and Micah 4. Her streets bustle with life and her markets with the international flavors of people far and wide. As prophesied, Jerusalem is a city of great controversy and the reawakened site of the Feasts of the Lord (Zech. 12:3; 14:16).

God's promises still hold as the ancient and modern dwell side by side within her walls, a timeless wonder to the city's role in fulfilling God's plans for His people.

Psalm 122:6 instructs believers to pray for this eternal city. Zechariah 2:8 says that he who touches Zion (Jerusalem) touches the apple of God's eye. To miss this is to miss a central part of God's character.

Though many rise against her, may we be those who stand with Jerusalem as watchmen on her walls—both Jew and gentile. Jerusalem is more than a city; she is a way of life and a display of God's covenant.

iStock.com/miacniak

iStock.com/SeanPavonePhoto

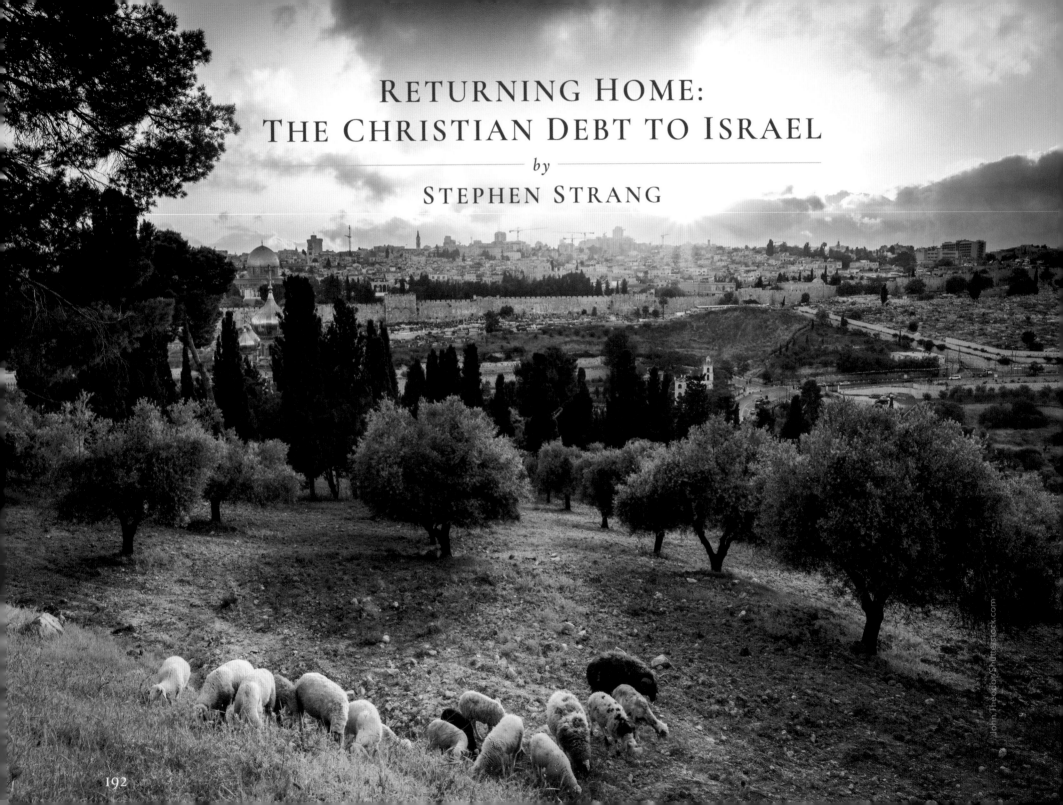

RETURNING HOME:
THE CHRISTIAN DEBT TO ISRAEL

by

STEPHEN STRANG

I have loved Israel and the Hebrew Scriptures all my life. My father was a Pentecostal pastor, and in our church (and home), I learned that the birth of Israel in 1948 was a fulfillment of the prophecy, *"Can a nation be born in a day?" (Isa. 66:8)*.

As a child, I understood that Jesus was Jewish and that He fulfilled the ancient prophecies. He was a Jewish rabbi, not a gentile savior. I always understood my Christianity within the context of its Jewish roots.

In Sunday School I learned about Adam and Eve, Abraham, Isaac, and Jacob. I learned to praise by King David's example and to dream based on Joseph's story. The wisdom of Solomon taught me how to live, and the prophetic instructions by Isaiah, Jeremiah, and Daniel warned me never to turn away from God.

My first trip to Israel in 1979 included a pilgrimage to Mount Sinai. I remember sitting atop that sacred mountain, rereading parts of the Torah, especially the Ten Commandments, and crying. I knew I had returned to where it all started. I was returning home.

Harold Kushner's *The Lord Is My Shepherd: The Healing Wisdom of the Twenty-Third Psalm* touched something profound in my heart, even though it was explained from the Jewish perspective—or perhaps because of it. This love for the Jewish roots of my faith comes naturally because I love God and have spent my life trying to live out His purposes for my life.

We wouldn't know God without the Bible, and we wouldn't have the Bible without the Jewish people. The world would still be pagan. Christians have a debt to pay to God's chosen people. The late Christian Bible teacher, Derek Prince, agrees. In his book, *Our Debt to Israel*, he wrote:

> All other nations of the earth owe all that is most precious in their spiritual inheritance to the Jews. This is true of all of us—whether we be Arabs, Africans, Asians or Europeans—Russians, Americans or Chinese. We all owe a spiritual debt to the Jews that cannot be calculated.

Saint Paul sums up the Christian responsibility toward the Jewish people with these words: *"… by the mercy shown you they also may now receive mercy" (Rom. 11:30)*. In other words, because of the mercy Christians have received from God, Christians show mercy to Israel.

So, how do we do this?

First, we can express sincere love for Jewish people. I share my deep and heartfelt love for the Bible, Israel, and the Jewish people with my Jewish friends. I love Israel in the same way I love being an American. But my devotion to my own nation pales compared to my love for Israel and Jews.

Second, we can pray for the good of Israel as the Bible commands: *"Pray for the peace of Jerusalem! May they be secure who love you" (Ps. 122:6)*.

Third, we can repay our debt to Israel through practical acts of kindness and mercy. One of the "gifts of the Spirit" Christians are taught is "showing mercy." Christians should exercise this gift not merely toward individual Jews but toward Israel as a nation. I do this by raising money for Israeli charities and hosting numerous "Nights to Honor Israel" to stir up love among my Christian brothers and sisters to support God's chosen people.

I'm appalled not all Christians share my perspective. Some are critical when I describe myself as a Christian Zionist and say terrible things, even spouting antisemitic clichès. *What's wrong with them*, I wonder. *Can't they see our entire religion is based on Judaism and that Jesus Christ Himself was a Jew?*

Thank God for revealing Himself to the Jews, which brought morality and sanctity of life to the world. And thank God that the prophecy was fulfilled: Israel was born in a day.

CELEBRATING ISRAEL'S INDEPENDENCE:
SOUTH AFRICA'S MESSAGE OF SOLIDARITY
by
MP STEVEN SWART

South Africa was one of the thirty-three countries that voted in favor of United Nations Resolution 181 in 1947, paving the way for the establishment of the State of Israel in 1948. This was the first time in almost two thousand years that the Jewish people had the chance to establish a sovereign Jewish State in its historical homeland.

Renowned biblical scholar, author, and teacher, the late Derek Prince, reminds us of our spiritual debt to the Jewish people in his booklet, *Our Debt to Israel:*

Without the Jews, we would have no patriarchs, no prophets, no apostles, no Bible, and no Saviour!

Deprived of all these, how much salvation would we have left to us? None! The nations of the earth owe all that is most precious in their spiritual inheritance to the Jews. This is true of all of us—whether we be Arabs, Africans, Asians, Europeans, Americans, or Chinese. We all owe a spiritual debt to the Jews that cannot be calculated…. I owe my whole spiritual inheritance, and every spiritual blessing I have ever enjoyed, to the Jewish people.

Israel is a living testimony of the Bible, including many prophecies regarding the ingathering of Jewish people from all nations. A visit brings alive our Christian faith.

My wife and I experienced this personally. Our twin girls were stillborn in 1988. We were overjoyed by the subsequent birth of our daughter in 1989 and visited Israel in 1991. My wife, Louise, prayed at the Western Wall in Jerusalem to restore our lost twins (Joel 2:25) and subsequently gave birth to twin boys.

Our message to the people of Israel is one of love and comfort (Isa. 40:1). This requires taking an active stand against antisemitism.

Rev. Dr. Kenneth Meshoe, founder and president of the African Christian Democratic Party (ACDP) in South Africa, is one of the most outspoken advocates for Israel, speaking out against detractors who try to label Israel as

Painting by Udi Merioz

an apartheid country. Rev. Meshoe has visited Israel numerous times, enabling him as a victim of apartheid to discredit the arguments that Israel is an apartheid country. He finds this narrative deeply offensive, given the hardships he and his family suffered under apartheid.

It's concerning that the present South African government, while purporting to hold a neutral stance on Israel, has increasingly adopted a biased approach to the country.

The UN World Conference Against Racism, Racial Discrimination, Xenophobia, and Related Intolerance held in South Africa in 2001 (the Durban Conference), aimed at becoming a "landmark in the struggle to eradicate all forms of racism." However, it degenerated into a forum for antisemitic and anti-Zionist declarations. This does not represent the millions of South Africans who love and support Israel. More South Africans and Africans are embracing Israel and seeing the positive benefits of such relationships, spiritually and physically, in the many solutions Israel offers with water, agriculture, medical, and other sectors.

I had the honor of supporting Israel during the Parliamentary vote, which took place ironically on the day Purim is celebrated worldwide.

Sadly, on March 7, 2023, the South African Parliament adopted a resolution calling for the South African government to downgrade our embassy in Israel—while many African countries are strengthening diplomatic and trade ties with Israel.

We in South Africa, and particularly in the ACDP, understand the significance of Israel and continue to intercede for and stand with the Jewish people and Israel, understanding Genesis 12:3, *"I will bless those who bless you, and him who dishonors you I will curse, and in you all the families of the earth shall be blessed."*

On behalf of all South Africans who love the Jewish people and the State of Israel, congratulations, Israel, on your 75th anniversary of independence.

CHRISTIAN STUDENTS AND THE BATTLE AGAINST ANTISEMITISM

by
DR. DONALD W. SWEETING

Photo by Richard C. Lewis

Israel has fought numerous wars since her founding in 1948, simply defending her right to exist. Even today, Hamas, Hezbollah, and Iran want to eliminate Israel. This pervasive hatred, coupled with the miraculous survival of Jews through the ages, tells us that something unique is happening.

I believe this deep animus is because the Jews are God's chosen people—behind Jew-hatred is often a hatred of God.

American universities have become the new breeding ground for anti-Israel and anti-Jewish bias. "BDS" student activism (boycott, divestment, sanctions) easily bleeds into antisemitism. Nine student groups in the law school of the University of California, Berkeley, amended their bylaws to ensure that no pro-Israel speaker be allowed to address them.

Photo by Richard C. Lewis

The attitudes of Christian students should differ from their secular peers. Here are some reasons why young Christians should not only oppose antisemitism but also be supportive of the State of Israel.

First, in nearly every generation, forces try to eliminate the Jews. In ancient Egypt, Pharaoh tried to destroy them. Under Sennacherib, the Assyrians attempted to do the same. Then came the Babylonians under King Nebuchadnezzar II. Then the Persians. Remember Haman? Then the Romans. Then the Ottomans. And, of course, the Nazis attempted the most ambitious campaign of genocide.

Christian persecution of the Jews over the centuries is a sad reality as well. But Christians today should have no part in "the world's oldest hatred."

God still has a plan for Jews. Stand with them and bless them because God says, *"I will bless those who bless you, and him who dishonors you I will curse" (Gen. 12:3).*

Second, Israel is the guardian of worldwide Jewry and a homeland for the Jews today. She is America's best ally in the Middle East and a democratic beacon in a tumultuous region.

Third, without the Jews, we wouldn't have the Bible. Without the Jews, we have no church, Mary, Joseph, or Jesus, and no understanding of redemption! Highlighting the Jewish roots of our faith will reshape our understanding. Remember your Jewish heritage.

Fourth, this is the Land God promised to Abraham and his seed—where the patriarchs walked, where Moses led the children of Israel, where Joshua battled, the sons of Jacob settled, the judges delivered, David and Solomon ruled, where the northern and southern kingdoms were situated, where the Temple was built, and where God chose to make His glorious presence known. This is where our Messiah was born, worked, walked, taught, was crucified, and was raised in fulfillment of prophecy.

Although they were scattered for two thousand years without a homeland, they not only miraculously survived but were regathered and reborn as a nation in

Photos by Richard C. Lewis

1948. Historian Barbara Tuchman put it this way: Israel "has confounded persecution and outlived exile to become the only nation in the world that is governing itself in the same territory, under the same name, and with the same religion and same language as it did three thousand years ago."

Fifth, Christian students must come to grips with the historical and theological significance of the Jewish people, Land, and the process of bringing them back. This isn't to ignore the complexity and diversity of Jewish history or to endorse all the policies of the Israeli government, nor to minimize the importance of Arab or Palestinian Christians. It is to underscore their unique historical particularity and role.

Finally, Israel has made biblical holy sites more available than ever before and many of us have been blessed to visit them. In Roman Palestine, the emperor Hadrian covered them and built pagan shrines upon them. Muslim dominance of the Holy Land made Christian pilgrimage difficult. Seljuk Turks made it impossible. But in the past seventy-four years, numerous new sites have been discovered, excavated, and made public. Israel is amazingly hospitable to allow this to happen.

In April 2023, Israel celebrated another Independence Day, only this one commemorated the 75th anniversary of Israel's founding, its "Diamond Jubilee." I hope this milestone will also be a time for young Christians to fortify their beliefs about the uniqueness and blessings of Israel.

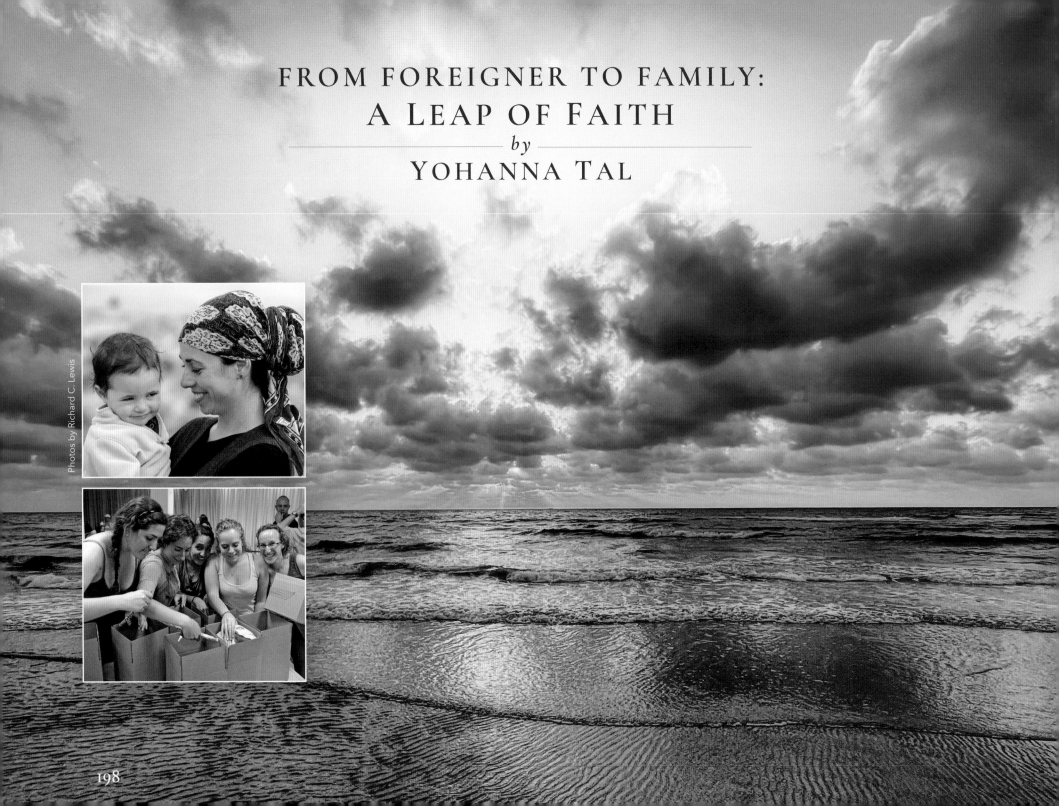

FROM FOREIGNER TO FAMILY:
A LEAP OF FAITH
by
YOHANNA TAL

Photos by Richard C. Lewis

While I was born in the Philippines, Israel is my spiritual homeland. Now I am an Israeli citizen and have the privilege of living here with my Boaz.

My first trip to Israel was in September 2015. My life changed immediately. Not only did I meet my husband, my soulmate, but God placed in my heart a deep, everlasting connection to the Land and its people. Though I heard clearly that He would bring me back, it was still painful to leave. Israel is not an ordinary nation. It's God's firstborn son (Exod. 4:22; Deut. 7:6).

As much as my return to Israel was the answer to my prayers, I had moved to a foreign land among a people I wasn't born into, who spoke a language I didn't speak. As a leap of faith, I left everything behind to embrace the future that awaited me in my new home. When God promised the Jewish people, *"I will bring you to the land flowing with milk and honey,"* none of them had ever been in the Land and didn't know what God had in store for them. Their return to Israel was a leap of faith, too, just as it was Abraham's.

Living in Israel, even with tensions and threats from enemies, my love for this Land grows abundantly. It's why I continually fight for the Land and her people.

The Land is where the Bible comes alive. I realize not everyone is as fortunate as I am to live in Israel, so my passion for sharing the wonders of Israel with Christians is one that drives my every waking moment.

The people make Israel so wonderful. Israelis are the bravest, toughest, and happiest people I have ever met. They have brought the Land to life and made the desert bloom, not just an agricultural feat but a fulfillment of prophecy. They have built one of the world's strongest and most powerful armies, serving as God's right hand in His promise to defend Israel. Israel has become a light unto the nations with world-class universities, medical innovations, and technology that blesses families worldwide.

Israel has built new cities out of sand while discovering archeological remains that prove biblical truth. Israel has revived the Hebrew language, fulfilling the prophetic ingathering of global exiles.

I am not Jewish or Israeli by birth, but I am grafted in as a Christian. The words of Ruth to her mother-in-law Naomi speak to my heart: *"For where you go I will go, and where you lodge I will lodge. Your people shall be my people, and your God my God"* (Ruth 1:16).

Moses only saw the Promised Land from afar. I have the indescribable privilege of seeing the prophecies come to life with my own eyes. I am forever grateful for all that the Lord has done for me.

Just as my eyes were opened on that first visit, I pray that all Christians come to visit to be enriched spiritually as I have been and to cast their lot with the Jewish people and Israel.

Israel's very existence and thriving is a reminder to the world that there is a God, and He keeps His promises.

Dear Israel, I am blessed to wake up each day to see you grow, evolve, and fulfill your role as the chosen nation God wants you to be. I am blessed to walk on your roads—the Land where our forefathers walked. I am blessed to be among your people and a part of the Land, both physically and spiritually.

My beloved Israel,

You have welcomed me.

You have taken me as your own.

You have protected me.

You have fed me.

You have clothed me.

You have loved me.

And for that, I will always be grateful.

FROM TOURIST TO ZIONIST:
A JOURNEY OF THE HEART IN ISRAEL

by

PASTOR SCOTT THOMAS

I had a heart transplant in November of 1992.

I was a twenty-five-year-old full-time youth pastor when I took my first trip to Israel. The experience exceeded my expectations. From sailing across the Sea of Galilee, floating in the Dead Sea, climbing up to Masada, praying at the Kotel, seeing the Temple Mount from the Mount of Olives, and visiting the biblical locations of Jesus' miracles, life, death, and resurrection … Israel was wonderful!

It wasn't until I shared my experiences with family and friends that I realized something had radically shifted inside my heart. I was hungry to learn more about the Land and people of Israel—not just of antiquity, but of

today. I spent late nights on my old dial-up internet researching everything I could to better understand Hebraic culture, customs, laws, and languages of the Bible. Before long, I had several binders of rabbinic teachings. I was an insatiably addicted closet Torah student.

Suddenly, I realized what had happened to me on that 1992 Israel tour—I had a heart transplant! God gave me a new heart for the Jewish people that has altered my life. I left home a Christian tourist and returned a Christian Zionist.

As I excitedly shared my heart for Israel and her people with pastors and church leaders, I ran into a wall called "replacement theology" or "Supersessionism." This doctrinal position touts that since the Jews' rejected Yeshua as Messiah, God removed His promises from them and gave them to the Church. God replaced the Jews with the Church.

Was it true? Had God changed His mind about the Jewish people? Had the Church now become the "apple of God's eye?"

After weeks of studying Scripture and Church history, I was convinced of God's unchanging plan for the Jewish people. Replacement theology was a vile attack propagated by antisemitic

leaders and teachers (Martin Luther, Justin Martyr, Origin, John Chrysostom, etc.). But I soon discovered that this twisted dogma was equally an attack on the very nature, character, and Word of God. Let me explain.

Unsolicited Promises

God's plans for Israel were displayed from the beginning in Genesis 12. God approached Abram and promised to make him a great nation, bless him abundantly, make his name great, and bless the world through his lineage. In Genesis 17:7, God assured Abraham that His promise was an *everlasting covenant*. God's promise to Abraham and the Jewish people

Photo by Richard C. Lewis

are unsolicited, entirely God's idea, without an expiration date. To the annoyance of Israel's detractors, God is still keeping His promise to Abraham and his children.

Unmerited Restoration

After God's promise to Abraham, Israel struggled with her faithfulness to God. Just when it looked as if God had revoked His promise, He declared His promise once again in Ezekiel

36. The prophet wrote about Israel's rebellion against God and the dire consequences they suffered as a result (vv . 16–21). Ezekiel then lists some magnificent promises to Israel. He states that God will *"gather you from all the countries and bring you into your own land"* (v. 24); *"clean from all your uncleannesses"* (v. 25); *"give you a heart of flesh* (v. 26); *"cause you to walk in my statutes"* (v. 27); *"you shall be my people, and I will be your God"* (v. 28); *"summon the grain and*

make it abundant and lay no famine upon you" (vv. 29–30); *"cause the cities to be inhabited, and the waste places shall be rebuilt"* (v. 33).

Even more astounding than these promises is the purpose that God gives for restoring Israel.

God's actions had *nothing* to do with Israel's worthiness and *everything* to do with *"for the sake of my holy name."* Israel, as a people and nation, is the recipient of God's undeserved grace and continues to be an illustrative picture of His relationship with the people He calls *"the apple of his eye"* (Zech. 2:8).

Unwavering Purpose

This powerful reality of God's grace toward Israel is further established by Rabbi Sha'ul (Paul) in Romans 11, where he wrote, *"Has God rejected his people? By no means!" (v. 1).* Then he added, *"…but as regards election [the Jews] … the gifts and the calling of God are irrevocable" (vv. 28–29).* In other words, despite Israel's failures and shortcomings, God's everlasting love, grace, and plan are still in full effect. God has not replaced the Jews!

The Trifecta

This simplified trio of the everlasting covenant with Abraham (Gen. 17:7), the restoration of Israel for God's "name's sake" (Ezek. 36:22), and Paul's reminder of God's commitment to the Jews (Rom. 11) all stand in lethal objection to the anti-grace dogma held by Supercessionists. God's action, plan, and covenants with Israel are unsolicited (God's idea), *unmerited* (God's work), and *unwavering* (God's faithfulness).

Why would one serve a God who changes His mind and breaks His "everlasting promises?" If God broke His covenant with Abraham and Israel, He can also break His covenant with Christians. God is either true or a liar, but He cannot be both.

Israel—A Picture of God's Grace!

Grace is typically defined as God's "undeserved favor" and is the predominant principle that underlines the Church's life-changing message of hope and redemption. Without God's grace, the Church would not exist. Yet, replacement theology claims to be the *recipients* of His grace

Photo by Richard C. Lewis

while working to depose the Jews of the same gift. Propagators of this twisted dogma have appointed themselves as the legislators of God's grace. Now, while the Jewish people are the target of replacement theology, the more egregious attack is actually against God's Word and character. This dogma is anti-Bible, antisemitic, and anti-Christ. God's relentless display of grace for the Jewish people is EXACTLY why the Church should be celebrating her. If grace for

Israel … then grace for all of us!

Israel is the model of God's grace-filled activity in *all* of our lives—unsolicited promises, unmerited restoration, and unchanging plan.

Am Yisrael Chai!

FROM THE HAGUE TO JERUSALEM:
PRAYERS, PROPHECIES, AND ISRAEL'S RESTORATION
by
FRANK J. VAN OORDT

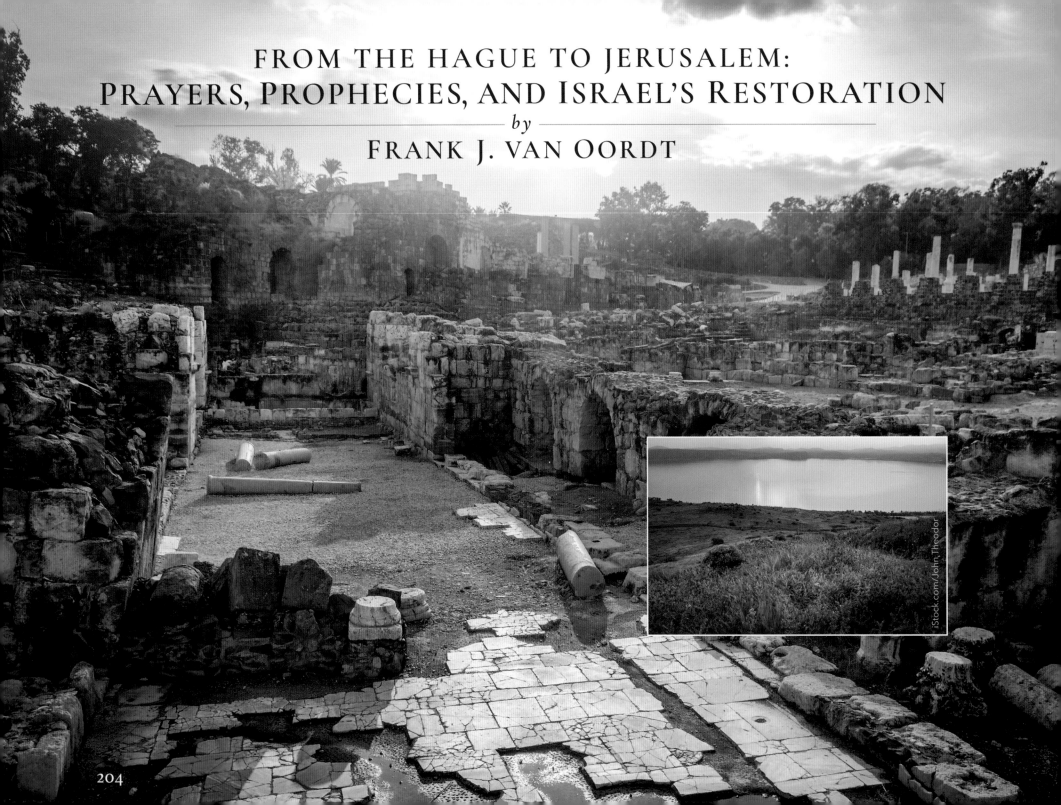

Around 1840, my great-great-grandmother was among those shocked by the French Revolution. She joined with other Christians in Europe to study biblical prophecies.

As they studied the prophets, they realized God's plan to bring His people back to the Land. *"I will take you from the nations and gather you from all the countries and bring you into your own land" (Ezek. 36:24)*. They gathered in the Hague and began to pray for the restoration of Israel. Since then, my family has prayed for this fulfillment. Here's one of our prayers:

> Accomplish for Israel, we beseech Thee, all the purposes of mercy and blessing which Thou hast yet in store for them; give unto them again the Land of their inheritance; build speedily the walls of Jerusalem, and make it to be the joy of the whole earth.

> Hear us, O Lord, for Thy name's sake, and answer us for Thine honour, through Jesus Christ. Amen.

When the State of Israel was established, my grandfather cried. He witnessed the fulfillment of prophecy. When Jerusalem became a Jewish city in 1967, my father visited the country and started business with Israel.

I stood in Amsterdam with the banner *"Let My people go"* because of the return of the Jews from the Soviet Union. Avital Sharansky was there calling for the liberation of her husband, Anatoly, who'd become Nathan after coming to the Promised Land. After him, millions followed.

The Lord protected them from assimilation. He protected their language. He protected His Word through the Masoretes' impeccable copies and the Talmudic's written oral interpretations. He protected His service through Synagogue and daily prayers. He was always there.

In 1947, a Bedouin shepherd boy discovered ancient scrolls in Qumran close to the Dead Sea. The scrolls included texts from almost all the books of Tenach. The Book of Isaiah was almost complete. The Lord uncovered His Word to the State that was proclaimed the following year.

Ezekiel 37 speaks about the different phases in the return of the people of Israel, including the return of bones to their rightful place. After all programs in Europe, persecution, and the almost extermination of the Jewish people, Zionism was heard. God brought His people back in groups of all sizes. Many came for safety or economic reasons, but as they gathered they remembered their history and tradition.

There they rediscovered the cave of Machpela, where their patriarchs were buried, Jerusalem, where their ancestors served God in the Temple, where David was their king. They start to speak their language, Hebrew. What was once reserved for many years for Tenach and Synagogue is now available to every Jew—the ability to read the Word of God.

Not all Jews have keep the 613 commandments, but it's a miracle to see the synagogues filled every Shabbat, to experience Jewish life all over the country, and to witness a country in silence at Yom Kippur. God connects His people to the Land and prepares Israel for the next step.

When the first Jews returned to the country, it was desolate, and Jerusalem was a dirty, empty city. Robbers made Jerusalem dangerous. People slept within the walls for safety. Nobody in the world was interested in the welfare of Jerusalem. Everything since has changed. When a stone is lifted in the city, the United Nations meets to talk about it. When a Jew visits the Temple Mount, the Security Council condemns it. We see Zechariah 12 becoming a reality.

Jesus says: *"Now when these things begin to take place, straighten up and raise your heads, because your redemption is drawing near" (Luke 21:28)*. Let us watch and pray as God fulfills all His promises.

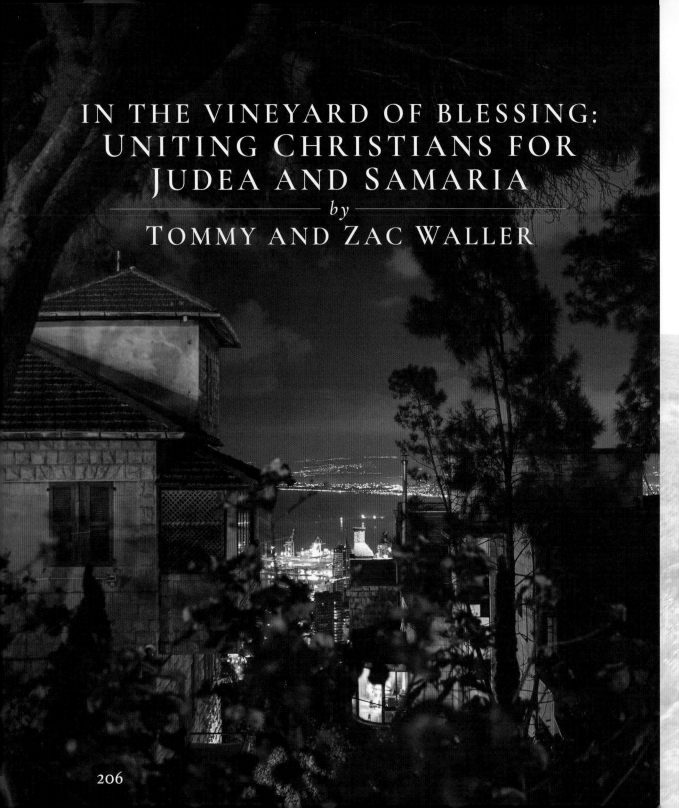

IN THE VINEYARD OF BLESSING: UNITING CHRISTIANS FOR JUDEA AND SAMARIA

by

TOMMY AND ZAC WALLER

We are Christian Zionists … but it hasn't always been this way.

We came to Israel in 2004. We didn't understand the significance of Israel or how our lives were about to change. Through a miraculous chain of events, we ended up on the Mount of Blessing—Har Bracha, Samaria, Israel. Nir Lavi showed us his new vineyard. He pulled out his Bible and explained the miracle of where we stood. Jeremiah 31:5 says, *"Again you shall plant vineyards on the mountains of Samaria; the planters shall plant and shall enjoy the fruit."* We got to see the fulfillment of this prophecy.

Nir explained that the harvest and pruning seasons were difficult. He needed many hands for a short period, and it was difficult to find Israeli laborers that had flexible schedules. We knew God was calling us to be part of what He was doing in Israel.

Upon returning to the States, we bought an old Bluebird school bus, sanded it down, painted it red, and put decals on the side that read, "Israel—the apple of God's eye." Thirteen of us—Mom, Dad, and all eleven children traveled the US and Canada, telling anyone who would listen that Israel was reborn and we could be part of its restoration. We educated, raised funds, and recruited volunteers to help Nir with pruning and harvesting his vineyard.

Since then, thousands of volunteers have come from more than thirty countries to support the valiant Jewish families living in Judea and Samaria. The Orthodox Jewish community of Har Bracha welcomed us, allowing us to repent for the evil ways of our antisemitic Christian forefathers and bring reparation to Yeshua's name.

Over the years, we've gotten to know the area and the people well. This gives us a vantage point to identify anti-Israel propaganda. There is so much good happening in Israel's biblical heartland, even with a misunderstood conflict causing a lot of pain and suffering in the entire region.

This conflict isn't new. Pharaoh, Amalek, Haman, Nebuchadnezzar, Antiochus, Titus, many popes, Martin Luther, and Hitler wanted to destroy the Jews. One after the other, the enemies of Israel were defeated. God promised to restore Israel to their Land.

"As I live, declares the Lord God, surely with a mighty hand and an outstretched arm and with wrath poured out I will be king over you. I will bring you out from the peoples and gather you out of the countries where you are scattered, with a mighty hand and an outstretched arm, and with wrath poured out" (Ezek. 20:33–34).

God chose Israel to represent Him and be a bright, shining light in a dark world. He

established them to bring redemption to the entire earth. Jeremiah, Isaiah, Ezekiel, and all the prophets speak of Israel's restoration as one of mercy, blessing, and a flourishing Jewish nation in their ancient homeland.

The miraculous re-establishment of the State of Israel, the miracles of the Six-Day War, the Jewish people returning, and the blossoming of the desolate Land all point to God's faithfulness to bless Israel and all the families of the earth.

The modern Hamans and Hitlers have targeted Judea and Samaria. We choose to stand here in that targeted area as a support and shield. We

stand unconditionally with God's chosen people.

Pro-Palestinian international pressure on Israel, however well-meaning, is causing incitement and bloodshed. Just a few days before writing this, my two young neighbors here in Har Bracha were brutally murdered. Their crime? Being Jewish.

It's time for Christian communities worldwide to leave Amalek's side and take a bold stand with God's chosen people. Let's encourage Israel to declare sovereignty over Judea and Samaria, the biblical heartland, today!

SECOND GENERATION BLACK CHRISTIAN ZIONISTS

by

JOSHUA WASHINGTON AND OLGA MESHOE WASHINGTON

Growing up Christian, our parents taught us to love, respect, and acknowledge the Jewish faith as the foundation of our own. As Black Americans and Black South Africans, we also learned how Blacks and Jews, both in South Africa and America, have a long and rich history, especially in some of the darkest parts of our stories.

In the United States, Dr. Martin Luther King Jr. expressed unequivocal support for Israel and the Jewish people as a matter of faith. Dr. King noted that even if Jews said they didn't need his support, he "would still take a stand against antisemitism because it's wrong, it's unjust, and it's evil."

Dr. King was unambiguous about supporting Israel: "Peace for Israel means security, and we must stand with all of our might to protect its right to exist…." He also made no distinction between anti-Zionism and antisemitism. In 1967, he rebuked a student's anti-Zionist comments by stating, "When people criticize Zionists, they mean Jews. You're talking antisemitism."

Decades later, Nelson Mandela was also clear about his support for Israel.

We recognize the legitimacy of Palestinian nationalism *just as we recognize the legitimacy of Zionism as Jewish nationalism*. We insist on the right of the State of Israel to exist within secure borders, but with equal vigor support the Palestinian right to self-determination.

Dr. King and Nelson Mandela had maintained strong relationships with Jewish leaders and lay members in their communities. In Mandela's autobiography, *Long Walk to Freedom*, he stated,

> In my experience, I have found Jews to be more broad-minded than most whites on issues of race and politics, perhaps because they themselves have historically been victims of prejudice.

This was regarding the struggle against apartheid South Africa and the South African Jews' crucial role in aiding Black South Africans.

Dr. King expressed warm sentiments about the Jewish community at the 68th Rabbinical Assembly for Conservative Judaism in March of 1968, just ten days before his assassination. When questioned by his dear friend, Rabbi Everett Gendler, about what seemed to be a growing anti-Jewish sentiment in the radical sect of the civil rights movement, Dr. King brought light to the situation while condemning

antisemitism as he had done many times. In his response, Dr. King stated, "Probably more than any other ethnic group, the Jewish community has been sympathetic and has stood as an ally to the Negro in his struggle for justice."

Dr. King and Mandela's voices are critical to remember at a time when no efforts are spared to drive a wedge between Blacks and Jews. Whenever we see attempts to obfuscate their words and intentions, we see it as an affront to our legacy. We see doctored videos attempting to paint Mandela as against the Jewish State. When Mandela spoke of the conflict, Mandela said, "I cannot conceive of Israel withdrawing if

Arab states do not recognize Israel within secure borders." He also expressed concern for the Palestinian Arabs and desired for them to have a state. We see pseudo-intellectuals either revising history to depict Dr. King as anti-Israel or trying to discredit him as weak and docile, a doctrine taught in public schools today.

In her infancy, struggling to survive, Israel's then Foreign Minister, Golda Meir, prioritized relations with the newly independent nations of Africa, something that was not only pioneering but prophetic.

Under her tenure, thousands of Israelis were sent throughout the continent to teach, invest, and build. Meir also oversaw Israel's 1962 vote at the United Nations condemning South Africa's apartheid policy, noting that it would be contrary to Jewish values for Israel to fail to raise her voice against apartheid.

While no less a pioneer, Meir's policy was derived from the visionary founder of modern Zionism, Theodor Herzl. While working tirelessly to establish a Jewish State, Herzl took on another important mission that Meir fulfilled and still speaks to us today.

There is still one other question arising out of the disaster of nations which remains unsolved to this day, and whose profound tragedy, only a Jew can comprehend. This is the African question. Just call to mind all those terrible episodes of the slave trade, of human beings who, merely because they were Black, were stolen like cattle, taken prisoner, captured and sold. Their children grew up in strange lands, the objects of contempt and hostility because their complexions were different. I am not ashamed to say, though I may expose myself to ridicule for saying so, that once I have witnessed the redemption of the Jews, my people, I wish also to assist in the redemption of the Africans.

Countless Israeli and African NGOs, businesses, and government-to-government programs understand that what Africa needs is not a handout but a friend who sees Africa's incredible potential and wants to help her reach it. Israel has been that friend since its rebirth.

Israel is a diverse, multi-ethnic society with people of many ethnic backgrounds and religious traditions. Through the restoration of the people of Israel to the Land of Israel, God is bringing Jews and Christians together uniquely. This deepens our understanding of Scripture and the roots of our faith and deepens our love for Yeshua.

We proudly celebrate Israel.

iStock.com/Subodh Agnihotri

Church of the Holy Sepulchre, Jerusalem

ISRAEL: A HOMECOMING TO HISTORY

by

PASTOR PAULA WHITE-CAIN

Ancient Jaffa and Modern Tel Aviv

When you first visit Israel, it is like coming home to a place you've never been. The Bible comes alive to you. You are quickly filled with awe and wonder as you can picture Jesus standing on a hillside that creates a natural amphitheater. You easily imagine Him sharing the parable of the sower—as not too far off in the visible distance is farmland.

We will never know our destiny if we don't know our history. Israel is a miracle and full of history; it is God's chosen people and nation. It gives us the opportunity to explore some of the oldest cities on Earth. Israel allows us to experience the Bible and our history. It's not enough to have knowledge of God; we must experience Him.

If you love God, you'll love His story, people, and Land. My deeply held faith and conviction have aligned me to stand with and support Israel in every possible way.

The God of Abraham, Isaac, and Jacob made a covenant with the Jewish people and promised them a nation. That nation, Israel, is the foundation and birthplace of our Christian faith. It holds our biblical heritage in which we honor God and partake of His blessings.

We are responsible for playing a crucial role in shaping the future of the State of Israel as a Jewish homeland. I also stand with Israel for geopolitical reasons. Since 1948, the nation of Israel has been America's staunchest ally in the Middle East. I proudly support Israel and the Jewish people.

Israel holds prophetic significance in our past, present, and future. During President Donald Trump's presidential campaign, he told Americans that he would move the US Embassy to Jerusalem and recognize it as the nation's capital.

Jerusalem is more than a capital city; it was the site of the Jewish Temple. Jesus went to Jerusalem with His parents every year for the Passover feast. Years later, Jesus died on a hill outside of Jerusalem. He became the Passover Lamb, whose blood atoned for the sin of the world. It was in the Temple in Jerusalem that the veil separating man from the presence of God in the Holy of Holies was torn from top to bottom.

I don't have words to describe the emotions that flooded me as I sat with President Trump in the Oval Office discussing Jerusalem as the rightful capital of Israel. Though highly controversial, it was the right thing to do. I remember telling the president, "It's right, and God has you." That moment is etched into my soul. President Trump fulfilled his campaign promise. I don't think I will be able to fully comprehend the magnitude of it all until I am in eternity.

I fell in love with God, His people, and His nation as a young woman when I experienced the reality of God's love, the faithfulness of His forgiveness, and the power of His Word. I would never have imagined God allowing me to play a role in fulfilling biblical prophecy.

You can fulfill biblical prophecy too. Here are just a few ways:

• Prayer: We are to *"Pray for the peace of Jerusalem" (Ps. 122:6)*. Prayer changes things, transforms people, and impacts nations.

• Visit: You can visit Israel and support Jews who want to visit.

You'll understand the significance of landmarks, walk the paths that Jesus walked, and fall in love with Him all over again. You'll get a fresh understanding of passages that you've read a million times. It's one of the reasons I love Israel so much!

• Support Israel's economy: Purchase products made in Israel, invest in Israeli companies, and promote tourism to Israel. This strengthens Israel's economy and supports her people.

• Advocate for Israel: Speak up for Israel in your community and on social media. Combat misinformation and negative stereotypes about Israel by sharing accurate information about the country's achievements and contributions to the world.

Every time I visit Israel, a deep sense of gratitude for who God is and what He has done overtakes me. Israel isn't just a place on the map. It's the center of God's heart, the apple of His eye. And, since Israel is important to God, it must be important to His people.

THE IMPACT OF PROFESSOR DAVID FLUSSER:
A JOURNEY INTO THE PRESENT TENSE OF ISRAEL

by

DR. BRAD H. YOUNG

Painting by Udi Merioz

Professor David Flusser was my Ph.D. in Comparative Religions advisor at the Hebrew University. I wanted to understand the Jewish roots of my Christian faith.

Flusser taught me the importance of understanding Israel in the present tense. The theology of contempt by the later Church recast Israel into the past tense for rejection and replacement. The past cannot be changed. The future is uncertain. The present tense miracle of Israel is full of promise. Flusser believed that the Israel experience would bring Christians and Jews together for study, learning, and life transformation. Israel, in the present tense, could bring healing to deep wounds and build relationships through reconciliation.

Flusser took me under his wing and did everything to help me. I was an outsider, but he brought me near to his work on the inside. At the end of my studies, Flusser recommended me to the Comparative Religions Department for a teaching position, which also provided financial help while I completed my dissertation. I became his research assistant and his driver. I learned more working side-by-side with him, editing his book, *Judaism and the Origins of Christianity*, than in all my years of formal education. I was trained by a master. He was like a father to me. He wrote the foreword to my book, *The Parables: Jewish Tradition and Christian Interpretation*.

He taught me how to think about research issues and how to approach a comparative study of Judaism and Christianity. He encouraged me in the Hebrew Heritage Bible Newer Testament (HHBNT) translation project. His friendship and encouragement have impacted my life, my career, and my family.

Flusser was a larger-than-life scholar with an eccentric personality. As an academic, he was characterized by his keen wit, infinite knowledge of primary sources, brilliant analysis, original thought, careful objectivity, philological comprehension, and critical-thinking skills. These character traits were all combined with a comedic sense of humor, robust energy, and a deep spirituality. Flusser immersed himself in the Dead Sea Scrolls, where voices with direct evidence from antiquity were now communicating with the modern world. Israel is a destination that promises intense discovery. Archaeology, history, and manuscript evidence converge together in present tense Israel.

Flusser prized the Judaism of ethical monotheism preached and practiced by Jesus of Nazareth. Jesus taught that the foremost commandment in the Jewish faith was, *"Hear O Yisrael the Lord our God, the Lord is one. And you must love the Lord your God with all your heart"* (Mark 12:29 HHBNT).

The second most important commandment is to love your neighbor—even your enemy—as yourself. The earliest stratum of Christian belief presented a Jewish Jesus who was authentic for the first century. Sadly, the Christ of the Church came to replace the authentic Jewish Jesus with a dark antipathy toward Israel. The faith in Jesus replaced and canceled the faith of Jesus. Flusser challenged Christians to not only believe in Jesus but also to believe Jesus.

Paul used the imagery of a branch grafted into a tree. The theology of replacement canceled the theology of engraftment. Instead of honoring the root that nourishes the branch, Christians cut off the branch they were sitting on.

Flusser helped me to recognize the significance of Israel. Paul acknowledged the people of Israel who did not believe in Jesus (Rom. 9:2–3) as an essential entity for all of salvation history. Their unbelief created an opening for the non-Jewish peoples of the world to believe in the one true God of Israel and to live in ethical monotheism. Flusser pointed out that Israel remains Israel because of the present tense!

In Romans 9:4–5, Paul settles the dispute. Israel cannot be forced into the past tense of replacement theology. The believers who follow Jesus in faith constitute a community. So the Church remains the Church, but Israel remains Israel—in the present tense.

*For The Hebrew Heritage Bible Newer Testament, translated by Dr. Brad H. Young, see www.hebrewheritagebible.com

THE CENTER OF LIFE:
A COMPASS IN THE HEART OF JERUSALEM
by
AMY ZEWE

My first trip to Israel was in 2006 when I was a young mother, leaving my children for the first time for over a night or two. A providential opportunity to study for twelve days in the Holy Land presented itself, and I dared to take it.

My sense of direction had always been keen, and finding my way around a city, or a forest, usually came relatively easy to me.

This honing capability of mine came to a halt when I arrived in Jerusalem. For whatever reason, I could not orient myself. North did not present itself (nor did east, west, or south). I always felt like I was already in the center—but of what, I couldn't discern.

After seeing a few sunrises and sunsets and walking in the footsteps of biblical figures, it dawned on me that what I felt was as though the magnetic center of life itself rested in Jerusalem.

Maybe the center of the earth, the center of the universe, or the center of the compass was Jerusalem. It sure felt that way.

In addition to being geographically disoriented, though surprisingly centered, the people of Israel revealed to me the various ways God makes Himself evident in today's world. When visiting biblical sites around Israel, it was through the insights of Jewish guides that I found unexpected revelation and insight.

Small insights into the nuances of the Hebrew language and the beauty of the surroundings revealed that the entire spectrum of human attributes (feminine and masculine) is demonstrated in the way God interacts with us. The material world always seems to reflect a spiritual truth. The poetry of the psalms suddenly made sense, and the words were not mere literary devices but descriptions of a physical world maintained by a personal Spirit.

In 2008, I took a second trip to Israel to complete my research for a master's thesis on human rights in the Middle East, particularly the unique position Israel holds in the region for championing and protecting human rights. Through firsthand interviews with refugees from Darfur, officials within the Knesset and various other ministries, and visits to help-oriented organizations, I was not only able to learn the truth of Israel and its people, but I was also able to articulate with firsthand evidence and expert testimonials the reality of life in Israel. Testimonies from Arab Christians trying to raise their children safely and refugees from Darfur sharing nightmarish stories of fleeing their homes and the journey to Israel revealed the common glimmer of hope in the surrounding doom and danger in Israel.

How do I generate a contagious curiosity and love for Israel—the Land, the Scripture that documents its history (and future), and its people to the next generation in my field of influence? This duty is part of my purpose and partially quelled in my work with The Jerusalem Connection and its various projects and outreaches.

Today's youth are compassionate and yearning for a magnetic center point—a purpose and a passion outside themselves. They may wane from their faith because it doesn't seem tangible. If only I could help every young person to visit the Land and people of Israel so that the words of their Bible jump off the page and become a real-time experience for them.

I've scaled the peaks of the Rocky Mountains and the Swiss Alps. I've trekked the shorelines of the Pacific and the Atlantic. I've beheld the vistas of palms on the shores of the bulge of West Africa and the shores of the Nile and traversed the deserts of Sedona. The handiwork of our Creator never lacks my awareness or awe, yet somehow, I still find the cobblestones of Jerusalem streets in the shade of Olive Trees amidst dry Israeli trade winds to be the center of my compass.

Kidron Valley and Valley of the Kings

Photo by David Kiern

What's Your Israel Story?

Pastor E. A. Adeboye

Enoch Adejare Adeboye holds a PhD in Applied Mathematics, from the University of Lagos, Nigeria in 1975.

As a teacher of holiness, he became the General Overseer of The Redeemed Christian Church of God, in 1981.

Daddy G.O., as he is fondly called, has a number of honorary doctorate degrees, including, doctor of divinity by Oral Roberts University.

In 2009, Newsweek Magazine named him as one of the fifty most influential people on earth.

Adeboye is the host and convener of a myriad of programs, including the annual Holy Ghost Congress, where millions of people gather for a week to worship God.

As a pastor of one of the largest Pentecostal churches with branches in over 180 nations, he has over fifty books to his credit.

Kay Arthur

A four-time Gold Medallion winner and author of more than one hundred books and Bible studies, Kay Arthur founded the ministry of Precept with her husband Jack in 1970. Through the Precept Bible Study Method she pioneered, Kay has spent her life championing biblical literacy as the path to a life-changing, personal relationship with God. Kay currently serves on Precept's board of directors and continues local and international ministry outreach as a Precept ambassador.

Honorable Michele Bachmann

Honorable Michele Bachmann, JD, LLM is a former member of Congress and current dean of the Robertson School of Government at Regent University. In 2006, Bachmann became the first Republican woman from Minnesota elected to the House of Representatives. She won reelection in 2008, 2010, and 2012. Bachmann quickly garnered national prominence as an outspoken advocate for conservative causes, particularly against the national debt and opposed deficit spending. Bachmann and her husband of forty-five years, Dr. Marcus Bachmann, have five children. They also parented twenty-three foster children during the 1990s. Bachmann extensively researched American public K-12 education and spoke nationally on the topic. Her political career stemmed from her interest in educational reform.

David Barton

David Barton is founder of WallBuilders, an organization dedicated to preserving truth in history. He is a nationally and internationally known speaker, historian, and *New York Times* best-selling author. He has written a number of best-selling books, with the subjects being drawn largely from his massive library of tens of thousands of original writings from the Founding Era. He also addresses hundreds of groups each year. David has received numerous national and international awards, and a national news organization has described him as "America's historian," while *Time Magazine* called him "a hero to millions — including some powerful politicians."

Ken Barun

Ken Barun is an accomplished and respected senior executive having served in the White House under the Reagan administration, on presidential committees under both Bush administrations, at the McDonald's Corporation, with Ronald McDonald House Charities as president/CEO, and most recently as chief of staff for the Billy Graham Evangelistic Association, where he was responsible for overseeing the day-to-day operations of the ministry, working closely with Franklin Graham. Ken is a long-time and an outspoken supporter and advocate for Israel, which is evident throughout his charitable work. His faith guides this and is evident throughout his personal and professional life.

Pastor Mark Biltz

Pastor Mark Biltz, founder of El Shaddai Ministries in Washington State, is a well-known and popular commentator on the Feasts of the Lord and has produced books and DVDs on the Feasts that have gone around the world. He has authored four best-selling books. Pastor Biltz has spoken at congregations and conferences all over the world including twelve countries on five continents. He has a local congregation in Washington State and live-streams their weekly service on their website as well as on Facebook and YouTube to over two hundred cities in twenty nations.

Pastor Boyd Bingham

Pastor Boyd Bingham has served as assistant pastor and co-pastor at the Binghamtown Baptist Church for more than a decade, taking up the mantle of the third generation in his family as spiritual leader, in partnership with his father who is senior pastor, and his grandfather before that. He teaches and is a senior administrator at the Gateway Christian School. Pastor Boyd also continues his family's long tradition of support for the Jewish people as God's chosen people, and for Israel where he has visited many times and has many deep personal friendships and projects that the church has supported.

Dr. Billye Brim

Dr. Billye Brim, president of Billye Brim Ministries, aka Prayer Mountain in the Ozarks, in the US has traveled internationally in a Bible-teaching ministry since 1980. From 1980 to 1991 she traveled regularly in the former Soviet Union teaching in underground churches. There she became aware of the refusniks. In 1986, after her husband's passing, she studied Hebrew at Ulpan Akiva in Netanya, Israel. Working with its founder she began seminar tours to Israel which continue till now. She is a regional director of Dr. John Hagee's CUFI and works with the Jerusalem Prayer Breakfast.

Rev. Rebecca Brimmer

Rev. Rebecca Brimmer is the international president and chairman of the board for Bridges for Peace. She is a spokesman for BFP and a published author. In 2023 she was awarded the Yakir Keren HaYesod award in honor of her lifetime of activities for Israel. In addition to education and *hasbara*, Bridges for Peace has projects in Israel showing practical support from Christians. BFP helps with *Aliyah*, immigrant absorption, and giving food to over 22,000 people each month through municipalities and the Social Welfare. Mission statement: Bridges for Peace, Christians supporting Israel and building relationships between Christians and Jews in Israel and around the world.

Dr. Michael L. Brown

Michael L. Brown is host of the nationally syndicated talk radio show, *Line of Fire*, and the author of more than forty books and 2,500 op-ed pieces. He has served as a visiting or adjunct professor at seven leading seminaries and has contributed to numerous scholarly publications, including the Oxford Dictionary of Jewish Religion and the Theological Dictionary of the Old Testament. He has preached around the world, bringing a message of repentance and reformation, and as a Messianic Jew, he has urged the Church to recognize its Jewish roots and God's ongoing purposes for the nation of Israel.

Stephen W. Brown

Steve Brown was born and raised in Asheville, North Carolina. He is the founder of Key Life Network, Inc., and Bible teacher on the national radio program, *Key Life*, and *You Think About That*, which are heard on over six hundred outlets. He also hosts a talk show, *Steve Brown, Etc.*, which is aired on the Salem Radio Network. Steve is a widely respected speaker, and widely published author. He teaches Practical Theology at Knox Theological Seminary and at Westminster Theological Seminary. He is also the former pastor of Key Biscayne Presbyterian Church, First Presbyterian Church, Quincy, Massachusetts, and East Dennis Community Church, East Dennis, Massachusetts. Steve is married to the former Anna Williamson, the father of two and grandfather of three.

Dr. Juergen Buehler

Dr. Juergen Buehler, serves as president of the ICEJ, overseeing the global ministry from Jerusalem and traveling extensively around the world to preach on God's purposes for Israel, the Church, and the nations in our day. A trained physicist (doctorate in chemistry from Israel's esteemed Weizmann Institute), Buehler is also ordained with the German Pentecostal Federation (BFP).

Shirley Burdick

Founder of Ten Gentiles, Shirley is a fifth generation Christian born in China. She immigrated to the US with her family at age 17. Her background was in software development. In 2000, she and her husband Bill came to Israel for the first time and were astonished by the restoration of Israel by God and the Jewish people. From 2008–2018, she volunteered in the Land for seven years. Afterwards, she and Bill created the nonprofit organization Ten Gentiles in Israel with their Christian and Jewish friends. The organization was inspired by Zechariah 8:23 to equip and engage Christians to participate in God's restoration of Israel alongside the Jewish people.

Nathaniel Buzolic

Nathaniel Buzolic is an Australian-born actor who is best known for his role as Kol Mikaelson in *The Vampire Diaries* and *The Originals*. His other film and TV credits include *Hacksaw Ridge, Deep Blue Sea 3, Saving Zoe, Supernatural, Pretty Little Liars*, and *Significant Mother*. Nathaniel has over four million followers across all his social platforms where he shares his photography, Christian faith, and his support of Israel's right to self-determination and sovereignty. Since 2019, Nathaniel has been operating and leading tours through Israel to bring people from the nations to experience the beauty and mysteries that God has slowly revealed through His Word in the Land of the Bible.

Laurie Cardoza Moore

Laurie Cardoza Moore is founder and president of Proclaiming Justice to The Nations (PJTN), and a respected voice on the frontlines as a tireless pro-Israel advocate and in the global war on antisemitism. PJTN was founded to educate, motivate, and activate Christians on the biblical mandate given by God to support Israel and the Jewish brethren, with a particular focus on the next generation. Laurie is host and executive producer of *Focus on Israel* reaching over 2.6 billion potential viewers through two dozen TV affiliates and satellite carriers globally. PJTN produced three Emmy Award winning documentaries. Laurie has received the "Goodwill Ambassador to Israel Award" by Israel Consul General, named among the "Top 100 People Positively Impacting Israel" by Algemeiner, and received the "Friend of Israel Award" by the Center for Jewish Awareness.

Dr. Ben Carson

Dr. Benjamin S. Carson, Sr., M.D., is founder and chairman of the American Cornerstone Institute, a think tank whose mission is to promote the founding principles which are cornerstones of the United States: faith, liberty, community, and life, and to pursue common sense solutions that challenge conventional groupthink. He most recently served as the 17th Secretary of the U.S. Department of Housing and Urban Development. For nearly thirty years, Dr. Carson served as Director of Pediatric Neurosurgery at the Johns Hopkins Children's Center, becoming the youngest major division director in the hospital's history at 33. In 1987, he successfully performed the first separation of craniopagus twins conjoined at the back of the head. He also performed the first fully successful separation of type-2 vertical craniopagus twins in 1997 in South Africa. Dr. Carson graduated from Yale University and earned his M.D. from the University of Michigan Medical School. He and his wife are proud parents and grandparents.

Pastor Doug Clay

Pastor Doug Clay is general superintendent of U.S. Assemblies of God. As chief executive officer, he serves nearly 13,000 churches in the US with over 3.2 million adherents. Previously, he served the church as general treasurer for nine years. He has also served as district superintendent, pastor, youth pastor, and youth director at the national and district levels. Clay has a passionate love for the local church; he is a church health enthusiast, and he effectively equips leaders to grow in their calling. He and his wife, Gail, have two grown daughters and seven grandchildren.

Pastor Terri Copeland Pearsons

Pastor Terri Copeland Pearsons and her husband, George Pearsons, are senior pastors of Eagle Mountain International Church, where they have pastored for over 30 years. She serves as chief visionary officer of Kenneth Copeland Ministries and is the president of Kenneth Copeland Bible College. Pastors George and Terri have been members of Christians United for Israel since its inception, standing firm in support of Israel, the Land and the people. For further information, visit www.emic.org.

Earl and Kathleen Cox

Earl Cox is an international Christian broadcaster and journalist who served in senior level positions with four US presidents. Due to his outspoken advocacy for Israel, he has been recognized by Prime Minister Netanyahu as an Ambassador of Goodwill from Israel to Christian and Jewish communities. He was named by Israel's former Prime Minister Ehud Olmert as "the voice of Israel to America." For over three decades, Earl Cox and his wife, Kathleen Dahl-Cox, have worked side by side in support of Israel. Among her many undertakings, Kathleen is a successful real estate investor and Zionist philanthropist.

Dr. Tony Crisp

Dr. Tony Crisp, PhD, DD, a native Tennessean, presently serves as an evangelical advisor to The Museum of the Jewish People, (ANU) in Tel Aviv, Israel. He serves as vising professor of Israel Studies at Brewton-Parker College, Mt. Vernon, Georgia. Dr. Crisp also served on the National Council of the American Israel Public Affairs Committee (AIPAC) in Washington, DC, for more than a decade. He hosts *On the Way, with Dr. Tony Crisp* daily podcast; heard in seventy nations and over 2,500 cities worldwide. He and his wife, Karen, live in the Tri-Cities area of East Tennessee and have three grown children and five grandchildren.

Pastor Rafael Cruz

Pastor Rafael Cruz is a powerful example of the American Dream. Born in Cuba, he began fighting Batista's regime as a teenager and was imprisoned and tortured simply because he wanted to be free. Rafael arrived in Texas in 1957. He got a job as a dishwasher, making 50 cents an hour, and worked his way through the University of Texas, while learning English. In 1980, Rafael joined the State Board of the Religious Roundtable, mobilizing millions of people of faith during Ronald Reagan's presidential campaign. He is an ordained minister and the Director of Grace for America, sharing the Word of God in churches and pastors conferences throughout the United States. He is the author of *A Time for Action, Empowering the Faithful to Reclaim America*. His son, Ted Cruz, is US senator from Texas.

Christine Darg

Christine Darg is presenter of the Jerusalem Channel on TV platforms worldwide. She first visited Israel in 1975 and helped her husband to start the Christian Broadcasting Network's Jerusalem bureau in 1982. For bringing many pilgrims to Israel, Christine received Israel's annual tourism award from the Knesset Christian Allies Caucus. She co-chaired five Jerusalem Assemblies in the Knesset and has twice been named among Israel's "Top 50 Christian Allies" by the Israel Allies Foundation. She has authored many books and is an advisory board member of UK Christian Friends of Magen David Adom and the Genesis 123 Foundation.

Pastor Jerry Dirmann

Pastor Jerry Dirmann is the founder and senior pastor of The Rock Network, a multi-site church based in Anaheim, California. Jerry is also the founder and president of Solid Lives, a disciple-making and church-planting ministry. He authored the "Operation Solid Lives" discipleship program as well as the "Jesus' Way Discipleship" system. Jerry's love for Israel and the Jewish people began in 1998 when he visited Israel for the first time. He has since led over fifteen tours to the Holy Land, including a pastors tour and several young adult tours. Jerry also served on the board of the International Christian Embassy Jerusalem–USA branch.

Pastor Richard Diyoka

Pastor Richard Diyoka Nsanguluja was born, raised, and educated in the Democratic Republic of Congo (formerly Zaire). He has been pastor of the Shekinah Tabernacle in Kinshasa since 1990. Pastor Diyoka founded the Shekinah Foundation in 1996. They have translated and printed Christian books of the Reverand William Marrion Branham, which are distributed around the world. Pastor Diyoka has been connected with the Centre Historique du Temple de Jerusalem, and has commissioned unique art from Israel for Shekinah Tabernacle where Israel's anthem, "Hatikvah," is sung each week as he connects his Congolese ministry with Israel. Pastor Diyoka is married to Madame Kapinga Diyoka Kyria. Together they have four children and fourtreen grandchildren.

Pastor Don Finto

Pastor Don Finto and his wife, Martha, spent the first eight years of their marriage ministering to the broken in post World War II Germany from 1952 to 1960. After their return to the US, Don pursued a PhD at Vanderbilt University, also teaching German and Bible at Lipscomb University until 1971. For the next twenty-five years, he was the pastor of Belmont Church in Nashville, after which he founded Caleb Global with a goal to "ignite revival in Israel, the Middle East and the nations." Martha (who died in 2016) and Don have three children, seven grandchildren, and eleven great-grandchildren.

Priscilla Flory

As Priscilla Flory enters her eighth decade, she is going strong, motivated by her love of God, people, and life. She has traveled the globe serving widows and orphans and teaching the seminar, "Good Mourning, Thriving through the Storms of Life." Priscilla authored the book *Going with God, Letters from Our Travels*, and is passionate to share about Israel everywhere. In addition to her three biological children and their precious spouses, and six grandchildren, Priscilla has also enlarged her family with numerous bonus children, grandchildren, and even great-grandchildren, in Israel and around the world. Priscilla lives in Virginia where she loves to extend hospitality to her worldwide family and friends.

Diego Freytes

For more than twenty years, Diego Freytes has been engaged in preaching the Word of God. He is also an intercessor with a strong prophetic call and has served in the local church leadership. After a season joining the International Christian Embassy Jerusalem prayer calls, he was asked to head up the ICEJ's Argentina Branch. With a background in technology and sales, he has always been passionate about working to extend the kingdom of heaven. He and his wife, Carolina, live in Córdoba, Argentina, with their two children, León and Serena.

Rev. Willem J. J. Glashouwer

Reverend Willem J.J. Glashouwer was born in the Netherlands during World War II into a Dutch Reformed family that was active in the Resistance Movement. His father was a well-known pastor, who was imprisoned several times, and was actively involved in hiding Jews. He is an ordained minister in the Dutch Reformed Church. Rev. Glashouwer is president of Christians for Israel International, with branches in over forty nations, a "Holland Choir," and supports charity projects in Israel, including helping to bring over 150,000 Jews to Israel from the former USSR. He is honorary president of the European Coalition for Israel. He has served as a producer, host, and executive director of the "Evangelische Omroep" (Evangelical Broadcasting Company) which is now part of the Netherlands State Broadcasting system, one of its larger broadcasting companies. He also pioneered the Institute for Evangelical Higher Education in the Netherlands, and the Christian School for Journalism. Rev. Glashouwer published several books, articles, and Bible studies on Israel. He has been married to Marianne for over fifty years and they are blessed with four children and eight grandchildren.

Pastor Trey Graham

Pastor Trey Graham is an author, speaker, radio host, and pastor of First Melissa Church in Texas. He is a graduate of the United States Military Academy at West Point and Southwestern Baptist Theological Seminary. Pastor Graham is the founder and teacher for Israel by the Book whose mission is to bless the people and the Land of Israel by studying, following, and teaching the Book, God's Word, including sponsoring multiple Bible study tours of the Holy Land each year. Trey and his wife, Bretta, have six amazing children. Learn more at www.TreyGraham.com and www.IsraelByTheBook.com.

Darrin Gray

Darrin Gray is a thought leader and public speaker on strategic philanthropy, fatherhood, mentoring, and leadership. In 2012, Darrin co-authored *The Jersey Effect, Beyond the World Championship*. *The Jersey Effect* demonstrates how to pursue the ultimate prize—less to do with winning a championship ring, and everything to do with how one can positively affect those around us through sports. Darrin serves professional athletes, coaches, alumni, and business leaders with godly leadership. He maintains a broad fellowship of NFL players and alumni for whom he leads annual trips to Israel in partnership with CUFI.

Tristan Hall

Tristan Hall is the international executive director of Jerusalem-based Christian Friends of Israel. He is originally from the UK, and first moved to Israel in 2006 to serve as an organizer of community projects across the towns and cities of Israel, with groups of short-term volunteers from the nations. Having loved every minute of this work for several years, Tristan continued to support Israel from the outside through fundraising, education, and *hasbara* amongst both Jewish and Christian communities. Following a season working for the Zionist Federation and WIZO, Tristan and his wife, Galya, returned to Israel in 2022 in order to serve at Christian Friends of Israel.

Pastor Malcolm Hedding

Pastor Malcolm Hedding is an ordained minister of the Assemblies of God of Southern Africa and has been involved in Christian ministry for forty-eight years. He has planted many churches in the country of his birth and has supported church plants in other countries including Finland, the United Kingdom, and the USA. He has served as the executive director of two biblical Christian Zionist organizations: Christian Action for Israel and the International Christian Embassy Jerusalem. Malcolm is a prolific writer and has authored seventeen books on various biblical themes including prayer, Israel, the Minor Prophets, and the Gospels; the latest of which being, *Understanding Hebrews* and *Understanding Revelation.* He serves on the International Board of the International Christian Embassy Jerusalem, and as its international spokesperson. He and his wife, Cheryl, have three children, all of which are in full-time Christian ministry, and they live in Murfreesboro, Tennessee.

Bishop Timothy Hill

Bishop Tim Hill is general overseer for the international ministries of the Church of God, leading the ministries of approximately 7.8 million members of nearly 42,000 churches in 185 countries and territories worldwide. A graduate of Lee University, Hill previously served on the Executive Committee of the denomination, holding various positions. Bishop Hill is the author of numerous books and other publications including six books of sermons and 150 gospel songs, many of which have been recorded by top musicians. At the core of Bishop Hill's ministry is his passion for revival and completing the Great Commission. Hill is married to Paula; they have three daughters: Melinda, Brittany, and Tara, two sons-in-law, and five grandchildren.

Dr. Wayne Hilsden

Since 1983, Dr. Wayne Hilsden is the co-founder of King of Kings Community, the largest evangelical congregation in Jerusalem. Additionally, Hilsden is the co-founder and president of FIRM: Israel Fellowship of Israel Related Ministries, an association of over seventy organizations that provide practical assistance to the citizens of Israel. Dr. Hilsden is a frequent speaker at conferences and churches around the globe. He highlights the remarkable restoration of Israel as a fulfillment of God's covenant promises in the Scriptures. He and his wife are parents to four sons and have eight grandchildren.

Pastor Larry Huch

Larry Huch is the founding and senior pastor of New Beginnings Church in Dallas, Texas. Over the past thirty years, Pastor Larry has become a recognized authority on the Jewish roots of our Christian faith. He is committed to standing with Israel, is a staunch defender against antisemitism, and actively promotes unity between Christians and Jews. In partnership with Keren Hayesod, Israel Allies Foundation, Magen David Adom and other organizations, his ministry has given nearly ten million dollars in the last ten years to support many vital charitable projects in Israel. In appreciation of this benevolent work and steadfast advocacy, Pastor Larry has been honored with many prestigious awards.

Rev. Kevin Jessip

Rev. Kevin Jessip is president of Global Strategic Alliance and an advisor to national and global business, political and faith leaders. As the co-chair with Rabbi Jonathan Cahn, he founded the global movement The Return, a cry for the nations to return to the Word, the will, and the ways of God. Global Strategic Alliance and The Return's mission is to proactively restore Judeo-Christian values to the moral and civic framework on a local, state, national, and international level, encouraging engagement through prayer, civic involvement and personal responsibility at every level of society. They stand with Israel to raise awareness of the importance of Israel in America's future, and the importance of America's stance against BDS, antisemitism, and efforts to delegitimize the nation of Israel.

Emily Jones

Emily Jones is a senior producer for CBN News in Jerusalem and works alongside a team of seasoned journalists covering stories in Israel and the Middle East. Before moving to Israel in 2019, she spent years traveling the region to study the Israeli-Palestinian conflict and raise awareness about Christian persecution and anti-Semitism. As an alumna of the Philos Project Leadership Institute and CUFI on Campus, she is passionate about promoting meaningful Christian engagement with the Middle East and pluralism in the region. When she isn't hunting stories, you'll find her practicing Krav Maga or listening to a podcast.

Pastor Becky Keenan

Pastor Becky Keenan is the president and founder of One with Israel, a movement of individuals, churches, and organizations to support Israel. Her love for Israel came from her father who served in the US military in North Africa and Europe where he witnessed the treatment of the Jews by the Nazis. Pastor Keenan has served in several capacities with AIPAC, IsraAID, Yad Vashem, the Texas Holocaust and Genocide Commission, and CUFI. She is the Spanish voice for Joyce Meyer and translates and records all JMM television programs in Spanish heard throughout Latin America. Pastor Keenan and her husband Pastor Joseph Keenan, are senior pastors of Living Hope Church, a non-denominational, multicultural congregation in Houston, Texas. She is the proud mother of two wonderful young adults, Katie and Joey.

Colonel Richard Kemp CBE

Colonel Richard Kemp CBE has spent most of his life fighting terrorism and insurgency, commanding British troops in some of the world's toughest hotspots, including Afghanistan, Iraq, the Balkans, and Northern Ireland, where he was wounded in a terrorist attack. Commanding British Forces in Afghanistan, he put together an unconventional force of British troops and US Marines that mounted successful counter-terrorist operations against key terrorist leaders. He served in Downing Street as head of the international terrorism team at the Joint Intelligence Committee assessing global terrorist threats for the Prime Minister and other cabinet ministers. He has been active in countering the anti-Israel narrative on the world stage including at the UN, the EU, and national legislatures e.g., Washington, London, and Berlin. He was appointed Member of the Order of the British Empire by the Queen for intelligence work in Northern Ireland and was promoted to Commander of the Order for counter-terrorist work in the U.K. and Afghanistan. He is a writer, prolific journalist, international speaker, and media commentator covering a range of issues including leadership, decision-making, crisis management, terrorism, intelligence, conflict, and the Middle East.

Anne Graham Lotz

Called "the best preacher in the family" by her late father, Billy Graham, Anne Graham Lotz speaks worldwide with the wisdom and authority of years studying God's Word. The *New York Times* named Anne one of five most influential evangelists of her generation. Her Just Give Me Jesus revivals were held in over thirty cities in twelve different countries, to hundreds of thousands. Anne is a best-selling, award-winning author of 21 books. Her latest releases are *Preparing to Meet Jesus* and *Jesus Followers*. She is president of AnGeL Ministries in Raleigh, North Carolina, and served as Chairman of the National Day of Prayer Task Force.

Pastor Conrado Lumahan

Pastor Conrado D. Lumahan is the assistant general superintendent/vice president of the Assemblies of God in the Philippines. He is the Christians for Israel (C4I) trainer and director of C4I Philippines, International Christian Mission (ICM) and Home Mission Department of the Assemblies of God. He is also the senior pastor of All Gospel Church, a vibrant and growing church in the Northern Philippines. Conrado is a sought-after conference and convention speaker. He is married to Amelia Mercado and they are blessed with one daughter and two sons, and two grandchildren.

Dr. Robert Mawire

Dr. Robert Mawire, a direct descendant of King Solomon with Queen Sheba, Prester John. He is vision driven; he founded Nehemiah Operation Worldwide (NOW) to sponsor *Aliyah*, established Good News Ariel radio FM 106, and partnered with the late mayor of Ariel Ron Nachman in the creation of Ariel Smart City, by sponsoring Russian scientists to Ariel. He assisted in the founding of the Christian

Allies Caucus and the Jerusalem Prayer Breakfast to raise worldwide support for Israel. He is the founder of WRNO Worldwide radio, Gerizim Group, and Hope for Africa humanitarian initiative. He is an author and international conference speaker. He is married to his Australian wife for forty-three years and has three sons and seven grandchildren. He lives in Texas, USA.

Pastor Tod McDowell

Pastor Tod McDowell was ordained as a pastor in Hawaii at Calvary Community Church in 2002. He served for fifteen years with Youth with a Mission at the University of the Nations in Kona, Hawaii. He was on the President's Council with Loren and Darlene Cunningham serving from 1992-2007. In 2010, he became the executive director for the ministry Don Finto founded called Caleb Global. Tod travels around the world teaching in missions and ministry schools, as well as in churches and conferences. He currently resides in Nashville, Tennessee. He has been happily married since 1993 and has four amazing children.

Chris Mitchell

Chris Mitchell established the CBN News Middle East Bureau in August 2000. Since then, he's covered the major events in the region including the Second Intifada, the 2006 Second Lebanon War, the Arab Spring of 2011, the rise of ISIS in 2014, the historic Abraham Accords, and told the story of the persecuted Christians from the Middle East. Mitchell also serves as executive director of *Jerusalem Dateline*, a bi-weekly program covering the Middle East seen in many countries around the world and broadcast on Daystar, GOD TV, and the NRB networks. He's also the author of *Dateline Jerusalem: An Eyewitness Account of Prophecies Unfolding in the Middle East.*

Chief Justice Mogoeng Mogoeng

Chief Justice Mogoeng Mogoeng is the fourth Chief Justice of the Republic of South Africa. He holds Bachelor of Law (B Juris), Bachelor of Laws (LLB), and Master of Laws (LLM) degrees. He is also a recipient of two honorary degrees of Doctor of Laws degrees and an honorary degree of Doctor of Humane Letters. During his term as Chief Justice, Mogoeng was elected as the president of the Conference of Constitutional Jurisdictions of Africa (CCJA), and also served as the chancellor by the Council of the University of KwaZulu-Natal for four years. He is married to Mmaphefo Anna Mogoeng and together they are blessed with three children and two grandchildren.

Rev. Johnnie Moore

Rev. Johnnie Moore is a popular speaker, author, and acclaimed human rights and religious freedom activist known for his consequential work at the intersection of faith and foreign policy, especially in the Middle East. He is president of JDA Worldwide and president of the Congress of Christian Leaders. Rev. Moore's many awards and honors include the Simon Wiesenthal Center's prestigious Medal of Valor. He was twice appointed to the US Commission on International Religious Freedom, and in 2020 was named one of America's ten most influential religious leaders. He is the vice chairman of the board of the International Fellowship of Christians and Jews and serves on advisory board of the Combat Antisemitism Movement. Rev. Moore is also a founding member of the ADL's Task Force on Protecting Minorities in the Middle East.

President Jimmy Morales

President Jimmy Morales served as president of Guatemala from 2016-2020. He is a prominent Guatemalan communicator, businessman, and politician who has risen from a working-class family to become one of his country's top leaders. President Morales credits his evangelical Christian faith to his success, as well as his strong position on Israel. In addition to being a leader in his own country, he has honorary degrees from Hebrew University in Jerusalem and Sun Monn University in Seoul, South Korea. He has also been a leader in international affairs, particularly as creator of the First Continental American Customs Union, within the Central American Integration System and the Dominican Republic.

Pastors George & Cheryl Morrison

Pastor George Morrison is senior pastor emeritus of Faith Bible Chapel, a non-denominational church in Arvada, Colorado, where he was senior pastor for over thirty-three years. Pastors George and Cheryl were leaders in supporting the Jewish community and Israel in the Denver area. They supported and led numerous interfaith, pro-Israel rallies as well as an annual Israel Awareness Day. For more than three decades, Pastor Cheryl Morrison led the International Singers and Dancers to Israel to perform and demonstrate unconditional love and support to the Israeli military and civilian population. Pastors George and Cheryl are executive board members, regional directors, and congressional liaisons for CUFI. Pastor George and Cheryl founded Truth & Life Ministries to mentor leaders, teach and preach throughout the world, and help believers understand their biblical mandate to stand with Israel and the Jewish people. Combined, they have traveled to Israel more than 150 times taking thousands of people with them.

Shelley Neese

Shelley Neese is president of The Jerusalem Connection. Shelley is the author of *The Copper Scroll Project* and host of the *Bible Fiber* podcast. She studied in Israel from 2000-2003, where she received her MA in Middle Eastern Studies from Ben Gurion University. Shelley is currently a graduate student studying biblical history and archaeology and consults for an upcoming documentary on the Tabernacle. Shelley has dedicated her life to sharing the story of Israel and the Jewish people. She currently resides in Arizona with her four children and her husband, a physician in the US Air Force.

Allison Ngo Griffin

Allison Ngo Griffin, a former Buddhist, worked for the Texas House of Representatives before a radical encounter with Jesus in 2015. Her first trip to Israel in 2019 to attend the Jerusalem Prayer Breakfast led to ongoing involvement with Israel. Allison is now an event coordinator for conferences and events that support Israel. She is married to Peter, whom she met in Israel, and lives in Miami, Florida.

Bob O'Dell

Bob O'Dell is a co-founder of Root Source along with Gidon Ariel. Bob is a writer, hi-tech entrepreneur and philanthropist, and a pro-Israel Christian with experience in different streams of the Christian faith. He has worked with Jews in Israel continuously since 1988, and in 2000 co-founded Wintegra (a successful high-tech Israeli startup) with an Israeli. Since 2013, Bob has worked with Orthodox Jews interested in entrepreneurial and philanthropic endeavors. His latest book, *Five Years with Orthodox Jews*, is available from Amazon and at root-source.com.

Lord Simon Reading

Lord Simon Reading is the Fourth Most Honorable Marquess of Reading. He was educated at Eton College and served as a Cavalry Officer on the Iron Curtain 1961-1964. Lord Reading was a member of the House of Lords from 1980-1999. Lord Reading has deep roots in and a history of support for Israel and links to the former Family Villa Melchett on the Sea of Galilee which is a center of dialogue and diplomacy. He is a Patron of JNF, and chair of the European and International Coalition Advisory Board for Israel. Lord and Lady Reading are focused on personal diplomacy to bring diplomats and others to Israel to show how important it is to support Israel at the UN and in general.

John Riley

John Riley has spent the last forty years as a prominent radio broadcaster and journalist. His coverage of the Middle East has been heard across the United States and around the world through American Family Radio as well as podcasts which are downloaded by thousands each month. He brings clarity and truthful reporting to the often-chaotic confusion of the Middle East. John has traveled extensively throughout the Middle East and has brought dozens of people to Israel over the last 30 years. He is married to his sweetheart, Lennie, and together they have nine children and nine grandchildren.

Gordon Robertson

Gordon Robertson is president and CEO of the Christian Broadcasting Network, a member of CBN's Board of Directors, executive producer of both CBN Films and CBN Animation, and host of CBN's flagship program, The 700 Club. He is also president of Operation Blessing, CBN's international humanitarian organization. The son of Pat and Dede Robertson, Gordon graduated from Yale and earned his law degree from Washington and Lee University. In 1996, he founded the Asian Center for Missions and created The 700 Club Asia in the Philippines, featuring local talent and guests. Following that model, he launched CBN centers in Indonesia, India, and other countries. Gordon and his wife, Katharyn, reside in Virginia and have three grown children.

Dr. Pat Robertson

Dr. Pat Robertson (1930-2023) was a renowned religious leader, philanthropist, educator, author, and former candidate for president. He was the founder and chairman of the Christian Broadcasting Network and hosted CBN's flagship program, The 700 Club, until 2021. He also founded Regent University, where he was chancellor; Operation Blessing, CBN international humanitarian organization; and the American Center for Law and Justice. His wenty-three books include *The Secret Kingdom*, which was the number-one religious book in America. Born March 22, 1930, he earned degrees from Washington and Lee, Yale, and New York Theological Seminary. In 1954, Pat married his beloved wife, Dede, who went to be with the Lord in 2022. Their family includes four children, fourteen grandchildren, and twenty-three great-grandchildren.

Curtis Robinson

Curtis D. Robinson is a presidential appointee on the United States Holocaust Memorial Council. He owns C&R Development Company, R&G Services, and eight shops at other businesses at Bradley International Airport. Dr. Robinson has honorary doctorates from Goodwin University and Lincoln College of New England. He received the ADL Torch of Light Leadership Award. He and his wife, Sheila, are philanthropists for the Curtis and Sheila Robinson Foundation, and co-founded the Curtis D. Robinson Center for Health Equity. Hebrew High School of New England launched the historic Curtis D. Robinson Center for Business and Innovation — a first-of-its-kind program teaching Jewish students business courses. He is completing his autobiography, *From the Back of the Bus, the Curtis D. Robinson Story*.

Bishop Jose Rodríguez and Dr. Vilma Rodríguez

Bishop Jose Rodríguez and Dr. Vilma Rodrí guez pastor Casa de Dios in Nashville, one of the largest Hispanic churches in the United States. In 1980, God put on their hearts to bless and pray for the peace of Israel, albeit with little knowledge of what it was about then. After pastoring for nearly forty-five years, Israel is always at the forefront of their ministry where they proudly display the Israeli flag and sing Israel's national anthem, "Hatikvah," at each service. God has blessed them with a beautiful family of five children and seven grandchildren, and many spiritual children in the United States and throughout the nations.

Joel C. Rosenberg

Joel C. Rosenberg is editor-in-chief of *All Israel News* and *All Arab News* and president and CEO of Near East Media. A *New York Times* best-selling author, Middle East analyst, and evangelical leader, he lives in Jerusalem with his wife and sons. Joel hosts *The Rosenberg Report* on TBN, the only prime-time weekly news and analysis program produced in Jerusalem on any US network. Joel writes for numerous media including The Jerusalem Post and Fox News, and has been interviewed on ABC's Nightline, CNN, C-SPAN, Fox News, MSNBC, the History Channel, CBN, TBN, and Daystar. He speaks frequently at churches and major Christian conferences around the world. Joel is founder and chairman of the Joshua Fund, to mobilize Christians to "bless Israel and her neighbors in the name of Jesus, according to Genesis 12:1–3." The Joshua Fund has invested more than $80 million in Christian ministries and humanitarian relief work in Israel, the Palestinian territories, Lebanon, Syria, Jordan, Iraq and Egypt. Joel has led seven historic and headline-making delegations of American evangelical leaders to meet with and open up on-going dialogues with senior Arab Muslim leaders, including Egyptian President Abdel Fattah el-Sisi, Jordan's King Abdullah II, Saudi Crown Prince Mohammed bin Salman, and United Arab Emirates Crown Prince Mohammed bin Zayed.

Ray and Sharon Sanders

Ray and Sharon Sanders are the co-Founders of Christian Friends of Israel Jerusalem, and have been based in Jerusalem at its headquarters since 1985. They have traveled to more than fifty nations, speaking among Christian groups of all backgrounds. They have written extensively, including many articles and books, about the imperative to stand with and bless Israel for decades. They provided the vision and leadership for CFI which has representative offices across the world. Over the decades, they have established deep roots in Israel, and are highly regarded among Israelis of all walks of life. Among their collective and diverse academic and Christian degrees, both are graduates of Christ for the Nations Bible College in Dallas.

Dr. Victoria Sarvadi

Dr. Victoria Sarvadi received her ThM and ThD from the former Center for the Study of Biblical Research in Glendora, California, now under the auspices of the Hebraic Christian Global Community. She is a certified minister since 2000, a frequent contributor to *Restore! Magazine*, and authored *Just a Little Girl*, an account of her life, coming to faith, and understanding the significance of Israel and the Hebrew language. She has been a speaker for conferences, congregations, women's ministry groups, Bible studies globally. She is also the executive director for the March of Remembrance Dallas. She has been a guest on major national and international radio and television programs including TCT, Daystar, and Upliftv Networks, seen worldwide. Her Precious Gems teachings on the Jewish roots of Christianity have appeared widely, and can be viewed at victoriasarvadi.com. She has six children, twenty grandchildren, and is married to Paul Sarvadi, chairman, CEO, and co-founder of Insperity, Inc. As co-founders of the Nathaniel Foundation, the Sarvadi's philanthropic contributions support numerous charities in the US and abroad.

Dr. Jim Garlow and Rev. Rosemary Schindler Garlow

Dr. Jim Garlow is co-founder and CEO of Well Versed, which brings Biblical principles of governance to government leaders in the US, Europe, and Latin America. He has led numerous trips to Israel, is a respected author of twenty-one books, commentator, historian, and pastor. His one-minute, "The Garlow Perspective," is heard daily on nearly eight hundred radio stations. Rosemary Schindler Garlow is an Israel specialist, having hosted dozens of trips to Israel, integrating her heritage as part of the Oskar Schindler family legacy as depicted in *Schindler's List*. She is an international advocate, building support between Christians and Jews, and is committed to exposing and combatting the evils of antisemitism. They co-direct Well Versed, and co-host WPN, the World Prayer Network. Together they have eight children and thirteen grandchildren.

Dr. Jim Showers

Dr. Jim Showers is the executive director and president of the Friends of Israel, a worldwide Christian organization headquartered in Deptford, New Jersey, founded in 1938 by Christians determined to help Europe's beleaguered Jewish population caught up in the Holocaust. Dr. Showers speaks at conferences, churches, and schools nationwide. He leads the semi-annual Friends of Israel "Up to Jerusalem" tours bringing hundreds of Christians to the Promised Land. He authors "Inside View," a regular column featured in the Friends of Israel magazine *Israel My Glory*. His popular series, "The Black Sheep of Christendom," exposing the dangers of replacement theology, was originally published in *Israel My Glory*.

Ricky and Sharon White Skaggs

Ricky is a fifteen-time GRAMMY® Award winner credited with twelve hit singles, thirteen IBMA Awards, nine ACM Awards, eight CMA Awards (including Entertainer of the Year), and has been inducted into the Bluegrass Music and Country Music Hall of Fame. His music career spans over 60 years. As a Grand Ole Opry member, he has released more than 30 albums and performed thousands of live shows with his band, Kentucky Thunder. Skaggs Family Records has released twelve consecutive GRAMMY®-nominated albums. His autobiography is *Kentucky Traveler*. Sharon White Skaggs is a member of beloved country-gospel family band, The Whites, and making music alongside her father father, Buck, and sister, Cheryl, for more than five decades. Together they have won many GRAMMY®, CMA, and Dove Awards, among others. They began as a Bluegrass group and became well-known for their string of country hits in the 1980s. The Whites are Grand Ole Opry members and were involved in the 2001 hit movie and soundtrack, *O Brother, Where Art Thou?*

Ann Stacy

Ann Stacy was born in 1948 in the Texas panhandle, months after Israel was reborn. Ann is a teacher by training, but most of her adult life has been associated with their family business. A new chapter of her life began in 2011 when she started hosting Israelis to share their stories in 2011. She sometimes thinks of their home as the Wayside Inn, as in Longfellow's *Tales of a Wayside Inn*. Ann is married to the love of her life, John, for nearly fifty-one years, and she's the proud mother of three grown children, and they have ten grandchildren, and five great-grandchildren.

Bishop Robert Stearns

Bishop Robert Stearns is the founder and executive director of Eagles' Wings in Buffalo, New York, a global movement of churches, ministries, and leaders; and president of the Israel Christian Nexus in Los Angeles, California. He has ministered in more than 30 nations around the world, with a central focus on the nation of Israel. Bishop Stearns is the visionary of the annual initiative, "The Day of Prayer for the Peace of Jerusalem," with participation of over 500,000 churches globally. He is at the forefront of educating Christian communities regarding the role of Israel, the Jewish people, and our shared Judeo-Christian values.

Stephen Strang

Stephen Strang, author of *Spirit-Led Living in an Upside-Down World,* is a long-time Christian Zionist and has raised hundreds of thousands of dollars for Israeli charities. For several years he was a regional director for Christians United for Israel. The founder of Charisma Media, and host of *The Strang Report* podcast, he was cited by *Time Magazine* as one of the twenty-five most influential evangelicals in America. He has interviewed four US presidents and has been featured on Fox News, CNN, MSNBC, CBN, the *New York Times*, Politico, and *Rolling Stone.*

MP Steven Swart

Steven Swart represents the African Christian Democratic Party (ACDP) in the South African Parliament. He holds degrees in law and economics and practiced as an attorney before being elected to Parliament in 1999, where he is serving his fifth term. He has visited Israel a number of times, and is regarded as a true and faithful friend of Israel and the Jewish people. As a member of Parliament he and his colleagues in the ACDP continue to advocate for Israel, whenever necessary. He is married to Louise, has three grown children, and resides in the Western Cape, South Africa.

Dr. Donald W. Sweeting

Dr. Donald W. Sweeting currently serves as the chancellor of Colorado Christian University. He is an ordained pastor in the Evangelical Presbyterian Church. Over the past seven years, CCU has sent dozens of students to Israel to do fieldwork in biblical archaeology and to learn about the Land and people of Israel. CCU has an active chapter of Christians United for Israel (CUFI). Dr. Sweeting has led or co-led five Holy Land tours with orty to one hundred people on each and was invited to travel to Israel to celebrate the nation's 75th Anniversary.

Yohanna Tal

Yohanna Tal was born in Lemery, Batangas, Philippines. She lived in Singapore for five years and moved to Israel after she got married in September 2016. She also published her first book, *The Journey*, in 2019. She is an active vlogger, maintaining her own YouTube channel that is dedicated to defending and showing the world the truth about Israel. Through her engaging and informative content, she provides a unique perspective on the political, cultural, and social aspects of Israeli life. Currently, she is working as a team manager for a tourism company in Israel, playing an integral role in bringing large numbers of tourists to the Holy Land.

Pastor Scott Thomas

Pastor Scott Thomas is the founding and lead pastor of Free Life Chapel in Lakeland, Florida, and president of Excel Christian Academy. He is the Author, Director, and lead instructor of ACTIVATE Christian Leadership Institute; a college accredited internship. Scott has served in full-time ministry for over thirty years and is an avid and outspoken supporter of the State of Israel and the Jewish people. He has been leading tours to Israel for decades, hosting pro-Israel events and is a noted speaker for various Jewish organizations. He serves on the Executive Boards of CUFI, and Operation LifeShield. Scott is a lifetime learner. He holds degrees in Psychology, in Biblical Studies, and a Doctorate of Divinity. Informally, he is in his twenty-sixth year of Hebraic and rabbinic studies. Scott and Cindy have been married for twenty-nine years and have a son, Caleb, who is married to Elizabeth, and one grandson.

Frank J. van Oordt

Frank J. van Oordt is the director of Christians for Israel, the organization started in 1980 by Frank's father, Karel. The roots of the love for Israel go back to his great-great-grandmother, who attended in 1840 prayer meetings for the restoration of Israel. Frank has also been brought up with this hope. He has been active in education, lastly director of Christian schools. Since 2018 he has been active for Christians for Israel. He leads the organization and gives Bible studies in the Netherlands. Frank is married to Hillianne and they have five children.

Pastor Paula White-Cain

Paula White Cain, a best-selling author, is president of Paula White Ministries and senior pastor of City of Destiny in the greater Orlando, Florida, area. She hosts a worldwide daily TV program, *Paula Today*, reaching 195 countries with a potential daily audience of more than six billion people. Paula's commitment to humanity is felt around the globe as she reaches out through numerous charities and compassion ministries, fulfilling her mission to transform lives, heal hearts, and win souls. She and her husband, Jonathan Cain, share their faith around the world and reside in Florida. You can learn more about Paula, her work, and her ministry by visiting Paulawhite.org.

Dr. Brad H. Young

Dr. Brad H. Young is emeritus professor of Biblical Literature in Judaic-Christian Studies in the Graduate School of Theology at Oral Roberts University. After experiencing Israel and exploring the historical beginnings of his Christian faith, he devoted his life to a career in research and education. He has taught advanced language and translation courses, and the Jewish foundations of Christianity to graduate students for over 30 years. In addition to his well-known research on the life of Jesus, he as devoted much energy to Jewish-Christian dialogue. He is the author of numerous books, including *Jesus the Jewish Theologian, The Parables: Jewish Tradition and Christian Interpretation, Meet the Rabbis*, and *Paul the Jewish Theologian*. He is the translator of the *Hebrew Heritage Bible Newer Testament*. In addition to teaching full time and speaking at seminars and conferences around the world, Brad has maintained a strong commitment to his family, the church, and the community.

Tommy and Zac Waller

Tommy and Zac Waller are the founders and executive directors of HaYovel. They have tirelessly worked with their entire family (of which Zac is one of eleven) to educate Christians and invite them to volunteer on the beautiful farms in Judea and Samaria. Since 2004, thousands of volunteers from more than thirty countries have harvested tons of produce and planted entire forests. When people talk about getting their hands dirty, nobody's hands are dirtier than the Wallers. The Wallers have been celebrated among members of Knesset and other government leaders, and they are firmly committed to loving, blessing, and serving God's chosen people, and to help Christians realize the redemptive potential of connecting with the Land and people of Israel, and making that possible.

Joshua Washington and Olga Meshoe Washington

Joshua Washington is the director of the Institute for Black Solidarity with Israel (IBSI). He is a composer and world touring recording artist. Joshua lectures on topics such as the historic Black and Jewish Relationship and the Africa-Israel Alliance. His album, *Zion*, has received national acclaim as he continues to tour and promote it all over the world. Olga Meshoe Washington is originally from South Africa. She is the CEO of DEISI (Defend Embrace Invest(in) Support Israel), a faculty member and Regional Director at Club Z, and board member of the IBSI. Olga is an internationally sought-after speaker on African relations with Israel and the Christian mandate to stand with Israel. Olga received the 2016 Jerusalem Award from the World Zionist Organization, in recognition of advocacy for Israel. Together they have two beautiful sons, Ezra and Judah.

Amy Zewe

Amy Zewe is the vice president of the Jerusalem Connection, an adjunct university professor, and runs a consulting business. Amy's work to advocate for the Jewish people and for Israel is a life-long passion. She enjoyed two study tours in Israel, completing her master's thesis on human rights in Israel. Amy generates a weekly "Red Alert" report on YouTube to inform on and combat antisemitism. She is a contributing author to *The Casualty of Contempt: The Rise of Antisemitism and What Can Be Done to Stop It*. Amy and her husband live in Virginia and their three grown children reside nearby.

We extend our heartfelt gratitude to the exceptional photographers and artists whose dedication breathed life into the pages of *Israel The Miracle*. Your incredible work has captured the essence of Israel's beauty and significance, making this a timeless and memorable book.

Laura Ben-David
www.laurabendavid.com
Twitter: @laurabendavd
Instagram: @laurabendavd
Threads: @laurabendavd

David Kiern
I Am Israel
www.IAmIsraelFilm.com
@iamisraelfilm

Rebecca Kowalsky
Images Through Time – www.imagesthroughtime.com
www.facebook.com/ImagesThroughTime1/
YouTube: @RebeccaKowalskyFineArt
Instagram – rebeccakophoto

Alex Levin
Art Levin Corp, Inc.
www.ArtLevin.com
www.facebook.com/Alex.Levin.Studio

Richard C. Lewis
Richard C. Lewis is a professional sports photographer in Miami for almost fifty years

Udi Meiroz
Blue and White Gallery
Jewish Quarter, Old City, Jerusalem, Israel
www.blueandwhiteart.com

Our Sponsors

We extend our heartfelt gratitude and sincere appreciation to all the generous sponsors who have made the publication of *Israel The Miracle* possible. Your unwavering support and commitment have been instrumental in bringing this transformative book to life. To those whose commitment as sponsors happened after publication, we look forward to recognizing you in future editions.

PATRIARCH SPONSORS

Binghamtown Baptist Church
www.binghamtown.org

Dr. Michael L. Brown

AskDrBrown Ministries

ASKDrBrown.org

Priscilla Flory

This sponsorship is gratefully given to lovingly honor Priscilla's mother, Harriett Buckingham Ripperger, Ruth Feldstein, and Hon. Michele Bachmann.

P.O. Box 908, Bellmawr, NJ 08099 • 856-853-5590

www.foi.org

The Friends of Israel Gospel Ministry is a historic Jewish ministry founded in 1938 to proclaim biblical truth about Israel and the Messiah while bringing physical and spiritual comfort to the Jewish people.

WRNO Worldwide Radio / Goodnews World

TAKING THE WHOLE TRUTH TO THE WHOLE WORLD

P.O. Box 895, Fort Worth, TX 76101 • 817-850-9990

wrnoradio@mailup.net

The Jerusalem Channel

Christine Darg and her husband, Peter, are founders of the Jerusalem Channel, www.JerusalemChannel.tv, your source of Good News for the Last Days. Christine is an advisor of the Genesis 123 Foundation and has been named among Israel's Top 50 Christian Allies by the Israel Allies Foundation.

Becky Keenan
President

www.onewithisrael.com
8012 Fuqua Street
Houston, TX 77075
281 - 503 - 4240

Education • Mentorship • Advocacy

20454 Old Orange Rd., Culpeper, Va. 22701

Basil Guralnick Bernstein MD

Christian Friends of Israel - Jerusalem
נוצרים ידידי ישראל-ירושלים
www.cfijerusalem.org
cfi@cfijerusalem.org
+972 2 6233778
https://www.facebook.com/CFIJerusalem/
PO Box 1813, Jerusalem 9101701, Israel

WallBuilders.com

wbcustomerservice@wallbuilders.com

Church of God
Bishop Tim Hill
General Overseer/Presiding Bishop

PO Box 2430 • Cleveland, TN 37320-2430

Rev. Linda V. Chandler
www.hostministries.org

International Christian Embassy Jerusalem
General Pierre Koenig 38, Floor 2
P.O. Box 1192 • Jerusalem • 9101002 • Israel
Office: +972 2 539 9700 • Fax: +972 2 539 9701
www.icej.org

Pastors Wives of America
Pastor Libia Duran

www.PastorsWivesofAmerica.org
Office: 202-983-4111

Curtis and Sheila Robinson

SALEM MEDIA GROUP™
6400 N. Belt Line Road
Irving, TX 75063
Phone: 469.586.0080
www.salemmedia.com

Texans For a Safe Israel

www.texansforasafeisrael.org

ABOUT

GENESIS 123 FOUNDATION

ואברכה
מברכיך
ומקלליך
אאר ונברכו
בך כל
משפחת
האדמה

The Genesis 123 Foundation has a simple but wide-ranging mission: to build bridges and strengthen relationships between Jews and Christians and Christians with Israel in ways that are new, unique, and meaningful. While many Jewish and Christian organizations work in this space, too many are transactional, viewing Christians as a faith-based ATM rather than genuinely building bridges.

This is a sacred relationship and responsibility that we do not take for granted. We strive to innovate and engage people, all around the world, and have done so through a variety of programs. We also strive to provide a resource for Christians around the world to bless Israel by funding programs that provide services to Israelis of all backgrounds with the highest integrity. Some of the programs that the Genesis 123 Foundation has innovated include:

Run for Zion
Run for Zion is the first Christian pilgrimage experience centered around the Jerusalem marathon, but not just for runners. It has a unique *"bless Israel and be blessed"* model that provides subsidies for travel along with hands-on involvement, connection to, and funding of a variety of non-profits in Israel. As one of Israel's largest annual community-wide sporting events, participants get to experience Israel as never before, while blessing Israel with every step.

Prayer and Biblical Based Programs
Often overlooked in building bridges between Jews and Christians are the essential things which we have in common: God and the Bible. We have launched programs such as Prayers for Zion and the Global Prayer and Virtual Pilgrimage series, to build connections at the most fundamental level that can engage Christians of all backgrounds everywhere.

Youth Engagement
Even in the most pro-Israel Christian homes and churches, there are few age-appropriate ways to engage Christian children with Israel. The Genesis 123 Foundation has launched initiatives to address this, filling a need, and as a critical way to engage the next generations.

Inspiration from Zion
In 2021, the Genesis 123 Foundation was blessed to be invited to host a podcast on the Charisma Podcast Network with Jonathan Feldstein as the first Orthodox Jewish host of a weekly program about and from Israel among hundreds of other Christian podcasts on CPN. Inspiration from Zion has been well received in some one hundred nations, connecting people with stories in and about Israel that they won't hear anywhere else.

Partnerships
Even among the biggest and most pro-Israel ministries, time and resources are limited. While the desire to support Israel is strong and sincere, sometimes managing resources limits the ability to do as much as one wants. To that end, we strive to create mutually beneficial, win-win relationships in everything we do.

Blessing the Nations
The verse, Genesis 12:3, ends with the mandate that Israel will be a blessing to the families of the world. Among all the programs that we do in Israel, we also strive to fulfill that mandate whether protecting Christians and Christian sites in the Arab world and Africa, advocating for Christians persecuted in Islamic nations, supporting Christians impacted by record flooding in Pakistan in 2022, providing baby formula to churches in the

US to ease the shortage that same year, speaking out against those who malign Christian support for Israel, and more.

Israel the Miracle is the latest of these programs. It made a wide global impact even before being published, including plans to translate the book into a number of languages to have the widest reach possible. There are other plans to follow the production of this as a book as well.

We invite you to connect with the Genesis 123 Foundation to be involved in your community and help us continue to build, widen, and strengthen the bridges we build, all to God's glory.

www.Genesis123.co

Gen123Fdn@gmail.com

To Learn More about the celebration of Israel The Miracle, please visit:

www.israelthemiracle.com